BLUE MAURITIUS

Helen Morgan trained as an art historian and archivist. She lives in Melbourne, Australia. This is her first book.

'Helen Morgan's book traces in great detail the stories of the twenty-six known "Post Office" stamps in existence in a scholarly but very readable fashion. She brings to life the collectors who hunted their quarry and the letters which the stamps adorned.' Peter Lewis, *Daily Mail*

'Helen Morgan's enthusiasm for these stamps is catching.' Ludovic Hunter-Tilney, *Financial Times*

'Fascinating... This is a very well and extensively researched book, not only of the stamps, but also of the various personalities, dealers, collectors and others who have discovered, handled or possessed them... Mauritius in 1847 is brought vividly to life, as is the stamp collecting world of the 1860s to the 1990s, the period of most activity and discovery of the 1d and 2d items.' *Philatelic Explorer*

Blue Mauritius

The Hunt for the World's Most Valuable Stamps

H ELEN M ORGAN

ATLANTIC BOOKS
LONDON

First published in Great Britain in hardback in 2006
by Atlantic Books, an imprint of Grove Atlantic Ltd.

This paperback edition published in
Great Britain in 2009 by Atlantic Books.

1 3 5 7 9 8 6 4 2

A CIP catalogue record for this book is available
from the British Library.

ISBN 978 1 84354 436 4

Typeset by Avon DataSet Ltd, Bidford on Avon, Warwickshire

Printed in Great Britain by CPI Bookmarque, Croydon

Atlantic Books
An imprint of Grove Atlantic Ltd
Ormond House
26–27 Boswell Street
London WC1N 3JZ

www.atlantic-books.co.uk

BLUE MAURITIUS

Il ne faut jamais désespérer en philatélie.
L'avenir nous réserve peut-être encore
des surprises heureuses.

(One must never despair in philately.
The future reserves for us yet, perhaps,
happy surprises.)

Georges Brunel,
Les Timbres-Poste de l'Île Maurice:
Émissions de 1847 à 1898,
Editions Philatelia, Paris, 1928

Contents

List of Illustrations   ix

Author's Note   xii

Introduction   1

1   Port Louis, Mauritius, September 1847   7

2   Message in a Bottle   16

3   To Philatelic Facts, Which Are Usually Dry   31

4   No Room in Madame's Lallier   41

5   Major Evans's Tour of Duty, Mauritius 1876-9   55

6   All, Alas! Discontinued by Death   65

7   Pretty Philatelic Fairy Tales   84

8   The Schoolboy and the Bordeaux Letters   105

9   The Blue Mauritius   122

10   The Big-game Collectors   155

11   Very Much in Love with Mauritius Stamps   177

12   Million-dollar Questions   201

Postscript   220

Glossary   225

Biographies of the Stamps   229

Notes and Sources   255

Bibliography   289

Acknowledgements   297

Mauritius Philatelic Society   301

Index   303

LIST OF ILLUSTRATIONS

Page

iii Two pence 'Post Office Mauritius' stamp. Copyright, Blue Penny Museum, Mauritius.

9 Ruisseau du Pouce, Port Louis, Mauritius. Postcard, collection of John Shawley.

13 Mauritian postage stamp commemorating Lady Gomm's ball and the 'Post Office' stamps. Collection of John Shawley.

19 'Mrs Lloyd's postman, Mauritius' by Owen Stanley, Voyage of the H.M.S. Rattlesnake: Vol. 1. MS, Mitchell Library, State Library of New South Wales, Australia. (PXC 281 f.24)

20 View of warehouses and the customhouse, Port Louis. Produced in 1847 as a hand-coloured lithograph by Deroy after an original work by Pierre Amand François Thuillier and printed in Paris by Lemercier. Copyright, Blue Penny Museum, Mauritius.

34 Mauritius page. Frederick Booty, *The Stamp Collectors Guide: Being a List of English and Foreign Postage Stamps with 200 Fac-simile Drawings*, 1862.

43 'La Petite Bourse des Timbres aux Champs-Élysées'. Arthur de Rothschild, *Histoire de la Poste aux Lettres et du Timbre-Poste Depuis Leurs Origines Jusqu'a Nos Jours*, Paris, 1880.

45 Bordeaux, Cours du Pavé-des-Chartrons. Postcard, author's collection.

59 Edward B. Evans. Frontispiece, *Philatelic Record*, Vol. 6, 1885.

63 One penny 'Post Office' on an envelope addressed to Monsieur Alcide Marquay. By permission of the British Library, The Tapling Collection, (6377).

71 Philipp von Ferrary. Frontispiece, *Philatelic Record*, Vol. 11, 1889.

74 Thomas Keay Tapling. Frontispiece, *Philatelic Record*, Vol. 9, 1887–8.

88 The Jerrom letter to Bombay, bearing two one penny 'Post Office' stamps. Courtesy of Investphila SA, Switzerland.

109 The Bordeaux letter, bearing both one penny and two pence 'Post Office' stamps. Private Collection. Courtesy of Richard Borek, Braunschweig, Germany.

117 Monsieur Théophile Lemaire. *Philatelic Record*, Vol. 21, No. 6, June 1899.

139 The original copper plate (perhaps) used to print the 'Post Office' stamps. Whereabouts unknown. Reproduced from *The West-End Philatelist*, 1912.

146 Fred Melville's *Rare Stamps: How to Recognise Them*, London, 1922. Held in the Royal Philatelic Society of Victoria Library, Australia.

157 Alfred Lichtenstein and Théodore Champion. Reproduced from *Balasse Magazine*, Brussels, No. 104, February 1956.

174 The one rupee Mauritius stamp issued to celebrate the centenary of the island's first British colonial postage stamps. Author's collection.

179 The original case containing two 'Post Office Mauritius' and other rare stamps. Courtesy of Museumsstiftung Post und Telekommunikation, Bonn, Germany.

194 Vernon Warren, *The Blue Mauritius*, Thriller Book Club, London, undated, first published 1954. Author's collection.

206 Jean-Baptiste Moens. Frontispiece, *Philatelic Record*, Vol. 15, 1893.

222 Bois Cheri, Blue Mauritius vanilla tea. Author's collection and the author's favourite tea!

Author's Note

In terms of prices paid for the 'Post Office' stamps I have cited currencies and amounts given in contemporary sources, such as philatelic journals, and, if available, followed conversions given therein. I did not attempt the onerous task of standardizing prices paid into one currency for comparative purposes. Historical conversions can be difficult to calculate, depending on what criteria are used as a basis (such as monthly salaries and cost of living). What did paying £1,450 for a stamp mean to George V?

The important thing to remember in this story is that while anybody could conceivably discover a 'Post Office' stamp, only the wealthy could afford to buy one. Their financial value remains a wonderment.

INTRODUCTION

*Probably the hostess would not have been flattered if
a guest had intimated that the entire interest and
enjoyment of the gathering would afterwards be
summed up in a square inch, unless she had reflected
that 'tis on little things great adventures hang.*

Rev. C. S. Morton, 'A Study of the Early Postal Issues
of Mauritius', *London Philatelist*, 1924

Winter in colonial Mauritius, from July to October, was a time of
balls and dinner parties. The 'gay season' usually began with the
return of the Governor and his family to the capital, Port Louis,
from their country residence in Moka. Then Mauritian society
stirred itself, eagerly anticipating the invitations to musical soirées,
picnics, race day at the Champs de Mars, and particularly to the
balls. Rejoicing in the cooler weather, the ladies readied their
wardrobes, shaking out their best dresses and venturing into the
well-supplied merchants' shops in town.

Lady Gomm was the Governor's wife and, while her ball was
neither the first nor the last of the season, it would be the grandest.
Elizabeth Gomm was well liked in the island and a great asset to
the Governor. She was charming and knew how to entertain to
advantage. She was also, it seems, happy to promote Port Louis's
newly organized town mail delivery on this occasion, using it to
send out the invitations (it is thought) to her ball. What better way

1

to introduce the local community to the concept of the penny postal system and the first postage stamps the island had ever seen?

The brilliant orange-red stamps were a great novelty and the profile of Queen Victoria printed upon them would immediately have caught the eye against the delicate buff colour of the envelopes. A few of the older French recipients might have raised an eyebrow resignedly for a moment at the sight of the head of the British monarch, as they prised open the envelopes to discover that a grand fancy-dress affair was to be held at Government House on the evening of 30 September 1847.

It was common practice to invite a slightly greater number of guests than were expected, for it was rare that everybody accepted. Yet on that mild Thursday evening, as a steady stream of soldiers in their military best strolled up the rue de la Chaussée from the nearby barracks, guests in their carriages continued to rattle in from all directions – along the rue Moka, up the broad tree-lined sweep of the Place d'Armes, the rue du Gouvernement and rue Royale. The carriages stopped briefly to set their occupants down, a bright splash of colour against the dark stone of Government House. It had been built by the French in another era, during their time as rulers of the island, and was periodically denounced by the British with a sniff as 'one of the most unsightly, inelegant structures in the place'.

It must have been a remarkable evening, but Lady Gomm's ball is remembered chiefly for one curious reason. Of the hundreds of invitations or admission cards sent out, three of the envelopes which carried them survived. These were the earliest items bearing postage stamps to pass through the Mauritian postal system. Not one of Lady Gomm's guests could have imagined that people the world over would soon be collecting these little scraps of paper, these postage stamps, and would even pay great sums for them –

that 150 years later the stamp-bearing envelopes they had chanced to keep would be worth more than a million dollars.

There were two versions, or values, of the stamps: the ONE PENNY used by Lady Gomm, printed in orange-red, and a TWO PENCE printed in deep blue. In addition to the value and the profile of the Queen, both designs carried the inscription POST OFFICE – MAURITIUS – POSTAGE. Up to 500, perhaps, of each denomination were issued in September 1847, engraved locally by Joseph Osmond Barnard. While some have found the stamps plain, they look as if care was taken over their creation, and the few surviving specimens are jewel-like. They seem almost to glow.

Mauritius was only the fifth country in the world – and the first British colony – to produce postage stamps. This fact would be enough to ensure interest in the island's first postal issue, but the stamps' fame and fortune flowed from more than this.

For a time, like Lady Gomm's ball, the first stamps of Mauritius retreated into obscurity, unknown and undocumented, until a two pence finally surfaced on the fledgling French stamp-collecting market in 1865. From the moment of the first announcement of this discovery in the philatelic press, mystery surrounded the little blue stamp. This specimen was ever so slightly different. In most respects it was similar to known examples of what was then thought to be the first stamp of Mauritius, except that it bore the words POST OFFICE instead of the expected POST PAID. Perhaps this particular specimen was an error, that quirk of manufacture beloved of the omnivorous collector? When had it been issued and how many more might there be? (These were already important questions for those who had taken up the world's strangest new hobby.) The stamp was evidently rare, and the lucky dealer who had acquired it priced it accordingly.

A handful of the so-called 'Post Office' stamps (also known as the 'Post Office Mauritius', and popularly as 'the Blue Mauritius') came to light in the following years. By the 1890s, surrounded by an aura of mystery and rarity, with the added spice of apparent error, they had taken hold in the public imagination as the most famous and expensive of their kind. Twenty-six (or perhaps twenty-seven) specimens survived the ravages of the waste-paper basket to become, along with the dodo and its tropical beaches, one of Mauritius's main claims to fame.

There was something intriguing in the idea of these plain little labels, intrinsically valueless, passing from hand to increasingly wealthy hand. Millionaire collectors were driven to bag the stamps as if they were big game. The discovery of a 'Post Office' was long the ultimate goal of collectors at both ends of the philatelic spectrum. Soldiers, schoolboys and stamp collectors everywhere (the entire German nation even) became obsessed with uncovering the mysteries of the stamps or, better still, finding another one. There was always the chance that an overlooked specimen might turn up in any place in the world that had communicated with Mauritius in the late 1840s.

Towards the end of 1903 this happened when a civil servant in London, sorting through his papers, came across a two pence 'Post Office' in perfect condition. It had lain forgotten in his childhood collection for some forty years. The find attracted international interest and philatelists came from around the world, crowding into the auction rooms of Messrs Puttick and Simpson.

More than an hour into the auction, the restlessness which had pervaded the room stilled. A hush descended as the auctioneer took a deep breath: 'Mauritius, lot 301, 1847 two pence Post Office, unused with large margins, a fine example'. The stamp was less than an inch in height and width, and was indeed a fine example. Despite its age, the rich blue ink was still brilliant. No marks defaced the profile of the young Queen and the whole was intact, with large margins clear of the design.

The bidding started at £500 and rose rapidly, by hundreds, to twelve, thirteen, fourteen hundred. Charles J. Phillips, representing the Reichspostmuseum in Berlin, declared himself out. The penultimate bidder threw up his hands in frustration at the record bid of £1,450, and lot 301 was knocked down to an agent, Mr J. Crawford.

Shortly afterwards, in conversation with the Prince of Wales, one of the royal courtiers remarked, 'Did your Royal Highness hear that some damned fool has just paid £1,450 for a single stamp?'

'Yes,' the future George V is reputed to have replied. 'I was the damned fool.'

Long before this, a London newspaper had described the auction prices of stamps as 'a contribution to the history of human folly'. Stamp collectors were thought a little strange. Yet the hobby soon eclipsed all others as the most popularly practised global pastime.

Its charms and benefits are indeed many. Stamp collecting can be instructive – encouraging a knowledge of zoology, history, geography, art, botany, languages and politics – as well as enjoyable. Part of the appeal is visual and part historical, both in the interest in the changing design aesthetic and stamp production, and in the reflections, in these miniature portraits, of people, places and events. Through the collecting of letters and envelopes bearing stamps and other postal markings, serious hobbyists (philatelists) research the development of postal systems and practices. There are many ways the hobby can be pursued. One collector dispenses with the terms 'stamp collecting' and 'philately' when he lectures on his favourite pastime, entitling his talks simply 'curiosity'.

Then there is the thrill of the hunt – the sense of achievement when gaps are filled. The pursuit and the find drive much collecting. For philatelists particularly, a desire for complexity linked to the challenge is also important. And ever present, underlying the pursuit, is the hope of discovering buried paper treasure – the rare stamp.

Ninety years after the Prince of Wales paid a record price for a schoolboy's 'Blue Mauritius', a consortium of Mauritian companies paid $2.3 million for two specimens of the rare 'Post Office' stamps. They have become one of the most documented of all postal issues, a byword for rarity, fame, wealth and mystery. Each new discovery inspired potted biographies, attended always by rumour and speculation. The most coveted scraps of paper in existence, this is their story, an adventure that began at a fancy-dress ball during turbulent times on a tropical island, taking them from Port Louis to Bordeaux, India and Great Britain, into the hearts and imagination of collectors everywhere.

Port Louis, Mauritius, September 1847

*Notice to persons attending Balls: – Monsieur F. has
the honour to inform the public and his clients, that he
will keep his hair-dressing room open on all such
occasions in the evening.*

Nineteenth-century newspaper advertisement,
Port Louis

Late in November 1842, Sir William Gomm was en route to take up the position of sixth British Governor of Mauritius. His party caught their first sight of the magnificent volcanic mountains of Port Louis – a riveting spectacle from any angle and particularly so from the harbour. The town spread from the seaboard to the green foothills of the mountains, Pieter Both and Le Pouce (the thumb), which stood out in bold relief against the jumbled rooflines of churches, forts and other buildings.

The news of the Gomms' arrival spread quickly, as the signal passed from their ship, the *Cleopatra*, to the signal station on Long Mountain and across the valley to Port Louis. Everybody knew the significance of the Union flag hoisted on Signal Mountain, clearly visible from the streets in the town: a frigate was approaching the harbour. At three o'clock in the afternoon, according to the pages of the local bilingual newspaper, *Le Cernéen*, the guns on the frigate sounded and Sir William 'crossed the Place d'Armes between a double file of soldiers extending from the Port to Government

House, and accompanied by all the authorities of the place, amidst the discharges of Artillery from the Citadel'. It was a grand arrival. High hopes were held for Sir William's governorship, based on the reputation that preceded him from his time in colonial administration in Jamaica (1839–42), and his military service during the Peninsular Wars and at Waterloo. The colony was certainly in need of a head, since the previous Governor, Sir Lionel Smith, had died of pneumonia ten months earlier.

High hopes were also held for Lady Elizabeth Gomm – 'la moitié gracieuse' (the charming half), as Sir William liked to call his wife. The editors of *Le Cernéen* anticipated that she would 'assemble around her the distinguished persons of our society and will thus be instrumental in establishing, between all parties, those bonds of sympathy and friendship, the formation of which the apathy of our former rulers has alone delayed'. Sir William, in a diplomatic gesture towards facilitating those bonds, gave his first address to the colony's legislative assembly in French.

Colonial Mauritius was still at this time, after more than thirty years of British rule, the 'Île de France' to many of its inhabitants. A small Indian Ocean island east of Madagascar, Mauritius was uninhabited before the arrival in 1598 of the Dutch, who named their new possession after their Prince, Maurits van Nassau. In little over 100 years, they had decimated the dodo, exploited the thousand-year-old ebony forests and founded the sugar industry on the back of black slavery. The island was abandoned by them in 1710, and annexed by the French East India Company a few years later, when it was renamed Île de France. Control eventually passed to the French Crown in 1764. Little more than an outpost settlement of several hundred inhabitants during the Dutch period, the island prospered under the French. However, despite defeating the British in 1810 in a famous naval battle at Grand Port in the

Ruisseau du Pouce (Pouce stream), Port Louis, Mauritius. Le Pouce,
the thumb-shaped mountain, can be seen in the background.

island's south, the French shortly after ceded Île de France to the
British. They were militarily outnumbered, the island was suffering
from the British naval blockades and the population was largely
indifferent to who ruled them, as long as normal trade was able to
flourish again. The victorious British renamed the island Mauritius,
and agreed to respect the culture, language, legal system and
religion of the incumbent French.

Mrs Fenton, an Englishwoman who spent five months in
Mauritius in 1829, noted that 'here the time of French ascendancy is
still too recent to be forgotten'. She observed the French influence
in the local inhabitants' general courtesy, 'which French politeness
has dispersed wherever they govern'. Charles Darwin, who stopped at Mauritius during the voyage of the *Beagle* in 1836, remarked
on the French character of Port Louis as particularly noticeable, he
commented, in the shops. By that he may have meant the European
origin of the goods, and their expense, or perhaps it was the

persuasive charm of the shopkeepers, who were often French or Creole – the latter an appellation for those of French origin born in the island.

By the 1840s the racial and cultural mix of Mauritius – a blend of French, African, Indian and Chinese, with a hint of British – was firmly established. Mauritius was a veritable Babel, whose different races were evident to the visitor disembarking at the Port Louis docks. Alongside a young man of French origin in the latest Parisian fashion walked a shopkeeper wearing the loose cotton frock and trousers of China. Beside him, hailing from Madagascar, was a man 'bare-headed, the hair twisted and worked into snake-looking points, which stick out and leave a very Medusa-like appearance'. And over there from Bengal, one of the recent immigrants wearing a cast-off soldier's coat and a cloth tied around his middle.

When the British took possession of Mauritius in 1810 the island's population consisted of approximately 7,000 people of European origin, 8,000 'free coloureds' and 63,000 slaves. Slavery was abolished in 1835 and replaced by an apprenticeship system. This reluctant workforce was supplemented by indentured labourers from India. But amid concerns that this was just another form of slavery, Indian immigration was suspended in 1839. The issue was one of the most pressing Gomm had to contend with on his arrival in the colony, for the labour market was critical to the island's export economy, and the established plantocracy – the Franco-Mauritian owners of the sugar plantations – were powerful. Indian immigration resumed under Gomm, and there was a mass influx of labourers – more than 33,000 men in 1843 alone. By 1847 the number of indentured labourers had outstripped the number of ex-slaves working as apprentices, but the Mauritian planters continued to press for increases in immigration. Gomm, however, correctly interpreted these urgings as evidence of the planters' desire to keep the upper hand in wage-bargaining, and found himself in great conflict with them.

These proved to be difficult years for Gomm and Mauritius, marked by financial crises caused by the labour problem, over-trading and an excess of imports – the ultimate (and perhaps most useless) being, in 1847, the importation of a rhinoceros. The Governor was unpopular in certain quarters. It was felt that a military governor would never be able to understand the best interests of a colony made up of merchants and planters. When the Gomms gave a levee to celebrate Queen Victoria's birthday in May of that year it was, noted local newspaper *Le Mauricien*, as in other years of late, badly attended.

The promulgation of an Order in Council to replace French with English as the official language of the courts in July 1847 was far removed from the conciliatory gesture of Gomm's maiden address. Due to come into effect on the 15th, it was noted in *Le Cernéen* of 8 July that of the 150,000 souls in Mauritius (not including those of English origin) only around 500 people knew the English language. It so happened that a young French lawyer, Célicourt Antelme, was presenting a case in Port Louis on the 14th and he prolonged the hearing until midnight, when he dramatically paused – it is said – and switched from French to English. But perhaps it is wise to remember of this anecdote that in Mauritian history (in the words of local historians) it is 'common knowledge', one of those good stories where fact and mythology are equally at home. There is a small paragraph in *Le Cernéen* of 17 July noting that Monsieur Antelme, in the Court of Assizes on the evening of the 15th (not the 14th), 'finished an eloquent plea with a touching goodbye to the French language, which was greeted by such loud and prolonged applause that the Chief Judge and the Substitute Procureur-General had much trouble in re-establishing silence.

Never, in the memory of the oldest members of the staff, had the crowd displayed such enthusiasm.' Each version of Antelme's story, whichever day the incident took place, has something to recommend it in the way of drama.

While the lawyer was inspiring the assembled crowd with his touching *adieu* to the French language, the second of the season's winter assemblies was getting under way. These were a series of seven subscription balls, held on the second Thursday of every month of the Mauritian winter, beginning in July. Similarly styled to the Almack's balls in London, they were managed by 'patronesses' (the Mesdames Stavely, Dick, D'Epinay, de Robillard and Lloyd) and 'commissaires' (the Messieurs Rawson, Barclay, Durant St André, Rudelle and Fraser). The Gomms were sure to have attended the winter assemblies, held at Port Louis's Masonic lodge – the Loge de la Triple Espérance – and undoubtedly they attended on the 15th.

Alas, on this occasion the Loge de la Triple Espérance was transformed into the Loge de la *Triste* Espérance. Although both the French and the British communities were well represented on the assembly's organizing committee, some of the French residents of the island chose not to attend the ball as a protest at its timing, coinciding as it did with the day deemed the 'death' of the French language in Mauritius. Four young men ranged themselves at the door of the lodge in a picket (perhaps inspired by Antelme's oration) and insulted those members of the French community who had put 'rejoicings and pleasure' above a proper regard for the gravity of the day. Their insults consisted of little more than groaning and hissing, and were more a case of bad manners than anything else (according to an editorial in *Le Mauricien* a week later). But the incident escalated when, in an overreaction by the government, the men were arrested and thrown into prison. They were soon set free but were then rearrested, and much bickering between the families of the prisoners and the magistrates ensued to secure their liberty again.

Sir William Gomm's growing unpopularity (with the French at least) is often advanced as the reason behind his wife's giving her famous ball of 30 September. Easing the tensions between the British and the French communities may well have been a motivating factor. However, poor Lady Gomm is popularly believed to have also been responsible for the infelicitous entertainment of 15 July, the aftermath of which long troubled the government. But it is evident from notices in *Le Cernéen* that she was not one of the earlier ball's patronesses. The July ball was a regular event, but in this case unfortunately timed, that was all. Five more assemblies would follow before Lady Gomm's famous fancy-dress ball, and the winter of 1847 was remembered – in British circles at least – as most enjoyable. Sir John Ewart, then a young soldier in the 35th Royal Sussex Regiment, recalled in his memoirs Lady Gomm's 'at

A version of Nash's lithograph of Lady Gomm's ball, along with a ball envelope, appeared together in 1978 on a Mauritian postage stamp commemorating the famous event and the issuing of the 'Post Office' stamps.

homes', the *jeunes gens* balls, the winter assemblies, two delightful balls given by a Frenchman named Vigoureux, the opera, a circus, picnics and garrison theatricals. Soldiering in Mauritius was not, it seemed, a particularly onerous duty.

Ewart remembered Lady Gomm's fancy-dress ball as a grand occasion. The large ballroom was decadently lit by the lamps, nearly 200 in number, which clustered about the ceiling. It seemed that the lights themselves were in costume and vying for attention as the best dressed. Monsieur Fouqueraux, known as the host of some of the best balls in the island and commonly referred to as 'Le Prince Charmant', would probably have been in attendance, nodding approval at the exhilarating scene before his eyes. The rich brocades of the dowagers' dresses reflected the mellow glow of the lamps, mingling with the younger ladies' silks, tulles and laces, while the dress swords of the soldiers were as dazzling as the jewellery and as shiny as the polished wooden floor. Recalling the ball in later years, Ewart remarked that 'for some weeks everybody was busy preparing for it… the dresses being magnificent, and the characters admirably sustained'. Guests who cared to dress according to the fancy theme chose from two groups of characters, the first from Walter Scott's *Ivanhoe* and the other from Byron's historical tragedy *Marino Faliero, Doge of Venice.* 'They marched into the room under a flourish of trumpets, presenting a most striking appearance.' Ewart himself wore a kilt, as he did at a ball held by one Colonel Blanchard soon afterwards. On that score Lady Gomm's ball triumphed too. The Colonel's rooms, unlike those at Government House, swarmed with mosquitoes, and poor Ewart, in his kilt, was 'exposed in a most disagreeable manner to the attacks of these voracious insects'.

Published in 1881, Ewart's memoirs – *The Story of a Soldier's Life; or Peace, War, and Mutiny* – would have been written up from diaries and from letters home, treasured and saved. Perhaps the soldier also had a copy – tucked away in a scrapbook, or fading in a frame somewhere – of the oft-reproduced image of the guests in fancy costume at Lady Gomm's ball, for he was able to describe it accurately thus: 'Nash, a very clever artist residing at Mauritius, made a capital sketch of these two groups, which was afterwards published.' And yet, his sporting and social life in Port Louis so well remembered, Ewart made no mention in his memoirs of Lady Gomm's stamped envelopes.

When a few of the ball envelopes finally surfaced, they were empty. How then was the connection between the ball and the birth of the stamps made? The popular version of the story holds that the envelopes contained invitations, but this is unlikely. According to the conventions of the day, Lady Gomm would have sent out her invitations at least three weeks, and certainly no later than a fortnight, in advance. Two of the envelopes later discovered bore the postmark 21 SEPTEMBER 1847 – less than ten days before the ball. Given Ewart's comment about everybody preparing for weeks beforehand, it is more likely that the famous 'Post Office' ball envelopes contained cards of admission, to be submitted by guests on the night at Government House. That the ball and the first use of postage stamps in Mauritius are related is an accepted connection in the island: a version of Nash's ball engraving and a one penny 'Post Office' appeared together in 1978 on a Mauritian postage stamp commemorating Lady Gomm's 1847 ball and her famous 'Post Office'-bearing envelopes. Yet there is nothing in the official post office archives and not a mention in either of the island's newspapers at the time to connect them. Indeed, there was no mention of the stamps in the press at all.

MESSAGE IN A BOTTLE

*Mauritius believed in having a new postal ordinance
about every year (on the same principle as a
horticulturist bedding out tulips) until they
discovered which kind did best on their own
particular soil, and what suited the public.*

Rev. C. S. Morton, 'A Study of the Early Postal Issues
of Mauritius', *London Philatelist*, 1924

In the early 1600s, Mauritius was still plentiful with giant tortoises
and the strange, fat, flightless dodos. The island provided food,
fresh water and safe harbour to the ships that plied the trading
routes from Europe around the Cape of Good Hope to the east. It
also provided news and information. On the Île aux Tonneliers, an
islet near the entrance to the main harbour on the island's west
coast (the future Port Louis), ships' crews deposited letters and
instructions in upturned bottles left hanging from trees, in the
hopes that others would collect and carry their mail to its intended
destination. Pieter Willemsz Verhoeff found a group of such letters
left by Dutch sailors at Mauritius during his expeditions of 1607–12.
Preserved in the archives of the Amsterdam chamber of the
Vereenigde Oost-Indische Compagnie (United East India Company), they are some of the earliest-known letters written from the
island.

This was the reality of communication in a maritime world. The carriage of mail depended upon the vagaries of shipping. There were no regular schedules and no guarantees that, once consigned to a ship, mail – or even the ship – would arrive intact. Emanuell Altham wrote at least two letters from the ship *Hopewell*, anchored in the waters off Mauritius in June 1628, to his brother in England. Similar in content, both letters noted that a certain Mr Perce would deliver up a jar of ginger, some beads and a live dodo to Altham senior. The duplication was undoubtedly an insurance against one of the letters going astray and they had probably been sent via different ships (a common practice that continued well into the nineteenth century). Both of Altham's letters arrived, surviving for a time in the family archives, but of Mr Perce and his charges, nothing more is known.

It wasn't until 1772, when Mauritius was in French possession, that an official postal service within the island was established. There had been an inland postal service under the French, but it had been tied to the delivery of the Port Louis newspaper, and only those who subscribed to the newspaper received their mail in addition for free. Through a combination of decentralization and the subsequent British blockade of Mauritius during the Napoleonic Wars, a general deterioration of all mail services to and within the island followed. The inland service fell into disuse and it was not revived by the British until 1834.

Before the advent of regular government-run mail services in 1848, outgoing mail relied on mercantile shipping interests. Masters of vessels were obliged by government ordinance to deliver up post office mail, packets, letters and newspapers to the postmaster within twenty-four hours of anchoring in the colony, or face a fine and imprisonment. Under British rule, all masters of British vessels about to proceed to sea were to give the postmaster at least twenty-four hours' notice of sailing dates and destinations, so these could be advertised and the mail made up. Missing the mail was a serious occurrence, obliging the postmaster to report to the Colonial Secretary, as in May 1847, when the mail came down to the HMS *Rattlesnake* too late, and part of the mail for Sydney was missed.

James Stuart Brownrigg had been Colonial Postmaster in Mauritius since 1843. It was the Irishman's first appointment under the colonial Mauritian government. When he had originally taken charge, it was, he later recalled, a post office in name only. With 'an indefatigability and zeal but few in a tropical climate would have done', Brownrigg strove to raise the department 'into one of utility to the public'.

By 1847, during what would later be recognized as a pivotal year of postal reform, the island's first postage stamps were issued. Brownrigg was supported by six clerks. There were also deputy postmasters located around the island, along with letter carriers, convict couriers and a few messengers. Most of the employees had been newly appointed in June of that year. Mail delivery was seen as a suitable alternative for those convicts unfit for hard labour and most of the post office's courier work was undertaken by convicts of Indian origin. While the legwork was done by Indians – brought in small numbers to Mauritius as convicts, servants and labourers from the mid-eighteenth century, well before the waves of Indian immigrant labour began in the 1830s – most of the clerks employed during the 1840s were of Franco-Mauritian or British extraction. However, there were two clerks born in Madras and the distinctively named 'Trusty Messenger' Grain d'Or (Grain of Gold) was an ex-government slave far from his homeland of Mozambique.

Brownrigg and his clerks worked a long day and a full week. Despite the wide streets of Port Louis and its location right on the harbour, the city absorbed the heat of the tropical days and held on

'Mrs Lloyd's postman, Mauritius'.

to it fiercely. Understandably, then, the post office day began in the cool of morning at 7 a.m., Monday to Saturday, but it was a long day, dealing with letters, newspapers and parcels for distribution, and the clarks could expect to finish at 5 p.m. in winter and 6 p.m. in summer. Sundays brought a little respite, the opening hours being from 11 a.m. to 3 p.m.

Close to the harbour's main landing place at the Place d'Armes, Port Louis's post office was situated in a rented building on the corner of rue Farquhar, a narrow street which ran directly into the lively bazaar, and had the advantage of proximity to Government House and other public buildings. Until a purpose-built post office was erected in the 1860s down at the harbour, the post office premises were the bane of the successive postmasters' lives. They were too hot and too small – 'Noxious effluvia coming from passages and stores on either side is constantly so intolerable as to be prejudicial to health,' wrote Brownrigg in 1849. On the day after Lady Gomm's fancy-dress ball in 1847, when the postmaster might happily have been reflecting on the successful introduction of postage stamps and the penny post to the town, he was writing an urgent request to the Colonial Secretary for a carpenter to do

View of warehouses and the customhouse, Port Louis, c.1847. The post office was not so far from here, and all buildings, except the customhouse, still stand today.

something to his office to stop mice eating the mail. All the clerks would eventually have special hand stamps on their desks to cover such miserable eventualities as EATEN BY RAT or MISSENT TO MAURITIUS.

And yet, despite the heat, the clerks worked in constant thrall to the myriad people who streamed through their doors – a black maid with coloured kerchief on her head, a near-naked Indian, soldiers in military dress and the sailors, as colourful as the flags on the ships in the nearby harbour. There were ships from all nations, for Mauritius by this time was an important stopping point on the routes between Britain and Europe and the Cape, India, Australia and New Zealand.

The stifling post office gave directly on to the Place d'Armes, the wide avenue which ran from Government House down to the landing place at the harbour. It was a beautiful walk at the height of the day, shaded on either side by large banyan trees and the flamboyant trees of Madagascar, with their vivid scarlet flowers and dark green foliage. Most of the merchant shops and places of business were to be found here, in the streets surrounding Government House and the Company's Gardens nearby. Commission agents, ship chandlers and general agents lined the rue de la Chausée and its continuation, rue Royale, and the streets which clamoured around the Place d'Armes. Charles Pridham, in his historical account of Mauritius in the late 1840s, wrote of the 'gay display of jewellers', cutlers' and milliners' shops', and noted the 'close proximity of the ships to the busy town', which gave 'a continued life to the scene'.

There was always something to see at the harbour, and if it happened that a new arrival was the monthly mail ship (or mail packet, as it was called) crowds soon gathered at the landing place. The arrival of the mail packet was always eagerly anticipated, as Nicolas Pike noted, writing in the 1860s:

… only those who have lived in the Colonies can realise the excitement of this one day. Telescopes are incessantly levelled at the signal mountains in city and country; and when the double balls are seen at the top of the signal mast, the Place d'Armes, quays and docks are gradually thronged. As soon as the steamer anchors, boats innumerable put off up the harbour, and only wait the signal that she has received pratique (that is, shown a good bill of health), when her decks are at once crowded to get the first item of news, and welcome the passengers. A rise or fall in sugar, war or peace news, flies like magic to the shore and spreads through the city. Then the tedious waiting for letters. Supposing the mail arrives early morning, it will be at least two or three o'clock before any letters are delivered, save Government despatches.

Mail day was of singular importance in the colony, and there were strict rules and regulations laid down in government ordinances which underlined this. Occasionally the arrival of a mail packet was signalled before the usual opening hours, requiring the postmaster and his clerks to 'repair immediately to the Post Office, and the delivery of letters, newspapers and parcels… commenced as soon as practicable'. If the delivery of letters received from the regular mail packet was begun before noon it would be continued until 6 p.m. If the delivery commenced after noon it was continued until 9 p.m. and resumed by 7 a.m. the following morning if not completed.

In 1828 Governor Cole had approved a new ordinance for naming (and renaming) the streets of Port Louis and its suburbs, and this served to complicate mail deliveries, even twenty years later. Only three streets retained their original names, including the Place d'Armes, the focal point of the town. Of the 194 street names listed in the ordinance, 50 per cent were completely new; the rest were anglicized forms of the French names (Gaiety Street for rue de la Gaité) or replacements of French names with those deemed more appropriate for a colonial English town – Rempart for Bonaparte, St George for Marengo and Wellington for Champ de Lort. Prosaic English names proliferated, such as Angle, Cork, Cotton, Milk and Pond streets (rue Descartes became Crooked Lane), while other names connected with the colony, such as Madras, Mosque, Pagoda, Nabob's and Ghoun streets, began to appear. Postmaster Brownrigg was again busy with his pen in September 1847, submitting to the Colonial Secretary the 'expediency of the houses in the town being correctly numbered to facilitate the delivery of letters'.

Then there was the issue of the dark streets during late deliveries (street lighting being barely adequate after dusk). Most likely on these days the light of the stars and the moon guided the letter carriers' footsteps. At 8 p.m. the military fired the evening gun, and 'its reverberations, after being caught up and repeated by the mountains behind', rolled like thunder over the town's rooftops. Dogs barked, donkeys brayed and everyone, it seemed, at least in the Anglo-Saxon part of town, was a pianist. For many years after these sounds had been replaced by others, Port Louis was remembered for 'the number of pianos heard in every street in an evening, from the Erard's grand and semi-grand to the humblest cottage instrument'.

The sound of these domestic pianos may have offered a comforting counterbalance to the Madagascar fir trees, which seemed to send forth a moaning sound when the wind was up. During daylight hours this was not unpleasant to the ear but, after the evening gun had signalled the day's end, pity the poor letter carrier as he neared the end of his round in the outer reaches of the town.

There is a long-held belief in the island that at night the trees harbour the dead, and as you pass beneath their branches a spirit might escape its shelter and begin to follow you home. The letter carriers would hurry their footsteps as the sound of the gun died away, and when they reached their own front doors, it was wise to turn and cross the threshold backwards, ensuring that the spirits didn't follow them in.

It was the custom in Mauritius, as it had long been elsewhere, to collect the fee for postage not from the sender but from the recipient upon delivery. Mail was delivered to the outlying districts by couriers. The various deputy postmasters dotted about the country were often shopkeepers and proprietors of businesses, while at Curepipe and Ville Bague the local overseers of convicts acted in this role. It was not an onerous task, for Mr Baird of Ville Bague received only seventeen private letters in the first half of 1848, dispatching a mere twenty-two.

For the most part, people called at the post office to collect their mail. They bustled into the little ground-floor office on the Place d'Armes and jostled for space at the small aperture through which letters were handed out. In 1849 *Le Mauricien* deplored the 'general rush to an opening of three inches wide' and wondered at the logic of such a system. Why not have five or six separate windows for deliveries arranged in alphabetical order by name? In response to this criticism a correspondent, signing himself 'Bayonet', proposed a better solution. On overland mail delivery days, he recommended, give the postmaster and his clerks the day off and a few intelligent corporals from the military would soon sort things out.

The situation continued to be lamented in the pages of *Le Cernéen* in 1852:

In a small shop where they sold salt fish, or in the shop of a shoemaker, a box is placed each day containing the letters received from Port Louis. When the box is emptied, its contents remain in the drawer... one, two, three, six months or even more, at the end of which time the whole is sent back to town if no one claims them. The papers go from hand to hand in the shop, and the real owner is indeed lucky if he ever finds an opportunity of claiming his property.

The frustration of the system was evident in the coloured hand stamps that accumulated on the bundles of lonely letters. *Le Cernéen* also noted:

We have traced by the aid of postmarks a long journey taken by a letter from Paris, addressed to a person in Mauritius. It was at sea two and a half months, arrived at Grand Port, returned to Port Louis, forwarded to Plaines Wilhems, carried back to town, taken on to Black River, and finally, after six months, its holiday ended, a lady whose name and position is known to all, except the post office, received it.

Upon receiving their mail, the newspaper remarked (tongue-in-cheek, one hopes) 'our doctors... called on their patients only to find them cured – or dead'.

The delay in communications with London due to the reliance on private shipping preyed on Governor Sir William Gomm's mind. This was particularly the case in the mid 1840s, when he was trying to contend with the financial crises caused by the Sugar Duties Bill. His own communications took several months to reach the decision-makers back home, where he was constantly being undermined by local lobbyists. With fine understanding, he wrote of these frustrations after reading of Stringfellow and Hensen's 'Aerial Steam Carriage', patented in 1842: 'The flying carriages will set all this to right, but I fear the art will not progress with sufficient rapidity to meet our time.' Gomm was right and the islanders would have 100 years to wait before the first regular air service to Mauritius. Wisely, he took matters into his own hands. The Governor would institute a government-run packet service in 1848, but not before he set about reforming the inland postal system and a town delivery service.

Both the Port Louis newspapers were particularly fond in these years of baiting the postmaster: 'Mr Brownrigg is responsible to the public for the irregularities of his office and we trust by continually pointing them out we shall succeed in obtaining a remedy.' In July 1847 *Le Cernéen* proclaimed, 'The Public complain of the Post, and the Post complain of the Public, and there is reason on both sides.' From the post office's point of view, under the old system it was irksome and uneconomical that many people chose not to receive their mail, reluctant to part with their pennies – 'a bad bargain' – if the sender was unknown to them. The storage capacity of the post office was stretched to the limit, blocked up with these 'worthless' letters, and 'letters written which have no object beyond perplexing the persons whose names they bear'. *Le Mauricien* in the same month deplored a spate of 'anonymous letters containing calumnies and scandals' and 'a great want of attention to the addresses of letters'. They cited an example of the latter: a letter posted in Port Louis in December 1846, postmarked February 1847, was finally received in July 1847 by the addressee, a Mauritian planter residing outside the capital; he paid eight pence for the privilege (six pence being the ship letter rate, plus two pence for the inland delivery, the letter, apparently having detoured via England). Another of the old system's defects was that anybody, regardless of whether they had title to them, could collect and pay for letters at the post office, resulting in a good deal of private information becoming generally known around the town. It was hoped that the innovation of pre-payment would solve some of these problems.

Late in 1846 a government ordinance providing for the conveyance and postage of letters had declared the tariff for local mail delivery within the capital at one penny and two pence for country deliveries. It was decreed that letters 'having a stamp or stamps affixed thereto... such stamps being provided by the Government... shall pass free of postage'. This was England's penny post, transplanted to Port Louis, and the birth of the first postage stamps of any British colony.

The charge of creating the stamps was given to Joseph Osmond Barnard, a local described as a watchmaker, jeweller, engraver, printer and miniature painter. Born in Portsmouth, England, Barnard had arrived in Mauritius in December 1838 aged twenty-three and a stowaway. He determined to improve his financial situation and pursue the profession of engraver. Whatever artistic leanings he possessed were sublimated in practical output and his daily living was earned through the production of business stationery, visiting cards, advertisements and the engraving of wedding rings. He is known to have engraved a view of Port Louis's Grand Hôtel d'Europe, but left no more substantial testament to his island life. Why, then, was Barnard chosen to engrave the first stamps of Mauritius? Perhaps it was his skill as a miniature painter – when he first advertised his services in March 1839, he counted miniature painting as one of his accomplishments. Or perhaps it was in recognition of the fact that postage stamps were as throwaway as the cards and stationery he produced.

Little is known about the 'Post Office' commission. The only record that exists is Barnard's handwritten estimate of November 1846 for producing 1,000 letter labels (postage stamps) in one penny and two pence values, along with a variety of hand stamps for cancelling the mail: PAID, FREE, TOO LATE and PENNY POST.

It is unlikely that Barnard was left to his own devices on the question of the stamps' design. He may have been instructed verbally or even given a copy of England's first stamp, the Penny Black, as a guide. The *Philatelic Record* would later conclude in the first full-length account of 'The Stamps of Mauritius' (1880) that 'the Mauritius stamps were no doubt copied from those in use in England at the time, and, if the side labels of the former were removed, they would be rude imitations of the latter'. The face and throat of Queen Victoria's profile were described as 'being shaded with rows of small dots, producing an effect somewhat similar to that caused by a severe attack of smallpox; the back of the neck is shaded with coarse lines'. Worse crimes of engraving were perpetrated against Queen Victoria's profile in succeeding Mauritian stamp issues, later designs by Barnard included. ('Mr. Barnard did not add a knowledge of dentistry to his other accomplishments, or he would not have omitted to draw Her Majesty's teeth!' the author of 'The Stamps of Mauritius' noted of one of the subsequent 'Post Paid' specimens.)

Around 500 of each value of the 'Post Office' stamps are thought to have been printed by Barnard in September 1847. Such a small number meant that the supply was quickly swallowed up. By June 1848, less than a year after their issue, Barnard had engraved new versions of the stamps as a series of twelve (in four rows of three stamps) for each value. These new stamps were similar to the design of the 'Post Office' issue, except that the words POST PAID had replaced POST OFFICE.

This change in wording would later form the basis of much

speculation. Was the 'Post Office' stamp an essay (in philatelic parlance) – a trial design, never officially issued? Or could the word OFFICE on the 'Post Office' stamps be a mistake? Barnard, for example, had made a slight slip with the engraving tool in one of the twelve specimens on the later two pence 'Post Paid' plate: the C in PENCE inadvertently becoming an O. Thus the famous PENOE error was born, and became a highly sought-after philatelic rarity, now worth tens of thousands of dollars. Such errors were understandable on so-called primitive stamps that were produced without the aid of mechanical process, where each stamp on the plate was hand-engraved. And they were also accepted: the stamps issued from Barnard's engravings for the 'Post Paid', PENOE error included, remained in use for around ten years.

For later collectors the rarity of the 'Post Office' stamps was heightened by the mystery of their discontinuation. That the word 'Office' was shortly after replaced with 'Paid' provided the opportunity for speculation along the romantic lines of Mauritian author Alfred de Pitray, who stated in 1975, 'Find the woman if you want... to know the truth.' He and others have imagined that it was Lady Gomm's desire to have those stamps for the 'invitations' to her ball, apparently already delayed in their delivery, which caused the Governor to allow the 'error' to pass. But given the length of time the PENOE error was in circulation, it seems unlikely that the 'Post Office' issue was replaced so quickly merely because it was born in error. There must have been another reason.

Some of the early hand-struck postal markings that preceded the use of postage stamps did incorporate the phrase 'Post Office'. At least six versions of these hand stamps have been recorded in use in Mauritius in the early period of British rule. These were the postal marks applied with hand stamps (engraved in reverse in metal, later in rubber) which the clerks used to cancel the mail and indicate its status: POST PAID PORT LOUIS, POST FREE PORT LOUIS, PORT LOUIS UNPAID, SHIP LETTER and – POST OFFICE MAURITIUS. The new postage stamps were also referred to colloquially and in government records as 'post office stamps' to distinguish them from the government revenue stamps.

Of the handful of stamps which preceded the 'Post Office Mauritius' into being, the world's first stamp, the famed Penny Black, bore only the words 'Postage' and 'One Penny' in addition to the Queen's profile (the sovereign's head, then as now, was thought sufficient to identify the issuing country). Brazil's stamps (1843) bore only the values. The Swiss stamps of Zurich, Geneva and Basle (1843–5) bore a variety of values, arms and the name of the canton, and the United States' first general issues (1847) bore values and the initials US, along with the words 'Post Office'. The art of stamp design was young and there were no rules.

The 'Post Office' stamps quickly faded from local memory, and most of the Port Louis locals, if they thought about these matters at all, probably believed that the 'Post Paid' stamps were the earliest postage stamps produced in the island. But perhaps a few specimens of the 'Post Office' issue were overlooked in their owners' writing desks; a pair might have been kept, unused, as novelties; or, affixed to envelopes and letter sheets, they were carefully or carelessly retained as mementoes.

To Philatelic Facts, Which Are Usually Dry

*Philately is the collection and study of any one or
more countries or issues whereby definite conclusions
are arrived at, in spite of the absence of official
records.*

A. Crippa, 'Stamp Collecting and Philately',
Stamp Collecting, 1924

An advertisement appeared in *The Times* of London in 1841 confirming that the hobby of stamp collecting, in one form at least, was not long in following the world's first postage stamps into being. Finding 16,000 used stamps insufficient to cover the walls of her dressing room, a much-quoted young lady wondered whether 'any good-natured persons who may have these (otherwise useless) little articles at their disposal, would assist her whimsical project'.

Women, it seems, were the earliest stamp collectors, using them to decorate walls, ceilings and furniture. In 1842 *Punch* magazine quipped that the ladies of England 'betray more anxiety to treasure up Queen's Heads than King Henry VIII did to get rid of them'. A number of British gentlemen claimed to have begun collecting stamps for reasons other than decorative during the 1850s. Almost from the day literature sprang up in support of the hobby, the claim to have been first was regularly debated.

By 1860 people of all ages, ranks and genders were to be found exchanging stamps, albums in hand, down Birchin Lane near London Bridge. The barterers of Birchin Lane attracted police attention. Surely such a peculiar mix of people swapping worthless scraps of paper down a back alley suggested involvement in something spurious or, at the very least, was evidence of alarming signs of mania? Indeed, on the Continent, stamp-collecting enthusiasts were described as timbromaniacs, from the French word *timbro-manie*, meaning a mania for stamps. Finding *timbromanie* a somewhat pejorative term, George Herpin, a French collector, coined the word 'philately' around 1862. Herpin put two Greek words together (*philos* + *atelia*) which combined meant a love of not being taxed, a reference to the innovation of pre-payment.

To its early practitioners the word philately had 'the double charm of being very euphonious as well as slightly incomprehensible to all but the learned', as the editors of the *Philatelist* put it in 1866. Study, classification and publication were the distinguishing characteristics of philately and philatelists over more amateur versions of stamp collecting and stamp collectors. Philately as a science – practised in a scientific spirit of research and understanding – originated in Paris, and was often referred to as the French school of stamp collecting. It went beyond the basic attractions of the hobby – the appeal of colour, design and shape, and the desire for completion – to the researching and documenting of all aspects of the stamp, including date of first issue, make up of the sheet, aspects of the production process, watermarks on the paper and the measuring of perforations. Based on their own collections and consultation of their fellow collectors' accumulations, the fledgling philatelists quickly poured the results of their researches into the first philatelic journals in the early 1860s.

By this time some seventy countries were issuing postage

stamps, but the number of stamps produced remained a matter for interested amateur speculation. The first stamp catalogue appeared in France in 1861 – Alfred Potiquet's *Catalogue des Timbres-Poste Crées dans les Divers Etats du Globe*, listing about 1,080 stamps. Yet collectors often came across stamps unknown to the compilers of those works and of uncertain authenticity. Postal authorities were often unable to answer with any certainty the questions stamp collectors and the new breed of 1860s philatelist began to pester them with. Philatelic facts had to be gleaned from the stamps themselves.

If the stamps had not been snipped or torn from their letters, envelopes and parcels, then it was possible to learn much from the postal cancellations and other markings about routes and rates, and in particular the dates of use. But often only the stamps were saved, the letters and envelopes discarded. The fragment of a cancellation – '... ct 185...' – on the edge of a stamp might be all that remained to indicate its period of use and its genuineness.

Philatelists found themselves piecing together their chronologies from chance remains, like archaeologists. Englishman Frederick Booty reportedly worked from a hoard of half a million stamps to produce the first illustrated stamp catalogue in 1862, the quaint and lovingly hand-drawn *The Stamp Collectors Guide: Being a List of English and Foreign Postage Stamps with 200 Fac-simile Drawings*. Booty classified and sorted until by dint of numbers he listed as much as it was reasonably possible to know about the number of stamps that had been issued since 1840 and the countries issuing them. He recorded the bare details and, in some cases better than others, produced sketches of some of the stamps. In the case of Mauritius, relatively few of the island's stamps appear to have found their way into British and European collections.

Although there had been seven separate stamp issues in

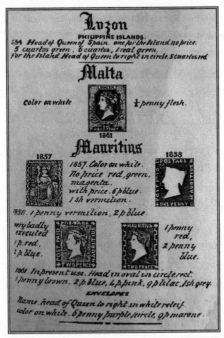

Mauritius page in Frederick Booty's *The Stamp Collectors Guide*, 1862.

Mauritius by the time of Booty's 1862 catalogue, nobody – collectors, cataloguers, even the postal authorities in the island itself – had recorded this. Most of these early stamps of Mauritius became popularly known by the names of their engravers. The 'Post Office' (1847) and the first 'Post Paid' (1848) were followed by the Lapirot, Sherwin and Dardenne issues, all locally engraved in 1859, and then the so-called Britannias (1858–62) – named after the figure of Britannia depicted on them – and De La Rues (1860–82). The latter two stamps had been produced in England and sent out to Mauritius.

The earliest date Booty assigned to a Mauritius stamp was 1856. Next he illustrated a 'Britannia', giving the date 1857. Then came a poor approximation of Barnard's one penny 'Post Paid' thought to date from 1858. Next in the chronology came, in Booty's opinion, a 'very badly executed' stamp, and indeed it was. The author was unable to date it, but the stamp he illustrated is identifiable as the charmless 'Lapirot' issue of 1859, in which Queen Victoria's head was likened by some to a monkey's. Lastly, Booty illustrated the 'Dardenne' issue, again unable to date it, and noted the De La Rues as the stamps currently in use. Mauritius was a jumble, the result undoubtedly of Booty lacking dated specimens to work from, and a paucity of Mauritius specimens generally. There is no evidence that Booty found a 'Post Office' among his great accumulation of stamps.

It was George Herpin, the Frenchman who had coined the term philately, who first remarked upon a 'Post Office' and its curious wording a few years later. Writing on the stamps of Mauritius in *Le Collectionneur de Timbres-Poste* of Paris in March 1865, Herpin considered the island's first issue to be the finer of the 'Post Paid', dating it to 1851. He also named Barnard as the engraver. The Frenchman thought the second issue of Mauritius was the coarser version of the 'Post Paid' (Sherwin's), dating it to 1852.

But then he noted a curiosity. 'Incontestably the most interesting variety,' Herpin stated in relation to this supposed second issue, was a two pence specimen in which the words 'Post Office' appeared in place of 'Post Paid'. Although he had not himself seen an example, Herpin had been assured of its veracity by a fellow philatelist in whom he had the greatest confidence. He even provided an illustration, cobbled together with the words 'Post Office' superimposed on to a coarse Sherwin 'Post Paid'. By 'variety', Herpin meant a specimen with an error. He believed the word 'Office' had probably been mistakenly engraved on one of the twelve individual designs (types) thought to make up the 'Post

Paid' plate. Other examples of mistakes like this were known: a 1 real stamp of the Philippines bore the word 'corros' instead of 'correos'. But how, Herpin wondered, could the substitution of a whole word – Office – have passed unnoticed by the Mauritius postmaster?

A few months later, in May 1865, the rival journal *Le Timbre-Poste* published a piece that was sceptical about the existence of such a variety. The editors of *Le Timbre-Poste* would believe it only when they themselves, Herpin 'or any other avowedly competent and authoritative person' had seen it with their own eyes. They consigned the 'Post Office Mauritius' to the 'too fertile imagination of fanciful collectors'.

Although the article in *Le Timbre-Poste* was unsigned, the writer was probably the Belgian dealer Jean-Baptiste Moens (the publisher of the journal), his brother-in-law Louis Hanciau or another contributor, 'Dr Magnus' (the pen-name of one Jacques Amable Legrand), any one of whom could have penned the words.

Jean-Baptiste Philippe Constant Moens (1833–1908) and the firm he established in Brussels were much esteemed in the world of philately. Obituary writers recognized him as the world's first dealer in stamps. He began to collect aged fifteen and was selling stamps from his small book business four years later. He joined the ranks of philatelic authors with the publication of a guide for collectors in 1862. All that is known of the discovery of the first specimens of the 'Post Office' issue, indeed of much of the history of the handful of those stamps eventually found, came from his pen in the late 1890s.

With a strong sense of public service, Moens garnered many honours and conducted his business along the same honourable lines – the word 'honour', and its variables, littered the public descriptions of the man and his business. Most astutely, the dealer, 'earnest in work, merry in relaxation', had purchased unused blocks of newly issued stamps from other continental countries to meet an ever increasing demand from collectors. Moens's purchases were credited with almost single-handedly guaranteeing the survival, in unused condition, of many stamps from the 1850s and 1860s. He was particularly adept at sniffing out a good stamp. Louis Hanciau recalled how Moens had once acquired a fine block of the first issue of the colony of New South Wales – the delightful one penny 1850, from the series known as the 'Sydney Views'. They had been 'found among the papers of an Australian who had died in a Brussels hospital'.

Moens's colleague Jacques Amable Legrand (1820–1912) was a French physician who found himself a philatelist by default. Like fathers before him and many to come, he had taken up a hobby to encourage his young son in the pursuit, only to find that his own passion surpassed and long outlasted that of the intended beneficiary. Legrand began collecting seriously around 1861–2, in his early forties. His abilities in the philatelic arena first became apparent in 1865, when he published an article on watermarks, followed a year later by his invention of the perforation gauge – a metric rule for measuring the space between the perforations on stamps – a version of which is still in use. (The number of perforations on stamps can differ from issue to issue and printing to printing. Establishing these can help to date a stamp or even to detect forgeries. As one philatelist has noted of the fascination with perforation, 'It is the nature of philately and philatelists, where any different aspect of a stamp, however small but repeated, increases and adds to the challenge of the chase.') Possessing a magnificent pair of sideburns to match the allusion to greatness, 'Dr Magnus' wrote prolifically, and was described as having a 'vigorous personality' and as 'always loath to be contradicted'.

The *Timbre-Poste* author, whoever he was, acknowledged that Mauritius was a hazardous field of inquiry. Like Booty and Herpin previously, he had gleaned his information from slim philatelic pickings. As a consequence, both Herpin and the unnamed author had supplemented their researches with letters to the postal authorities in Mauritius. Herpin mentioned that an employee of the Mauritius Post Office Department had helped him with his queries, and this employee must have confirmed that Barnard engraved the early stamps. Unfortunately, his rival at *Le Timbre-Poste* found the staff unresponsive to demands for precise dates of issue. Herpin was nevertheless a little wary of the information he did receive, believing it was given more in the spirit of willingness to oblige than from documentation or actual memory. This was almost certainly the case. Philatelists were not the only interested parties writing to the postal authorities in Mauritius at this time. Correspondence in the Mauritius Archives reveals that various postmasters from around the world, including New Zealand, France, Italy and St Helena, requested, and were given, specimens of current Mauritius stamps in 1865. Some also wanted specimens of discontinued stamps. It appears that no record of specimens of issues formerly in use had been kept, for the Mauritius postmaster was unable to supply this want and seemed to know little about them.

Towards the end of 1865, after continued speculation, Moens and Hanciau announced in *Le Timbre-Poste* that they had at last confirmed the existence of not only the two pence 'Post Office' (Herpin had mentioned the variety in relation to that value only) but a *one* penny specimen as well. A subscriber to *Le Timbre-Poste* had come forth with two used 'Post Office' stamps and the journal's editors had at last seen them themselves. This was news indeed. Moens could not bring himself to believe, as Herpin had wondered and others suggested, that the engraver had made the same mistake twice on both the one penny and two pence plates of the 'Post Paid' issue. 'This famous "post-office" did not find itself there accidentally,' he declared. 'It has, certainly, a significance which still escapes us.'

One method of testing the error theory was to plate the 'Post Paid' issue. Plating was a delightful occupation that sharpened one's powers of observation – the philatelic equivalent of playing 'spot the difference' – and involved the reconstruction of the make-up of the original plates used to print stamps. Of course, this was unnecessary when the physical plates still existed, but this was not always the case. The 'Post Paid' and other early stamp issues of Mauritius had been hand-engraved on copper plates. Each stamp on the plate was a unique engraving, which meant it was possible through minute study to detect slight differences between each stamp and determine its original position on the plate. Some of the earliest stamps produced, like those of Mauritius, were separated, not by tearing perforations, but by cutting them out singly or in strips, depending on how many were required at the time of sale. Some of these stamps survived as pairs, strips or even as block multiples, and became highly sought after by collectors; as a point of reference, they provided a means of reconstructing the engraved plates.

The task of plating the Mauritius 'Post Paid' issue fell to Legrand. With the aid of examples from fellow Mauritius collectors, from Moens and from his own holdings, he was able to sit down and successfully reconstruct the 'Post Paid' plates, publishing his results early in 1869. Legrand determined conclusively that there were twelve stamps on each plate (there were separate plates for the one penny and two pence values), and he was able to position them by identifying the subtle differences in their appearance and by using multiples.

In so doing, Legrand also established that the 'Post Office' stamps did not belong to either plate, speculating that they might be essays. Perhaps they had escaped the attention of the postal clerks in Port Louis all those years ago as they battled the heat and the stream of inquiries in a multitude of languages. A year later, in January 1870, Legrand had purchased both values of the 'Post Office' stamps from Moens. He sat down again to re-examine the 'Post Office' issue, with two other collectors' 'Post Office' stamps kindly offered for comparison. The doctor was certain that each value was printed from the same engraving: that is, one only for the one penny and one only for the two pence. The one penny specimens he examined were identical to each other, and the two pence were all identical too. Legrand was sure that the stamps were proofs (and *not* errors) which had passed through the postal system by accident.

Philatelic writers all agreed on one thing. The early stamps of Mauritius were rarely met with. Across the Channel the editors of the English journal the *Stamp-Collector's Magazine* dated the first appearance of the 'native' stamps of Mauritius to as late as 1858, wondering why, after only four years in existence, they should be so rare. The gentleman collectors of England, they stated, had certainly been unable 'to bring to light the old Mauritius' from their hiding places.

The *Stamp-Collector's Magazine* proposed the theory that the early stamps of Mauritius had only ever been for local use in the island, something about which Herpin had also speculated. But if so, then how had a collector on the Continent come by a pair? Could there be any more of these curious stamps out there and, most importantly, where should the hunt begin?

No Room in Madame's Lallier

*I am not a thief, Madame, I knew there was some
mistake… For a few minutes they were mine,
that is enough.*

'Monsieur Félix', stamp dealer, in *Charade*, 1963

In the latter weeks of September 1847, while the 'Post Office'
stamps of Mauritius were on sale for the first time in Port Louis, the
businessmen of Bordeaux sat twiddling their thumbs. The weather
on tropical islands was suitable for balls, but in France it was
proving disastrous for shipping, both becalmed and paralysed by
the persistence of the east winds.

Port Saint-Jean, at Bordeaux, lay many miles inland from the sea
on the River Garonne. Deep and wide, and perfect for shipping,
the Garonne sustained one of the busiest commercial ports in
France in the nineteenth century, a time when more than half the
local Bordeaux worthies were involved in shipping in some way.
Most maritime activity centred on the Quai des Chartrons,
picturesquely stretched along a magnificent curve in the river. John
Murray's *Hand-Book for Travellers in France* considered the Quai
des Chartrons to be the most splendid of its kind in all Europe.
Handsome Italianate buildings of pale stone lined the quay,
perfectly situated to catch the first and last rays of the day's sun.
Ships from all over the world jostled to unload their goods – sugar,
rum, rice, cocoa, coffee, spices and gum. Indeed, so numerous

were the vessels, large and small, that a contemporary observer wondered how collisions were avoided when the wind was strong.

The Quartier des Chartrons, which gave directly on to the quay, was the centre of Bordeaux's wine trade: the marvellous wines, spirits and liqueurs of the region were the main commodities the Bordelais exported to the world. But there were numerous other sundries on offer too. Alongside the butchers and bakers and clog makers providing the necessities of daily life, were fireworks manufacturers and makers of billiards equipment, tinder, mirrors, parchment and small clocks. The streets around the port were crowded with women of all ages balancing large baskets of bread, oranges and onions, while not so far away, in the older part of town, the *coffretiers* and *bimbelotiers* were busy creating sturdy yet beautiful little boxes for supply to perfumiers and chocolatiers.

Despite the weather, many ships did leave Bordeaux during the months of September and October 1847, their destinations including Dublin, New York, Guadeloupe, Montevideo, Senegal, Vera Cruz and the Indian Ocean islands of Bourbon and Mauritius. Once the winds began blowing in the right direction, the ships began arriving too.

With the ships came the mail, much of it business correspondence concerning the exchange of goods. The ships' captains were obliged to deliver their mail from abroad to the postal bureau at Pauillac, a little seaport town some miles from Bordeaux, before proceeding down the river to their eventual destination at Port Saint-Jean. A courier from Pauillac would then rush the mail by road to Bordeaux, prioritizing deliveries from the colonies to the businesses around port and the Quai des Chartrons. Most of the mail still arrived free of postage stamps, bearing the signs of travel in the form of handwritten postal markings or hand-stamped cancellations. The occasional English or Brazilian postage stamp may briefly

'La Petite Bourse des Timbres aux Champs-Élysées', from Arthur de Rothschild's *Histoire de la Poste aux Lettres et du Timbre-Poste Depuis Leurs Origines Jusqu'a Nos Jours*, Paris, 1880.

have distracted the merchants' eyes, before the letters were filed away as records of business transactions and largely forgotten.

By the early 1860s, stamp collecting in France, as in England, was a robust infant. Stamp dealers similar to Moens's firm in Brussels were already in business and scenes akin to those in Birchin Lane in London regularly took place in the Tuileries and Luxembourg gardens in Paris. Every Thursday and Sunday stamp swapping continued well into the fading light of day, involving between 300 and 400 collectors – men, women and children alike. Alfred Potiquet's catalogue of stamps was so successful that it soon ran into a second edition.

The new mania for stamp collecting had also spread to Bordeaux. Many merchants in the Chartrons area had accumulated considerable amounts of day-to-day business correspondence, and behind the façades of the Quai des Chartrons, overlooking the busy port, some of the inhabitants began to look through their old correspondence collections to find examples other than the by now more familiar French stamps (first issued in 1849).

At least one of these collectors may also have subscribed to Moens's journal for stamp collectors, *Le Timbre-Poste*, and seen the debate in its pages in 1865 about the existence of the curious Mauritius stamps bearing the inscription 'Post Office'. For by October of that year *Le Timbre-Poste* had confirmed the formerly doubtful existence of the 'Post Office' stamps, its editors having been shown two specimens by a subscriber.

Albert Coutures, a young man of twenty in 1865, was recorded by Moens as the owner, at the time of their discovery, of this 'Post Office' pair. Through an intermediary, a shopkeeper from Bordeaux, Moens bought Coutures's entire collection, valuing the two 'Post Office' stamps within it at 200 francs. This was a large sum – the face value of most of the French and Belgian stamps in use at that time could be counted in centimes.

The stamps had a traceable history. Moens noted that the two 'Post Office' stamps had originally belonged to a certain Madame Borchard – née Jeanne Heritzen – who also came from Bordeaux. She had exchanged them with Albert Coutures for two Montevideo stamps. The Montevideo 'suns', so called for the faces beaming out of the sun's corona in their centre, were among the first stamps of the South American republic of Uruguay, issued in the late 1850s in numerous values and shades of blue, green, red, yellow and purple. While attractive and important stamps, they would not prove a fair exchange for the 'Post Office' in monetary terms.

There is no record of a stamp exchange in Bordeaux. It is likely that Albert Coutures's and Madame Borchard's paths crossed simply because they both lived in the Chartrons area, close to Bordeaux's lively port. By 1869 Albert Coutures was listed in his own right in the Bordeaux *Annuaire*, residing in the rue du Palais-de-l'Ombrière in the centre of the town. This was the main address of Maison Coutures Frères, glassmakers and notable traders of Bordeaux. The Coutures brothers also had premises on the Quai des Chartrons, close to where the Quai began and the vast space of the grand Place des Quinconces ended. Here, too, running into the Quai was the Pavé des Chartrons, a wide street lined with grand buildings. Monsieur Adolphe Borchard, merchant and shipowner, could be found at number 26 on the Pavé. Albert, like his brothers, would have known most of the other merchants in the Chartrons area, and that, undoubtedly, is how he came to discover a like-minded soul in Monsieur Borchard's wife.

Why had Madame Borchard exchanged her 'Post Office' for the

Bordeaux, Cours du Pavé-des-Chartrons.

Montevideo stamps? Because, Moens explained, they had 'in the eyes of that lady, the supreme advantage of having a place for them in her Lallier', which the 'Post Office' stamps did not. The Lallier referred to was a stamp-mounting album, first published by the French dealer Justin Lallier in 1862. One philatelic writer later described the Lallier, in those early days of collecting, as 'second only in veneration and respect to the Family Bible'. The album was small, around 18 by 27 centimetres, and easy to hold. It was divided into sections – Europe, Asia, Africa, America and Oceania – with spaces reserved for the 1,097 stamps which the author believed to exist. Lallier's summation of the Mauritius stamps was as muddled as that in Booty's catalogue, but it was also vague enough to not preclude the inclusion of at least the two pence 'Post Office' stamp on the album's Mauritius page. Monsieur Lallier, in common with most collectors in those days, understood that the 'complete list' of all the world's postage stamps was not yet known. Madame Borchard surely understood this too. Was her exchange with Coutures a folly, as Moens's tone implied, or was it that she was happy to exchange these two 'Post Office' stamps because she knew she had a ready supply of the Mauritian curiosities at hand?

She found them among her husband's business papers: a two pence and a one penny, used side by side on a single piece of correspondence. They had been cancelled with a single boxed PAID hand stamp that would forever signal their common origin (tie them together, as philatelists would say). And they were not the only specimens Madame Borchard found at this time. In total, from the mid-1860s until the end of the decade, she would find half of the known 'Post Office' stamps. The majority of these would be handled by another Bordelaise, a certain Madame Desbois, who operated a bookshop, dealing in stamps on the side, and who later became the grande dame of Bordeaux philately.

Although women feature rarely in this story, their contribution was significant. Moens deferred to the superior knowledge of Madame Desbois on the issue of the stamps' provenance, publishing a letter from her which surmised that: 'The house of Borchard, which between 1847 and 1848 did a considerable trade in Mauritius, ought to have had among its correspondence a large proportion of the "Post Office" issue of Mauritius, perhaps even in one postal delivery.' Madame Desbois was probably correct in this assumption, given the limited time that the 'Post Office' stamps had been available for sale. (They had reportedly sold out very quickly.)

It could take two to three months for a ship to sail from Mauritius to France, so, having departed the tropics in late September 1847 (and feasibly carrying the first letters to bear the new postage stamps of Mauritius), the vessels could not have arrived in Bordeaux until late December. While there is no obvious connection to Adolphe Borchard in the list of maritime arrivals in the *Mémorial Bordelais* newspaper for this time, there is a clear-cut explanation for the existence and quantity of correspondence to Borchard from Mauritius. The English three-master the *Jane-Greene* was due to leave Bordeaux for Mauritius at the end of January 1848 and had ample room for more freight. Interested parties were directed to contact the ship brokers Messieurs Serizier and Laffitte for conditions, or Monsieur Adolphe Borchard, consignee.

In July 1847 Messieurs Serizier, Laffitte and Borchard advertised the departure of two English ships from Bordeaux for Mauritius, the *Reliance* and the *Norfolk*, which duly arrived at their destination in September and unloaded their goods. A new maritime arrival was almost always exciting, bringing passengers perhaps and always carrying a complement of news and goods. The French inhabitants of Mauritius (at least) certainly preferred their goods imported from France, and the local merchants in Port Louis wasted no time in advertising newly arrived shipments in the local newspapers. In early July furniture, opera glasses and a music box (a little damaged by sea water) were on offer, landed from the ship *Arab* of Bordeaux. The *Arab* also brought with it engravings of saints, crosses and reliquaries, straw hats and paisley muslins. Eight ships arrived in mid-September, a few days before the 'Post Office' stamps went on sale for the first time. They came from ports in France, Sweden, India, South Africa and the colony of Sydney, carrying animals, sundries, wine, deal plank and immigrant workers. Of these, both the *Sirène* and the *London* hailed from Bordeaux, the latter bringing a great number of live plants (such as nasturtiums and jonquils) and literary works including Lamartine's Bordeaux-related *Histoire des Girondins*. Goods newly received from the *Augusta Jessie* of Bordeaux were advertised on 30 September, the day of Lady Gomm's ball, and included fabrics, drapes, eau-de-Cologne, lavender water, hats for men and cadets, and six pretty hats for ladies. Between them, the *Reliance* and the *Norfolk*, under the management of Serizier, Laffitte and Borchard, unburdened wine, superb parasols (in all shades), fancy shoes, a choice of excellent pious reading, wallpaper, games for children, richly dressed dolls, chocolates and other confectionery, and beautiful little cardboard boxes, perfect for gifts, made by the Bordeaux *coffretiers*.

As one actively involved in the business of shipping and trade, of necessity Adolphe Borchard received and kept correspondence from agents, ship chandlers and merchants. From whom precisely, however, it is difficult to say. When Madame Borchard began to look through her husband's correspondence in the 1860s, she removed the stamps from the letters they had travelled on, destroying most of the evidence of their journey and the story behind them. This was usual in the early days of collecting, driven in some cases by the desire to fill blank spaces in albums, to save space generally and possibly also to protect privacy. The value, historically and financially, of keeping stamps on the items to which they were originally affixed (described by philatelists as 'entires') was not yet appreciated.

Adolphe Borchard died in February 1869 and Madame Borchard found herself a widow at the age of forty-two, with at least six children, ranging in age from five to fifteen, to look after. According to the stamp dealer Madame Desbois, as recounted to Moens in 1899, Madame Borchard had never searched her husband's correspondence thoroughly. When Adolphe Borchard died, 'the winding-up of his business, which was carried out very quickly, obliged the widow to leave her house and to go and live with some friends. All the papers were sent in pantechnicons to a waste-paper merchant, who undertook to pulp them… The time was not opportune for searching for stamps.'

How many of the 'Post Office' stamps received by Monsieur Borchard – and others – met this fate? In later years waste-paper merchants became more aware of the value of certain 'foreign elements' among the material they obtained. It is possible that this recognition was developing by the late 1860s, for Madame Desbois's tale of the Borchards concluded on a lucky note for the dealer. Paper was a valuable commodity and it is not at all surprising that some of the paper was sold rather than pulped. Some of the Borchard correspondence bearing postage stamps ended up wrapped around the wares of a hawker plying her trade in one of Bordeaux's public places. She called to some barefooted children playing nearby and bestowed the little images upon them, and they ran, those canny children, straight to the premises of

Madame Desbois. Seeing their admiration for a collection she had laying on a table, the equally canny Madame offered it to them in exchange. She had recognized that most of the children's stamps were of the first issue of India (1852) but there were also seven one penny 'Post Paid' of Mauritius among them. Almost as rare, she knew, as the 'Post Office', and extremely valuable.

Prior to her husband's death, over a four- or five-year period, Madame Borchard had found thirteen 'Post Office Mauritius' – seven of the two pence and six of the one penny. Ten of these passed through the hands of Madame Desbois. With some authority Moens in Brussels pieced together the chronology of these discoveries in his 1899 account, 'Encore les Post-Office de Maurice'. He had himself handled seven of Madame Borchard's finds close to the time of their discovery.

There were the first two found together, which Moens had by October 1865. Then there was another two pence, credited as having come originally from Madame Borchard, and sold by Madame Desbois for an unknown sum in 1866. Three years later, in 1869, Madame Desbois sent Moens one of the 'Post Office' stamps which Madame Borchard had saved from previous investigations into her husband's correspondence, a two pence described as 'almost unused' (it had a slight blue mark above the letters AU in MAURITIUS). Moens paid the Bordeaux stamp dealer 100 francs for it and, with access to more moneyed collectors, promptly sold it for 250 francs. Early the following year, 1870, Madame Desbois sent another three 'Post Office' to Moens, all from Madame Borchard: a one penny and two pence described as unused, and a one penny used. This time Madame Desbois charged 500 francs for the three. The value of the 'Post Office' stamps was rising slowly but surely.

Most of the stamps which Madame Borchard found were

damaged in some way, perhaps as a result of their travels through the Mauritian and French postal systems (often via the English too). Perhaps in those fledgling days of stamp collecting – and with a house full of small children on her hands – she couldn't be expected to be as circumspect with her scissors as later collectors would have liked her to have been. Moens was unnecessarily damning of Madame Borchard, suggesting that she 'was probably naturally highly strung, which explains why, among the thirteen stamps which she removed from her husband's correspondence, there are four which have a missing corner'. But why was it Madame's fault? The 'Post Office Mauritius' stamps had been made before perforations were introduced. Might it not have been one of the postal clerks, in the cramped and stuffy conditions of the Port Louis post office back in 1847, whose trimming technique was a little untried?

Several of the stamps were heavily cancelled with postmarks in the form of parallel lines, with the boxed PAID hand stamp or with a circular date stamp. On one used two pence the cancellation was intact, reading 'Pauillac 2 Janvier 1848', confirming the postal procedures listed in the Bordeaux *Almanach* and *Annuaire* for 1847, that ship mail was unloaded at the postal station at Pauillac. Madame Desbois – an observant woman – would later point out, in correspondence published in the *Gazette des Timbres* in 1874, that this was evidence that the date of issue of the 'Post Office' stamps was closer to this date – by implication 1847 – than to 1850 or 1851, which various gentlemen of the philatelic press had supposed.

Six of the thirteen ex-Borchard stamps were described as unused, but how would the Borchards have come by unused specimens of Mauritius stamps? In philately the description 'unused' sometimes meant merely unmarked, rather than new. Often the ink of cancellations was removed, as collectors at this time preferred clean stamps. Perhaps, given the novelty of postage stamp usage in Mauritius, it was, again, rather a case of the postal clerks there (by accident or design) failing to apply the hand cancellations directly on to the stamps, so preserving their fresh appearance.

This was the state of play in 1870. Madame Borchard presumably left her home on the Pavé des Chartrons, since no more is known of her. In addition to the ten 'Post Office' stamps that found their way on to the stamp-collecting market via Madame Desbois and Jean-Baptiste Moens, there were three remaining 'Post Office' stamps with a Borchard provenance. These would not appear on the market for some years, Madame Borchard apparently having exchanged them directly with other collectors in Bordeaux, as she had with Coutures. Madame Desbois came across one of these in 1872, a used two pence said to have been exchanged by Madame Borchard with a collector named Martineau. The Bordeaux stamp dealer duly sold the stamp to Moens, again for only 100 francs, and Moens sold it four days later to the renowned French collector Arthur de Rothschild for six times that much. Madame Desbois, in correspondence with the Parisian dealer and publisher Pierre Mahé, noted in 1874, 'I have entirely given up the hope of being able to meet with those rarities which I had the honour of discovering.' She was still looking, however, and found a specimen the very next year, 1875, when she purchased the collection of another Bordeaux collector with whom Madame Borchard had exchanged one of her earlier finds. Madame Desbois bought this collection in its entirety for 500 francs, then promptly sold the single unused two pence 'Post Office' to Moens for a savvy 300 francs. Her Belgian confrère sold it immediately for twice that amount.

It would be the last 'Post Office' stamp to pass through Madame Desbois's hands, but she continued to enjoy her self-appointed status as discoverer of the Mauritian rarities for many years, sharing her stories with the generations of Bordeaux philatelists who visited her little shop. Madame Desbois's name still appeared in the 1902 Bordeaux *Annuaire*, listed as operating a reading room and a bookshop (selling books old and new), and as dealing in rare stamps. She died early in 1912 in her nineties.

Neither Madame Borchard nor Madame Desbois made great sums from their Mauritian sales, but Moens sold the stamps soon after purchasing them, usually for double, quadruple or even six times the price he had paid. The 'Post Office' stamps were acknowledged to be rare – practically non-existent in comparison with the millions of the world's first stamp, the Penny Black, circulating in collections. They were also fast on the way to becoming desirable objects for the stamp-collecting world's elite, those with a keen interest in the origins of stamp issuing and production, and especially those collectors who aimed to gather an example of every stamp ever issued.

The first 'Post Office' stamp found outside of Bordeaux and in the island itself, by a Monsieur Noirel of Port Louis, surfaced in 1868. According to Moens, the stamp was given as a gift to Noirel, having been found originally by a local merchant on a letter bearing specimens of both the one penny 'Post Office' and one penny 'Post Paid'. A Mauritian philatelist, Albert Rae, subsequently corrected the record, claiming that Noirel's 'Post Office' was found by Noirel himself among an auction lot of old newspapers purchased at a public sale. Stamps were commonly affixed to newspapers and sent through the post, and examples of Mauritian newspapers bearing the early stamps of Mauritius still exist.

Whatever the circumstances of Noirel's discovery, he had sold the 'Post Office' to a Monsieur Lionnet by April 1870, a busy year for 'Post Office' sales, when five of the known specimens changed hands, some more than once. Noirel's two pence soon found its way on to the European stamp-collecting market, having been purchased by Moens. Several months later the Belgian sold the stamp, again to Arthur de Rothschild, for 500 francs and made 400 francs clear profit from the sale. The 'Post Office' stamps would never know their days of penny value again.

That a specimen had been discovered in the island itself was encouraging, for it seemed that the 'Post Office' stamps had been used on more than a few choice letters to Bordeaux. Yet curiously, despite the escalating interest in and value of the stamps, it seems that nobody at this time thought to pursue the obvious whys and wherefores of the Borchards' abundance of early Mauritian stamps – shipping interests, commerce and business correspondence. The ship brokers Serizier and Laffitte, who were working in partnership with Adolphe Borchard in 1847–8, *must* have had similar quantities of the Mauritius 'Post Office' and 'Post Paid' among their correspondence, but certainly no 'Post Office' were ever traced back to them. (Louis Laffitte's correspondence may well have suffered the same fate as Adolphe Borchard's, and ended up at a waste-paper merchant's. He died in 1851, well before the stamps were known and the Bordeaux discoveries were made by Madame Borchard.) There were other Bordeaux families involved in commerce with Mauritius through shipping, such as the Widow Fabre, Sons and Company, and a Monsieur Delmestre, who were advertising room for consignments on Mauritius-bound ships at the same time as Adolphe Borchard. But neither their names nor their stamps have the good fortune to appear in the 'Post Office' story.

Major Evans's Tour of Duty, Mauritius 1876-9

*In 1876 he exchanged into a battery ordered to
Mauritius, being in no small measure instigated to
take this step by the hope, which was so completely
crowned, of being able to do something for
philately in this sugary isle.*

Philatelic Record, January 1885

Across the channel a young man who became one of England's
most distinguished philatelists, known to all the philatelic world as
Major Evans, was looking forward to his next assignment with the
Royal Artillery. Edward Benjamin Evans was born in November
1846, almost simultaneously with the postal ordinance which
foreshadowed the birth of postage stamps in Mauritius. He began
collecting stamps as a schoolboy and his first article, 'On Stamp
Collecting', was published in a philatelic journal when he was just
eighteen.

While on commission with the Royal Artillery in Malta in 1867
his passion for stamps, if it needed any encouraging, was strengthened by a certain Lieutenant Speranza, soon to be a founding
member of the Philatelic Society in London. A few years later,
while stationed in Plymouth, Evans met the dealer Edward Stanley
Gibbons (founder of the stamp firm which still bears his name)
and the dealer and philatelic writer Edward Loines Pemberton;

from that moment his philatelic fate was sealed. Motivated by his interest in the early stamps of Mauritius, the soldier managed to combine his philatelic passion and work duties, and some time in 1876 arrived in Mauritius with the Royal Artillery.

Evans was an indefatigable and dogged researcher, whose soldiering duties, like Ewart's in the 1840s, do not appear to have taken a lot of his time. Writing under his philatelic pseudonym 'Cheth' in Port Louis's *Mercantile Record and Commercial Gazette* in 1878, Evans reported on at least one entertainment performed at the Line Barracks by the Bohemian Dramatic Club, the overall impression being given that a good time was had by all, especially those, like Cheth, who were fond of their whisky.

But the pull of philately was also strong. In preparatory comments to his classic article 'The Stamps of Mauritius', published in the *Philatelic Record* (1880) after his return from the island, he put his finger on the lessons and benefits of original research:

> When I commenced my researches in Mauritius, I was not very sanguine as to the result. I thought it impossible that there could be much information to be obtained. I took it for granted that the dates given for the various issues were correct; I knew that there had been doubtful points, but I imagined that they had been cleared up as satisfactorily as they were ever likely to be, and I was astonished both at the amount of fresh information I obtained, and at the fact that so much of the information was fresh.

On a fine August afternoon in 1878 – the very next day in fact after the performance of the Bohemian Dramatic Club so enjoyed by the whisky-laden 'Cheth' – Evans addressed the annual meeting of the Royal Society of Arts and Sciences in Port Louis. Presentations

on the benefits of planting eucalyptus and medico-legal con-
siderations on the ruptures of the spleen were followed by an
examination of natural specimens from the nearby Seychelles.
Then it was Evans's turn, and he informed the assembled crowd
that the early stamps of Mauritius had 'always excited very great
interest among collectors' (for his audience, however, this might
have been hard to imagine in comparison with the more obviously
voluptuous nut from the Coco de Mer palm they had just seen,
also a collectable). The reason for this interest, he suggested, was
'partly as very curious specimens of engraving, partly on account
of the great rarity of some of the varieties of them, and partly no
doubt on account of the want of accurate information as to their
origin and dates of issue, which led to all sorts of conjectures being
formed about them.'

Evans had had little reason to trust the oral testimony he
encountered. Thomas Henry Thompson – the fifth postmaster
since Brownrigg in 1847 – was at first sceptical about the existence
of the 'Post Office' issue, stating it as his opinion 'that they had been
made in Europe for the benefit of collectors'.

Joseph Barnard had wound up his engraving business a few
years after producing the colony's first postage stamps. All the
stock from his little shop on the Chaussée was sold at auction in
1851. To support his growing family, he successfully moved into
lighterage (the loading and unloading of goods from ships), and
by 1862 was able to purchase a sugar estate, complete with factory,
in the south of the island. But in May 1865, a decade before the
arrival of Major Evans, Joseph Barnard died at the age of forty-
eight.

The widow Barnard, who with their ten children survived the
engraver, was only in her fifties when Evans was conducting his
researches on the island in the 1870s. But nobody, it seems, thought

to ask her if she knew why her husband engraved the first stamps 'Post Office' and afterwards changed the wording to 'Post Paid'.

Brownrigg, who had been the Colonial Postmaster in 1847, had been forced to resign from his position in 1853 after certain accounting irregularities had been revealed. He had also, the previous year, been challenged to a duel by his head clerk. ('If your aim be as true as you boast,' wrote this mutinous challenger, 'and mine the same, there will be no need of a doctor.') The problems at the Port Louis post office had clearly escalated beyond the mundane issues of noxious effluvia and mice eating the mail, and make sad reading in the dispatches and correspondence later published in connection with the postmaster's removal. Brownrigg left the colony in 1853 and never returned.

Of the other postal employees, there was Mr Lumgair, who had worked in the Mauritius Post Office Department from 1862 to 1875. Many years later, in 1909, Lumgair's memories of Mauritius were published in the *Stamp Lover*, but having missed the birth of stamps in the colony by some fifteen years, the former clerk was unable to shed much light on the 'Post Office' story. However, when Lumgair began working in the post office in 1862, one of the clerks who had been in the service in 1847 was still employed there, Moutoussamy Appavou. Did they ever talk about the early days?

Moutoussamy, originally from Madras, had been appointed (in the language of the day) to the position of Malabar clerk at the Port Louis post office in January 1839. Possibly one of the longest-serving postal employees at this time, Moutoussamy was put forward for retirement in 1877: 'Now totally unfit for the duties required from age and impaired vision... Mr Appavou is 59 years of age, and has been 39 years in the service, having joined the Department in 1839, when the Post Office was in the Chaussee, and the staff consisted of the Postmaster and Mr Appavou.' It was not

Edward B. Evans.

true that Moutoussamy had been the only postal employee besides the postmaster back in 1839 (there were in addition two clerks, the Trusty Messenger Grain d'Or, several other messengers and seven convict couriers), but the notion that he had been reflects at least the recognition of his longevity in the position – he was an elder postman, so to speak. Despite the island's chief medical officer returning a positive verdict on Moutoussamy's health and the admonition that 'The state of the eyes did not escape notice. Mr Appavou can see perfectly well, if he likes, and may [benefit from] the use of spectacles', Moutoussamy was allowed to retire on two-thirds of his annual salary in January 1878. The only momentous thing which seems to have happened to him during those thirty-nine years of service was an unfortunate incident when riding the mail cart home late one evening during a severe storm in 1861. He was thrown out of the cart, broke his arm and was laid up for three months, the injury eventually hampering his ability to sort the mail.

Moutoussamy, the one employee from 1847 still working at the Port Louis post office while Evans was undertaking his investigations there, would undoubtedly have handled the 'Post Office' stamps in the course of his daily work. But what he may have had to relate of this important period in the island's postal history is anybody's guess, because again it seems that nobody thought to ask him. Evans lost the perfect opportunity to supplement his rigorous and valuable searches through the records of the Post Office Department with the oral testimony of one at least who had a direct connection with the events of thirty years before.

Despite his scepticism, Mr Thompson, the postmaster, was friendly and gave Evans 'all the information in his power; but that did not amount to very much, and he was quite unable to tell me where I could get any more'. This proved Evans's chief difficulty, but undeterred by a postmaster who appeared to have little concept of government record-keeping, he pushed on. Evans spent much of his leisure time based in the Colonial Secretary's offices and was fortunate in the assistance he received. The Colonial Secretary 'allowed me every facility for examining the official correspondence preserved in his office; gave me permission to copy or take notes of anything I wanted; and offered to have copies made of any letters I wished for in full'. He also put Mr Lumgair at Evans's disposal. As Evans tells it, both he and the Colonial Secretary were clearly aware of their responsibilities in relation to the official documents before them, and Evans assiduously made copies of the information he required.

And yet he returned to England with a key original document in his possession – Joseph Barnard's handwritten estimate for the production of the 'Post Office' stamps (referred to in the estimate as letter labels). It was undoubtedly found among the government records of which it rightly formed part, but in the acquisitive tradition of the British collector it remained in Evans's possession until 1898, when the major graciously gave it to the British Museum. (It is now on semi-permanent display in the British Library.) Perhaps through his persistence and obvious flair for philately, Evans won the admiration of the government officials – all of whom 'were most kind in their endeavours to assist me' – who may have made him a gift of Barnard's estimate. Or from the vantage point of more than a century we might rather say simply that he took it.

Evans also uncovered a letter from the Colonial Postmaster, Brownrigg, to the Colonial Secretary apprising him that as at 20 September 1847 (ten days before Lady Gomm's ball) 700 postage stamps had been printed. The second letter Evans uncovered from Brownrigg to the Colonial Secretary, dated 2 May 1848 (both letters still, happily, preserved in the Mauritius Archives), clarified once and for all that the 'Post Office' were a legitimate issue (not 'escaped' proofs). Brownrigg wrote:

Sir, – (1) I have the honour to report for His Excellency the Governor's information, that improved plates containing twelve impressions of each postage label (one penny and twopence) are now finished and ready to be worked whenever it shall please His Excellency to favour me with his instructions.

(2) Some delay in their delivery, it is true, has unavoidably occurred, in consequence of the engraver having been for some time under medical treatment for his sight, which had become impaired. This delay would not, however, have occasioned any inconvenience or disappointment to

the public had I been permitted to use in the meantime the original plates, the only objection against them – as I understand – being, that as there was only one impression of each label, too much time would be occupied in working off any large number. This objection cannot, however, apply to the new plates, as the engraver assures me that he can, within the hour, take off from 1000 to 1500 impressions.

(3) When first these labels were introduced 1000 were struck off, and so desirous were the public of availing of them, particularly for town letters, that in the course of a few days they were all disposed of.

This was the key to the first issue's rarity and evidence that they were not part of the 'Post Paid' plate. (This accorded with Legrand's previous findings.) Only a small amount of these stamps were printed and they were so popular that they are supposed to have sold out a few days after going on sale. There is no mention of the change in wording from 'Office' to 'Paid', but it is unlikely that the 'Post Office' stamps were viewed at the time as mistakes. Because only one impression of each stamp could be printed at a time, the original plates had been discontinued from use. The references to poor Barnard's eyesight problems were seized on by some later writers on the 'Post Office' stamps in support of the theory that it was this incapacity which led to the 'wrong' inscription.

While the original stamps Brownrigg referred to weren't explicitly identified as those bearing the inscription 'Post Office', Evans concluded that they were, citing the example brought to the philatelic world's attention by Madame Desbois a few years earlier of a two pence blue 'Post Office' date stamped January 1848. This usage predated Brownrigg's letter of 2 May 1848 announcing the

One penny 'Post Office', used on an envelope that probably contained an
entry card to Lady Gomm's ball and which was addressed to Monsieur
Alcide Marquay. Acquired by Major Evans in Mauritius in 1878.

production of the stamps engraved twelve on a plate (the 'Post
Paid').

In early 1879 Evans left Mauritius the proud possessor of some
fine examples of the island's early postal rarities, including a small
buff-coloured envelope bearing a brilliant orange-red one penny
'Post Office'. The stamp itself was cancelled with a circular MAURI-
TIUS POST OFFICE hand stamp, dated 21 September 1847. Here was
evidence that the 'Post Office' stamps were a legitimate issue and
not erroneously used proofs. The contents of the envelope were
long gone and there was nothing inside to alert Evans to the
purpose of the little missive originally addressed to Monsieur
Alcide Marquay. It would be another twenty years before something similar was discovered.

Evans was probably the first – and certainly the luckiest – of the
philatelic gleaners to pick over the island. Lumgair recalled in his

1909 article that the locals tended to destroy envelopes, and undeliverable letters returned to the post office were periodically ordered by the Dead Letter Committee to be taken away and burned. Many of these letters, he was sure, had borne philatelic gems.

ALL, ALAS! DISCONTINUED BY DEATH

*... be content with nothing short of perfection, and
your stamps will be a joy to yourself and a satisfaction
to your executors.*

Rev. H. C. Bond, 'Collectors and their Stamps',
Stamp Collecting, 1920

'Looked upon,' stated Frederick Booty in his 1862 guide, 'as
hopelessly but harmlessly insane on the subject', stamp collectors
had increased in numbers from handfuls to hundreds in the first
few years of the 1860s. To some there was a latent beauty in the
postage stamp. To others stamp collecting was an instructive and
entertaining pursuit whose goal was enjoyment. Others evinced
stranger reasons for collecting stamps: Dr Gray, a reptile expert at
the British Museum, did so primarily, it seems, because he believed
it was he, and not the famed philatelic reformer Sir Rowland Hill,
who first proposed the introduction of a uniform inland postal rate.
Many early practitioners of the hobby aimed to gather all-world
general collections, and while there were only around 500 stamps
in existence, this was thought possible. But the discovery and
recognition of rarities such as the 'Post Office Mauritius' soon put
the achievement of this desire beyond the reach of all but the
fortunate few.

Madame Borchard was not to be one of these. When she first
came across the 'Post Office' stamps among her husband's

correspondence in the mid-1860s, their value was untested and their status as a legitimate issue was uncertain. She was a collector, plain and simple, with an abundance of old stamps from Mauritius which more than met her needs. Unfortunately the circumstance of her widowhood intervened before she could fully realize the value of the seven specimens she had kept. Albert Coutures, owner (courtesy of his exchange with Madame Borchard) of the first two 'Post Office' stamps known to the wider philatelic community, had made a large sum from the sale of his collection to Jean-Baptiste Moens late in 1865. Coutures was twenty, according to Moens, when he sold his collection, and the amount realized probably helped put the young man on a good financial footing. Perhaps that was why he sold his stamps, or perhaps other interests had crowded stamp collecting out of his life. Then there was the un-named Bordeaux collector who sold the dealer Madame Desbois his collection in 1875. This had contained an unused two pence blue 'Post Office', obtained some time in the 1860s through an exchange with Madame Borchard. The motive for selling this collection, Moens wrote wonderingly, was the need to raise funds to attend a fair in Paris. The Bordeaux collector Émile Lalanne, on the other hand, was serious about his stamps. Moens described him as the first, or most important, collector in Bordeaux at the time. Lalanne had gathered the perfect set of 'Post Office' stamps (used and unused specimens of each value), and would not part with his collection until 1893, almost thirty years after having started.

First among the fortunate few was the purchaser of Coutures's one penny and two pence 'Post Office' stamps. Frederick Adolphus Philbrick (1835–1910), a judge, was a client of Moens and bought the two 'Post Office' specimens for 500 francs in February 1866, a few months after they had come into Moens's possession. Philbrick was an astute and serious collector, a founder member of the

Philatelic Society of London in 1869 (later the Royal Philatelic Society London), and its second president (1878–92). He was also a bibliophile and a horticulturist, specializing in orchids. His philatelic proclivities encompassed the collecting of essays and proofs, telegraph stamps, entires and postcards, but his great passion was for unused stamps. He aimed for completion and his tastes were broad, taking in Great Britain, Europe, the Confederate States of America, Hawaii, Mauritius, British Guiana and the Australian colonies. Also typical of the more serious early collectors, Philbrick wrote up and published his research. He, along with the Bordeaux collector Lalanne, was one of the 'Post Office' owners who made the stamps available for Legrand's study in 1870. By the close of the 1870s the judge's collection was complete in most of the rarities. The obligations of the judicial life increasingly took up much of his time, and in 1881, a few years into his presidency of the Philatelic Society of London, Philbrick sold his collection, including the two 'Post Office' stamps, for the enormous sum of £8,000. It was then reckoned to be one of the greatest philatelic collections in England, possibly even the world.

Baron Arthur de Rothschild (1851–1903), another long-term 'Post Office' owner, began collecting stamps in his teens, around 1865, perhaps inspired by his older brother James-Edouard, a collector of books and manuscripts from an early age. Arthur's merchant banker father, Nathaniel, was a member of the wealthy Rothschild family. The budding philatelist was fortunate that both his father and his grandfather had numerous correspondents around the world who were only too happy to oblige them by sending new issues of stamps for young Arthur's collection. In 1870, Arthur, recently removed to Brussels on account of the Franco-Prussian War, paid Moens 500 francs for the used one penny 'Post Office' discovered by Monsieur Noirel in Mauritius. He completed the set a few years later, paying the Belgian dealer 600 francs for the ex-Borchard used two pence 'Post Office' acquired by Madame Desbois in 1872.

For both the French baron and the English judge, owning the one penny and two pence 'Post Office Mauritius' was important in the context of their pursuit of completion. Both were clients of Moens, and Rothschild was a founder member (later president) of the Société Française de Timbrologie. His collecting tastes ran to unused stamps if he could acquire them, and to postcards, envelopes and other entires. The Baron also contributed articles to the philatelic press and wrote a book, *L'Histoire de la Poste aux Lettres*, first published in 1873, which bespoke a genuine love and affection for his hobby. Rothschild enjoyed his philately until around 1892 (he also collected stationery, ties, cigars and hair ribbons), but when his health began to fail his doctor ordered him to spend the winter months in the South of France. The charms of philately waned as Rothschild spent time frequenting the Monte Carlo casino and pursuing the sport of motor-car racing. 'I no longer want to see these albums,' he declared to his secretary one fine day in March 1893. 'They must be gone within forty-eight hours.' Those in the know believed that Rothschild's collection, like Philbrick's before, was the greatest assembled up to that date. Still, it was unclear whether his collection had been sold after all. In 1899 Moens still believed the Baron to be in possession of his two.

When Major Evans returned from his tropical interlude in 1879, fourteen specimens of the 'Post Office' stamps were now known, seven of the one penny and seven of the two pence. All of these (perhaps barring Evans's) had now passed at least once through dealers' hands and reposed in collections considered serious: Judge Philbrick in England, Baron de Rothschild and Dr Legrand in France, and a collector named Perinelle (of whom nothing beyond his name is known) each had two, a specimen of both values. Émile Lalanne of Bordeaux had four, and Major Evans had the first example of a 'Post Office' stamp known still on cover (on its original support) – the envelope addressed to Monsieur Alcide Marquay. The remaining stamp, and second last discovered, was the uncancelled two pence Madame Desbois had purchased in 1875 from the Bordeaux collector desirous of attending the fair in Paris. Although defective (a part of one corner was missing, thanks perhaps to Madame Borchard and her scissors, or to Moutoussamy and his) it was still a fine example, unmarked by the heavy hand of a postal clerk. Madame Desbois sold this 'Post Office' to Moens for 300 francs, and he immediately sold it ('always without remorse') for 600 francs.

The new owner of this uncancelled two pence was a quietly obsessive young man in his twenties, destined eventually – as the greatest of his kind – to feature on a stamp himself. We shall call him Philipp von Ferrary. It would be another six years before he joined the ranks of his confrères in owning both values of the rare Mauritian stamps. These were Perinelle's two 'Post Office' specimens, the one penny and two pence described by Moens as uncancelled. Ferrary bought them from Moens for 5,500 francs in February 1881. Moens had paid Perinelle 3,000 francs for them a month earlier. Perinelle had owned the stamps for eleven years, originally purchasing them in January 1870 for 950 francs from Moens, who in turn had acquired them in the lot of three 'Post Office' stamps sent him by Madame Desbois, valued at 500 francs for the three. To what tune Madame Borchard originally benefited in this chain of commerce is not recorded. Perinelle received more than triple the amount he had paid in 1870, and Moens almost doubled his investment over a period of little more than a month. Ferrary had paid more than four times the sum for each stamp than he had paid for the unused two pence in 1875. He was a wealthy and committed collector with an appetite for rarities – it was he who, in 1881, purchased Philbrick's collection in its entirety.

Philipp was the son of the Duke and Duchess of Galliera, Raffaele de Ferrari and Maria Brignole Sale. Both his parents were born in Genoa in Italy. Philipp was probably born in Paris in 1850. It is difficult to know how much of what is written about him is true, for he was a private man and certain details of his life are confusing (he changed his mind several times about his birth date and only his death date appeared on his gravestone). What is clear is that nothing annoyed him more than misuse of his name. Being referred to as the Duke of Galliera, after his father's death in 1876, enraged him sufficiently to write letters of protest to the philatelic press, one of the few occasions his own words appeared there. He had, he said, 'abandoned all present and future claims' to that title, and apparently his father's money along with it (his mother was as wealthy as it was possible to be, so this hardly mattered). He wished simply to be known as Philipp von Ferrary, adopting a German sounding version of his name, because 'Although, unfortunately, it was not granted to me to be born on German soil, still my young heart was nurtured there, and I drew in love for Germany with the breath of my earliest years.' Along with his father's wealth and title, he had dispensed with the Italian part of his cultural heritage too. Nor was he fond of the French, even though he spent much of his life in Paris. In 1886, Ferrary underwent another name change. At the age of thirty-six, he became the adopted son of an Austrian soldier, Emmanuel la Rénotière von Kriegsfeld, and wished to be known as Philipp la Rénotière. Several photographs of him exist inscribed with the curious amalgam Philipp la Rénotière von Ferrary, but only Philipp Arnold – his first name and the name of one he called

Philipp von Ferrary.

'brother' – was inscribed on his gravestone. Ferrary's fluid identity would ultimately prove the undoing of his great collection.

Like Arthur de Rothschild, Ferrary began collecting stamps as a boy some time in the early to mid-1860s, when the hobby was starting to attract more practitioners. Perhaps, as with Rothschild too, stamps found their way into his collection courtesy of his father's business correspondents, for the Duke was involved in numerous agricultural, commercial and industrial enterprises, within and outside of France and Italy. The young Ferrary did venture out of the family's grand mansion on the rue de Varenne, accompanied (some say) by his mother, the Duchess, in search of stamps. His visits to the little shop of Pierre Mahé, one of Paris's first stamp dealers, began a life-long acquaintance and business relationship between the dealer and his prodigy.

The boy probably also tried his luck at the shop of Madame Nicolas, on the rue Taitbout. Mahé acknowledged Madame Nicolas

– like her Bordeaux contemporary Madame Desbois, a rarity, as a woman, on the commercial side of the philatelic fence – as the sovereign of the Parisian stamp world at this time. Many of stamp collecting's elite, such as Herpin and Legrand, would assemble in her shop to buy and discuss her wares. She was a small, thin woman, lively, intelligent and good at business – sometimes she fleeced her customers, but with such a light hand and an agreeable smile, according to Mahé, that no one dared protest. Her husband sold stationery, while she dealt in old stamps, also working as Moens's French agent. Ferrary no doubt found his way to her and perhaps in her shop met those early philatelic luminaries, their earnestness a great example to him. But it would seem he preferred Pierre Mahé; in 1874 he employed the dealer as the curator of his private stamp collection, charging Mahé to make it the best in the world.

Ferrary was 'a magnet for rare stamps' and was obsessed with completion. He collected everything – every variety possible of every stamp ever issued, used and unused. While not, apparently, fond of blocks and multiples of stamps, or stamps on covers (they took up too much room), his collection did contain fine examples of these. But Mahé deplored Ferrary's habit of cutting the stamps from envelopes and letters, long after the value of keeping entires intact was understood by the philatelic community ('unpardon-able!'). Attainment of completion and perfection required constant attention, and Ferrary travelled regularly throughout Europe and Britain searching for stamps (he spoke at least eight languages). He engaged directly with dealers, rather than leave everything to Mahé (in contrast to many of today's wealthy collectors, who leave such transactions to their secretaries and their agents), and as a consequence his philatelic knowledge was strong. This didn't mean he was never duped and he knew that he had been on occasion.

However, he told his friend, the Stanley Gibbons dealer Charles J. Phillips, 'I would sooner buy one hundred forgeries than miss that variety I could not find elsewhere.'

Ferrary purchased his first 'Post Office' from Moens in 1875, the newly discovered unused two pence from Bordeaux. No other 'Post Office' stamps came on to the market again until Moens obtained Perinelle's specimens in January 1881. The Belgian dealer would have known Ferrary's wants and offered him the two 'Post Office'. When Ferrary purchased Philbrick's collection later that year it was probably irrelevant to him that Philbrick's albums contained two 'Post Office' stamps, given that he already possessed three, although the used specimens he obtained made the perfect set of used and unused 'Post Office', which only Émile Lalanne had possessed until then.

Ferrary's acquisitions encompassed more than most other collectors were willing or able to include in their collections – except for one other: Thomas Keay Tapling. Inevitably, when Ferrary began purchasing the collections of serious philatelists in their entirety, he accumulated duplicates, but he would only part with these in exchange for stamps he wanted. Thomas Keay Tapling had such a stamp (or stamps; what exactly is disputed in the literature) and in turn he required a two pence 'Post Office'. Since 1881 Ferrary had owned five of the Mauritian rarities. Some time in the mid- to late 1880s he parted with the spare unused two pence (his first 'Post Office', purchased back in 1875) to satisfy his own and Tapling's wants.

Born in 1855 in Surrey, Tapling too had collected stamps from an early age; at sixteen he was already a member of the Philatelic Society of London. Called to the Bar in 1880, his philatelic enthusiasm only strengthened with the increasing demands on his time, a reflection of the value of the hobby to him. Tapling took

Thomas Keay Tapling.

over the family business on the death of his father and was elected to Parliament in 1886. In 1881 he was made vice-president of the Philatelic Society to Judge Philbrick's president. Tapling was generous with his philatelic knowledge, in person and in print, and happy to make his stamps available for study. Working with his collection was a true recreation and source of pleasure, as was socializing with his fellow collectors.

London's philatelic fraternity was a very jovial one. Tapling hosted the annual meeting of the Philatelic Society over dinner at a Holborn restaurant in December 1884, and Ferrary and another leading French philatelist, one of the brothers Caillebotte, were his guests. Judge Philbrick, the old dealer Stanley Gibbons and Major Evans were among those in attendance. Monsieur Caillebotte replied to the toast on behalf of the guests – Ferrary was of a more retiring nature – and the evening ended with rounds of singing.

Nurtured by England's leading collectors at an impressionable age, it is not surprising, given his adequate financial means, that Tapling should have become so completely enamoured of stamps and willing to pursue the ideal of the all-world general collection. His first step in this direction was, like Ferrary's, the purchase in 1881 or 1882 of another great collection, that of fellow Englishman and 'born philatelist' W. E. Image (1807–1903), a Fellow of the Royal College of Surgeons. Image's collection was rich in rarities and far surpassed Tapling's efforts to that time. However, it lacked the 'Post Office', and philatelic obituaries of Image recorded the sad fact that he had passed up the opportunity to purchase two of the stamps. He had been offered first refusal of Perinelle's two 'Post Office', but deemed Moens's asking price of 6,000 francs too high. Ferrary subsequently paid 5,500 francs for them. When Image died, two 'Post Office' were worth in excess of ten times that amount. Tapling's first 'Post Office' – the used one penny on the envelope addressed to Monsieur Alcide Marquay – would not be acquired until 1884, through his purchase of Major Evans's collection of Mauritius.

Tapling never tired of purchasing from dealers and buying up whole collections. As the *Philatelic Record* put it, 'The changes of life are many, hence owing to death, removals, and other causes, quite a depletion of the older collectors in his favour took place.' Tapling absorbed at least eighteen major collections into his own. But in none of these did he claim the two pence 'Post Office' to complete his early Mauritius, a gap finally filled by the exchange with Ferrary (the deal struck, perhaps, at one of the Philatelic Society's boozy dinners). By 1890 Tapling's collection was as complete and perfect a story of the first fifty years of the postage stamp as he could make it, containing almost every stamp ever issued and including most of the rarities. Only Ferrary's collection was greater. (There seems to have been little rivalry between the two great collectors, although Ferrary, curiously, did not become a member of the Philatelic Society in London until after Tapling's death – six months later to be precise.)

But 'Sorrowful indeed!' were the collectors who picked up their black-edged philatelic journals in April 1891. Thomas Keay Tapling had died suddenly of complications from pleurisy at the age of thirty-five. Tapling was well liked – friendly, hospitable, modest – and committed to the greater good of stamp collecting. 'It will be remembered of him', noted one obituary, 'that from childhood to his latest days he never once wavered or faltered in his love of our science, and that he died as he had always lived – a true gentleman and philatelist.'

Tapling had 'fully contemplated and arranged for the disposal of his stamps, whenever the summons came'. He bequeathed the entire collection of over 200,000 stamps to the British Museum, along with money to fund its arrangement and description, stipulating that it be called the Tapling Collection and, importantly, that it never be broken up and sold. Despite the high monetary value of the collection (in 1891 reckoned to be around £50,000), the museum's trustees dithered for a time in accepting such modern items into their custody. Happily they relented and after years of preparation, the Tapling Collection was finally put on permanent public display in 1903. But some of the rarer stamps of British Guiana and Hawaii, and the two 'Post Office' stamps, were withheld from view, deemed too valuable and precious. On this the *London Philatelist* remarked, 'So great is the reputation of these latter two stamps as *the* great rarities... that to many collectors [the Tapling display] will seem like *Hamlet* without the Prince of Denmark.'

Albert Rae was a Mauritian public servant who collected books and documents relating to the history of the island. He was also passionate and knowledgeable about its stamps and must have hoped one day to encounter a 'Post Office' himself. In 1887 he finally did: a used two pence blue on a fragment of an envelope or letter, addressed to 'H. Caunten, avocat, au Port Louis'. A Monsieur Henri Adam Junior acquired the stamp in that year, perhaps from Monsieur Caunten himself, and Albert Rae purchased it soon after from Adam for a 'trifling sum'. A subscriber to Moens's *Le Timbre-Poste* (a postcard from Rae to Moens renewing the subscription in 1886 exists in a private collection in Mauritius), Rae would have been aware of the great value of early Mauritius stamps. He savoured his possession of the 'Post Office' for a year or two, then consigned his collection to a Parisian dealer in 1889.

The Caunten fragment changed hands several times that year, a certain Monsieur Perrissin paying 4,000 francs for it in November. What did this sum mean for the price of a 'Post Office'? Ferrary had paid 5,500 francs – the equivalent of £110 per stamp – for two unused 'Post Office' back in 1881. It is difficult to attach a monetary value to the only other 'Post Office' transactions that occurred between 1881 and the arrival of the Mauritian discovery on the market in 1889–90. The 'Post Office' stamps had appreciated in value, not quite doubling in price, and Perrissin might reasonably have expected a quick return on his investment, given the length of time since the last open sale of a 'Post Office'. He sent the stamp to a special exhibition held under the auspices of the Philatelic Society of London in May 1890 (Tapling was a major organizer), and his agents there, Whitfield King & Co., produced a special postcard advertisement featuring a photograph of the Caunten fragment. It was captioned 'photograph of the rarest stamp known'. The singular specimen was offered at £200 and the blurb on the reverse of the advertisement implied that the reason for the rarity of the first issue of Mauritius was that the stamps had been printed from single engravings (not a plate of multiples), and the word 'Office' was an error, soon corrected to 'Paid'. But on this occasion, the two pence 'Post Office' did not sell. Shortly after the exhibition Perrissin let the stamp go at a loss to another dealer for only 3,500 francs. This dealer in turn was able to sell the stamp a month later at a small profit for 3,750 francs.

The 'Post Office' stamps had increased in value, that value closely tied to the desire of collectors. With the two great collectors Tapling and Ferrary satisfied, the market for these expensive rarities appeared to have stabilized. They were 'unattainables' – beyond the reach of the ordinary collector. Ordinary collectors were, nevertheless, still perfectly happy to dream about chancing across as yet unrecognized 'Post Office' specimens in insignificant stamp or correspondence collections.

Smarting at the loss of Philbrick's collection to Ferrary, the *Philatelic Record* had expressed the forlorn hope back in 1882 that, 'Were the rarer stamps less hoarded and huddled in senseless reduplication into a few collections, they would pass more frequently through the dealers' hands, and be sold at lower prices.' But this had not occurred. The 'whim and rapacity' of the dealers, aided by publicity in the French and British daily press ('news-paper twaddle', according to 'An Old Collector' in the *Philatelic Record* in 1887), had only caused prices – and the fame – of rare stamps in general to increase.

Reflecting on this period as the century drew to a close, the gentleman of the *London Philatelist* detected a change in the practice of their hobby. It was certainly no longer possible to keep to the lines of a 'general collection of an inclusive and scientific nature', because of both the flood of varieties 'borne upon us with crushing effect' and the high cost of rare stamps. Even aiming for completion in Great Britain, one of her colonies or in the European countries was difficult. Tapling's collection would never come back on to the market and Ferrary was impossible to outbid. His collection too, it was surmised, was destined to find its way to a museum, because he, like Tapling, could not bear the thought of its dispersal.

Ferrary's mother, the Duchess of Galliera, had died in 1888. She willed much of her great fortune to the establishment of charitable institutions, including three hospitals and, along with her sizeable art collection, left two palazzos to the city of Genoa. The mansion on the rue de Varenne, the Hôtel Matignon, she gave to the Austro-Hungarian Emperor Franz-Joseph for use as the Austrian Embassy in Paris, stipulating that a wing be set aside for her son's use during his lifetime. The Hôtel Matignon, where Ferrary spent much of his life, had had a colourful history, previously belonging to Talleyrand during the years following the Revolution and then to the Emperor. After the restoration of the monarchy, the Hôtel Matignon passed into royal ownership, and a community of nuns was established there to pray for the souls of victims of the Revolution. It was turned back over to the government after the 1848 revolution and the Duke of Galliera became the next owner. It was a grand building and could accommodate upwards of 3,000 party guests. Charles J. Phillips, the English dealer who visited Ferrary in his apartments there, described the courtyard as so big that twenty coaches drawn by four horses apiece could manoeuvre easily within it. The entrance to Ferrary's rooms was guarded by 'several large and fierce dogs', which apparently roamed loose in the courtyard. Three rooms on the first floor housed the stamp collection.

Phillips was one of the lucky few allowed an audience with the great collection. Ferrary was not inclined to share his wealth of knowledge, either through publication (as Philbrick, Rothschild and Tapling were) or through exhibiting portions of it, as members of philatelic societies commonly did. Many viewed this as extremely selfish. But Phillips explained that Ferrary was protecting himself from being inundated, at absurd prices, with 'varieties' he didn't have. Everybody knew that it was outside Ferrary's power to refuse such stamps (for he truly had the *timbromanie*), and his family, becoming increasingly concerned at the manner in which their inheritance was being spent, are said at one point to have threatened to sue Ferrary for wasting money on stamps. The harassed collector supposedly undertook studies in law to prove that he was of sound mind.

Perhaps he was a little eccentric – Ferrary is said to have refused a request from the then Prince of Wales to view the stamps, because he had promised his deceased mother that he would never allow his stamps to leave their house on the rue de Varenne. 'I only saw him once,' wrote the philatelic journalist Fred Melville, 'but the recollection of him is still vivid. Looking anything but spick and span, rather dowdy in fact, apparently careless of his attire, except for the yachting cap he always affected, his hypnotic eyes fixed themselves upon my memory.'

He would shuffle into the dealers' shops and they would greet him, 'Bonjour, Monsieur Philipp!' (It was always wise not to attempt a surname.) The manner in which Ferrary bought his stamps was still a talking point years afterwards. The pages of the dealers' stock book turned under his seemingly casual glance, as he steadily removed the stamps to a pile on the counter until it had grown to a size he was happy with. He refused to bargain and placed a heap of gold coins next to the stamps commensurate with his opinion of their worth. Then, without a care, he would shove his precious purchases into the pockets of his tatty overcoat and trousers and leave without a word.

Quietly, and seemingly unknown to the philatelic world, Ferrary purchased Arthur de Rothschild's collection in 1893. In doing so, he became the owner of two more 'Post Office' stamps, bringing his total to six. Some would later say that he had a penchant for the 'Post Office', but it was probably no more than he had for other rare stamps. Acquiring Rothschild's two did give him a pair of very strong bargaining tools to use as exchanges in his quest for other stamps, but he held on to the six 'Post Office' for almost twenty years.

The sale of Rothschild's collection did not affect the 'Post Office' market, but in the same year, 1893, four 'Post Office' stamps came back on to the market, the first since the used two pence on the Caunten fragment had failed to sell for the asking price of £200 in London in 1890. Émile Lalanne, the Bordeaux collector and contemporary of the Mesdames Borchard and Desbois, had at last decided to part with his collection. It was bought in its entirety by a Monsieur Piet Lataudrie, who retained the used 'Post Office' specimens until 1896, but – 'judging two Post Office sufficient to his happiness' – immediately sold the unused specimens to the stamp-dealing firm of Stanley Gibbons in London. They paid £680 for them in 1893 and happily advertised their purchase as the highest price ever paid for two stamps. The value of the 'Post Office' stamps was again on the rise. Lataudrie obtained the equivalent of £1,600 for the two used specimens in 1896 (an incredible rise in value over a short time), and when Legrand too decided to part with the bulk of his collection in 1897, the two 'Post Office' it contained were extracted and fetched £1,860 (£1,920 in some accounts) – the equivalent of 46,500 francs. Moens marvelled at these sums, recalling that he had purchased these very same 'Post Office' stamps (a used one penny and unused two pence) almost thirty years previously from Madame Desbois for 200 francs. It was the ultimate example, for the *London Philatelist*, of the change that had been wrought since the early days of stamp collecting – the doctor's two 'Post Office' stamps had been purchased 'for a larger sum than he has expended on his whole collection!' With each new 'Post Office' sale from this period, a new record was set.

With Tapling dead, and Lalanne's and Legrand's collections broken up and sold, Ferrary was now almost the sole survivor of the traditional type of general, inclusive collectors. Certainly, his collection was the greatest still intact.

Jean-Baptiste Moens died in 1908 and Pierre Mahé died in 1913. Both losses would have been upsetting for Ferrary, who reputedly once said to a rival dealer that Moens and Mahé were his gods. The curatorship of Ferrary's collection was passed to Pierre Mahé's son Edward. Ferrary continued his stamp-related travels across the Continent until the outbreak of the First World War. He spent some time in Vienna early in the war, then returned to Paris, before leaving for Switzerland in 1916 (he had become a Swiss citizen eight years earlier). The French government would not allow him to return to Paris, so Ferrary asked Edward Mahé to send him a small portion of his collection (Sicily and Greece) to keep his spirits up.

In May 1917, in his late sixties, Ferrary died of a heart attack. There was immediate speculation about what would happen to his collection. His intention had been that his stamps should stay together. Ferrary's will made it clear that the collection was to go to Germany, there to be displayed as the 'Collection of Arnold'. (He had, at some point, also assumed the middle name of Arnold, a close friend.) This would never happen. The French government seized Ferrary's home in Paris, the Hôtel Matignon (which subsequently became, and remains, the residence of the French prime minister). The great philatelic collection was sequestered for sale to recoup war reparations from Germany. Monsieur Philipp could not have imagined a worse fate for his stamps.

PRETTY PHILATELIC FAIRY TALES

*A stamp collector, the possessor of a collection of
12,544 stamps, wishes to marry a lady who is an
ardent collector and the possessor of the Blue Penny
stamp of Mauritius, issued in 1847.*

Advertisement, *Monitor*, 1891

The reappearance of 'Post Office' stamps on the market in 1893 set philatelic fanciers thinking again about fortunes to be made and where to find them. New discoveries had been few and far between. The last two specimens had been found in Mauritius – a one penny by Major Evans in 1878 and a two pence by Albert Rae in 1887. To date, the stamps had been discovered only in the island itself and among the Borchards' single cache of correspondence in Bordeaux.

A new (or as yet unrecorded) 'Post Office' stamp surfaced early in 1897, with antecedents again going back to Madame Borchard. It was a heavily obliterated one penny cut into on the left side, the result apparently of a direct transaction between Madame Borchard, her scissors and a man named Schiller. Moens was unsure when this transaction had occurred, and thought perhaps it was as early as 1864–5, contemporaneous with Madame's dealings with Albert Coutures and predating her contact with Madame Desbois. Moens also recorded of this find, made by Bordeaux dealer Marcel Pouget, 'This stamp came from a wretched little collection, for only

100 francs, if we are to believe the first version given us.' The Belgian dealer knew the value of a discovery story like this, and knew that Pouget would know it too, continuing, 'On the contrary, it was in a lovely collection, for which thousands of francs were paid, according to another version.' Whatever the truth of these stories, that there were two versions – one more tantalizing, of the rags to riches variety – reflected a growing interest in the circumstances of the stamps' discovery.

The idea that these valuable scraps of paper might still be chanced upon had great appeal to a general public becoming more familiar with such stories, which were now finding their way from the philatelic into the daily press.

One rumour had it, back in 1893, that the original 'Post Office' plates had been found and that the Mauritius government were going to reprint from them. But they were only the plates of one of the later issues of the 1850s and they remained for the time being in the vaults of the Mauritius Treasury. Confused reports of fresh discoveries appeared a few years later in the hiatus between the Gibbons firm's high-priced purchase of Lalanne's unused specimens and Lataudrie's subsequent sale of Lalanne's used specimens for the extraordinary sum of £1,600 in 1896. In exasperation at having been sent the story so many times, in April of that year the London magazine *Stamp Collectors' Fortnightly* published an extract sent to them by some journalist friends, with the rider 'we at length strangle our dubiety and give it to our readers for what it is worth'. Under the heading 'A pretty philatelic fairy tale', the editors quoted the latest stamp-collecting story:

A friend of the editor of the Paris *Figaro* read a short account of the sale [an old collection of stamps to a Monsieur Victor Robert], and the prices quoted, notably those of the Réunion stamps, made his mouth water; for he had lived at the Mauritius about a score and a half or two score of years ago, and he regretted that he had not bought a few. Then suddenly, as if moved by an electric shock, he went to his writing-table or store cupboards and began searching among his old papers. It had flashed on him that in those days of yore he had on one occasion written a letter to Europe, which for some reason or other he had not despatched, and the envelope of which had not been torn up. And surely enough, he found the old wrapper with four absolutely new stamps of the Mauritius on it. These four tiny bits of paper are said to be worth close upon £1400.

The editors' scepticism was probably warranted; they were in a good position to judge the story on its merits and against the numerous similar stories which seemed by inference to be doing the rounds. Was there any truth to the tale? While not designating the stamps in question as the 'Post Office' issue (the editors of the *Philatelic Journal of Great Britain*, however, said the story as originally reported had done so), the article did describe them as 'said to be only fourteen specimens in existence', which is almost correct – fifteen were known by this time – and it also mentioned one of these fourteen stamps as having been 'sold in England last November for £340'. No sales of 'Post Office' stamps were recorded in either 1894 or 1895, so perhaps the narrator was thinking of the two 'Post Office' stamps which the Gibbons firm had purchased for £680 in 1893, just halving this total to reckon the price of one. Or perhaps the story is muddled and the stamps were the dazzling block of four unused one penny 'Post Paid' later owned by Henry Duveen, the London-based art and antiques dealer.

The sale of Legrand's two 'Post Office' stamps in 1897 – another heavily obliterated, ex–Borchard one penny and an unused ex–Borchard two pence – for the reported figure of £1,860 increased the public's curiosity about the stamps, particularly as to how many were known. Various philatelic journals published listings of the recorded 'Post Office' stamps and their owners from this time. With at least sixteen now known (the grubby one penny belonging to Schiller having surfaced in early 1897), they were not as rare as a few other stamps, it seemed, but, as the *London Philatelist* said, 'It is their prestige that has made, and always will make them the "king and queen of stamps".'

Would any more 'Post Office' stamps be found, previously unrecorded, in collections first started in the 1860s? Or would any new discoveries occur in Mauritius and France? Given that the Bordeaux discoveries of the 1860s were a direct result of trade with Mauritius, what about other places that the island's residents had had reason to communicate with? During September and October 1847, ships bearing goods from England, Ireland, Sweden, India, South Africa and Australia had travelled to and passed by Port Louis.

Perhaps the fabulous price fetched by Legrand's two 'Post Office' in 1897 did provide inspiration to philatelists and interested collectors alike, for some time in that year the first discovery of the 'Post Office' stamps occurred outside Mauritius and France.

Charles Howard had chanced upon his prize walking among the gilded birdcages, spices and rolls of shimmering textiles displayed on the stalls running the length of a Bombay bazaar. He may have belonged to the growing class of stamp collectors and been actively seeking the bright little scraps of paper, which often found their way on to the local market stalls, quite at home in the confusion of

The Jerrom letter to Bombay bearing two one penny 'Post Office' stamps.

objects and colours. There, one day in 1897, he came across some old stamps and began sorting through them, when two brilliant orange-red portraits of the Queen – a much younger visage than the old round-cheeked profile so familiar to him from her proud statue outside Bombay's Victoria Station – caught his eye. It looked like an envelope but was in fact a folded letter sheet: a single sheet of paper with the contents written on one side, folded up into a rectangle resembling an envelope with the address inscribed on the front. Side by side on the front were two one penny 'Post Office' stamps from Mauritius, both impressions still beautifully clear despite the dark lines of the cancellation. The letter was addressed to 'Thos. Jerrom Esqr., Secretary to the Bombay Auxiliary Bible Society, The Esplanade, Bombay'. A date stamp in the left-hand corner revealed that the letter had been posted from Mauritius on 4 January 1850 – a rare and interesting find.

Did Howard realize what he had stumbled upon? It is not clear what he paid for the letter, but the fact that he brought it with him to London to sell the following year suggests that he did.

None of the earliest owners of the Jerrom letter thought to unfold the sheet and reveal its contents, or if they did, no record was made. 'Post Office' experts repeatedly asked the owners to open the letter, but they were always refused, no doubt because of the fragility of the paper. It was not until 1968, when the letter was sold in New York for the highest price ever paid for a philatelic item, that more information came to light. The sale had attracted front-page headlines on both sides of the Atlantic, prompting a great-niece of Thomas Jerrom to come forward. It emerged that Jerrom was an Englishman who in 1847 had gone with the Church Missionary Society to Bombay, where he was ordained a priest the following year. He married in 1851 and died shortly afterwards at the age of thirty-five. In 1976 the letter had new owners, the Weill brothers, who agreed to its being opened for examination. The sender was revealed to be another cleric, the Reverend Langrishe Banks, who was working in Mauritius for the British and Foreign Bible Society. He would die in the island, succumbing to the cholera epidemic that decimated Port Louis in 1854. The letter acknowledged receipt of 'a box of Scriptures etc.' and was most apologetic for the delay in doing so, their having been sent without a return address. Banks hadn't known whom to thank until Jerrom followed up the box of Bibles with a letter inquiring whether they had ever been received. A gentle and unimportant slice of colonial life had survived its two communicants thanks to a pair of sharp eyes and two plain little stamps.

Was it curious that the letter was date stamped 4 January 1850, when, according to Brownrigg, Colonial Postmaster of Mauritius at the time, all the 'Post Office' issue had sold out within days of their September 1847 issue? Not if Mr Lumgair's 'Mauritius Memories' were correct. The former Port Louis postal clerk recalled that locals occasionally came across specimens of the 'Post Office' and 'Post Paid' issues, forgotten and unused, in drawers and went to the post office to inquire whether they could still legally be used for postage. (They could.) It is difficult to imagine that any of the small number of 'Post Office' stamps issued could have survived and been subsequently used like this into the 1860s (the period that Lumgair was writing about), but it seems a reasonable explanation for Reverend Banks's use of the stamp early in 1850. Or it might have been that Banks was in the habit of applying the stamps to his letters before completing them, and, not yet in possession of a return address for Jerrom, he put the letter to one side until he had it.

There were several versions of Howard's find circulating in the philatelic press. Moens reported in *Le Timbre-Poste* in September 1898 that Howard was a friend of Judge Philbrick, and implied that Howard was only passing through Bombay, where he bought some old correspondence. Moens revised his story in his 1899 account of the 'Post Office' stamps: 'It is said now that the discovery was made, improbably, it seems to us, in an Indian bazaar.' Why improbably? Some of the Borchards' old correspondence had ended up wrapped around a hawker's wares to be sold on the streets of Bordeaux. The *Monthly Journal*, meanwhile, claimed that the letter had been found in a sugar broker's office in Bombay.

Some seventy years later details of the story were still emerging. In October 1968, as the Jerrom letter went under the hammer in New York, a small note appeared in London's *Evening Standard* from H. G. Slater of Surrey. He was, he said, the son of a friend of Howard's from India days. In Slater's version, Howard had come across the philatelic treasure in the bazaar but hadn't enough cash on him to purchase the 'bag of stamps' and so 'went off borrowing from his friends', of whom Slater's father was one. Money obtained (five rupees, the equivalent then of around five shillings), Howard returned to the bazaar as daylight ebbed and only just beat somebody else to the stamps.

Stories like this always surfaced at the time of sales of the 'Post Office' stamps. They usually contained these elements of chance, luck and paltry original purchase prices, and smacked of exaggeration. Slater's story may have had its share of mythologizing, but was probably close to the mark when he speculated of Howard that he 'was a pretty shrewd chap. He knew he could not get a good market for the envelope in India, so he came to London. He had it photographed to show prospective purchasers and put the original in the bank.'

Less than a year after the Jerrom letter came on to the market in London, Moens stated that Howard had purchased the letter for £50, not five rupees. The Stanley Gibbons dealer Charles J. Phillips, to whom Howard first offered the letter when he arrived in London, also believed that Howard had paid £50 for it. Phillips was recalling this many years after the event, in 1939, and may have been using Moens's biographies of the 'Post Office' stamps to jog his memory. However, unlike Moens, Phillips was directly involved with the bargaining over the price of the item, so the figure of £50 may be accurate. Regardless of what he had paid for it, Howard certainly knew the letter and its stamps were worth much more than that. Phillips claimed that Howard offered it to him for the extravagant sum of £2,500 and, 'after much dickering backwards and forwards', sold it instead to the dealer W. H. Peckitt for £1,620.

'Post Office' stamps were now expected to sell for a large sum, but even Moens balked at the news: 'To buy a stamp for 25,000 francs, it is good, it is even an extravagance which not everybody would allow themselves; but to buy two other stamps, identically alike, it is no longer extravagance, it is insanity.'

*

The sensation of 1898, however, had been discovered and made known earlier in the year, heralding one of the most intense and concentrated periods of philatelic finds in the history of stamp collecting. It was another widow, this time in Mauritius, who made the lucky discovery.

Madame Duvivier, like most of the wealthier class of Mauritians in the nineteenth century, lived out of Port Louis itself, at Calebasses, to the north. Her husband, Edmond Duvivier, had been a solicitor in Port Louis during the 1840s and travelled to his offices daily, while his sisters, the highly regarded Madamoiselles Duvivier, ran a school for girls on one of the main thoroughfares of the town. As for many widows, there came a time when the house was too big for her and she could no longer live on her own. In preparing to move, she began to sort through the old papers which the family had accumulated. Perhaps she also consulted her nephew Aimé Duvivier about the best course of action. Aimé was the son of her husband's brother Emile, and worked in the civil service, attached to the archives since 1879. He had been appointed assistant archivist in 1885, rising to archivist in 1891, a position he would hold for the rest of his life. He had a fine and detailed knowledge of the history and topography of Port Louis, was involved with the island's *Revue Historique et Littéraire* and was also at one time treasurer of the Mauritius Institute. Who better to consult about old papers? While there is no written evidence that Aimé advised his aunt, he did supply the publishers of *Mauritius Illustrated* (1914) with a photograph of the item he may have been instrumental in saving from the waste-paper basket.

For Madame Duvivier had found a small buff-coloured envelope, addressed simply to her late husband – Ed. Duvivier Esq. – and bearing in the upper right-hand corner a beautifully clear specimen of the by now famed orange-red one penny 'Post Office' stamp of Mauritius. She may well have known of the existence, rarity and fame of the early Mauritian stamps herself, but Aimé is certain to have known, and may even in his first year of government employment been lucky enough to catch a glimpse of the envelope addressed to Alcide Marquay – strikingly similar if the visual memories could be stretched back that far – before it was taken away from the island by Major Evans in 1879.

Like the Marquay envelope, the Duvivier envelope was cancelled with a MAURITIUS POST OFFICE hand stamp, dated 21 September 1847. Discussing the find, the editor of the *Philatelic Journal of Great Britain* compared the handwriting on the Duvivier envelope with that on the Marquay envelope and declared, 'This almost proves what has been asserted, namely, that all the 1d. stamps were used to send out invitation cards to a dance at Government House.' The circumstances and myths surrounding the ball, the stamps, the invitations and the Gomms had yet to crystallize and be understood, but somebody had evidently made some connections between the stamps and the ball before Madame Duvivier's discovery.

Perhaps the first reference to a ball in connection with the stamps is that given by a gentleman signing himself 'Cerne' in the *Westminster Gazette* in 1897 (a gentlemen who knew his Mauritian history – the name originally given the island by the Portuguese in 1507 was Ilha do Cirne, Swan Island, and the island's oldest newspaper was named after this, *Le Cernéen*):

Sir, An explanation of the great rarity of the 1847 postage stamps of Mauritius may interest your philatelist readers. In that year the heads of departments, civil servants, and members of the Governor's staff agreed to give a ball in return for a like entertainment given by the officers of H.M.

12th Regiment. A consignment of stamps for the postal service in the island had been received some days previous to the issue of the invitations. This was the first time postage stamps were used there, and the Postmaster-General, who was on the ball committee, thought it right to have the envelopes containing the invitation cards stamped by way of introducing the system to the inhabitants. But the Radical element was then strong in the Legislative Council, and the chance of having a slap at Government House was too tempting to let slip. So at the next meeting of Council a resolution was passed declaring that postage stamps for a small island were quite unnecessary, and an order given that they should be destroyed. The only stamps used were those on the invitation cards, between two and three hundred in number.

Could 'Cerne' have been speaking from experience – his own or a story passed down to him – or was this version another of the muddled half-truths beginning to permeate the story of the 'Post Office Mauritius'?

The notion of the Legislative Council ordering that the bulk of the first issue be destroyed was not even then supported by the research published by Major Evans in 1880 in the *Philatelic Record*, but perhaps 'Cerne' was not a reader of the philatelic press. That the only stamps used were on the invitations to a ball was also clearly unsupported by the number of specimens already known that had turned up in both France and Mauritius. Might the postmaster sit on a ball committee? Despite the doubtful nature of some of these assertions, could there be a ring of truth to the use of the stamps on the invitations as a means of launching the new postal system? It was certainly an opportune time to do so. (Legrand had been told something similar in correspondence with a Mauritius-based collector back in 1869–70: that the one penny was used by the post office for a special reason.)

There was no mention in the press reports of an invitation or entry card being found with the Duvivier envelope, yet the suggestion that there was entered the literature some time after the publication of Moens's 1899 biography of the stamps. Perhaps this stemmed from a misreading of Moens's French – 'une enveloppe, contenant une invitation au bal donné par le Gouverneur et qui avait été conservée comme un "souvenir de jeunesse"'. The statement could be read two ways: an envelope, enclosing an invitation to a ball given by the Governor, which was kept as a souvenir of youth; or, an envelope, *which had contained* an invitation to a ball. Perhaps the reference to an invitation was general, to indicate the reason the envelope might have been kept as a souvenir. The ball envelopes now extant were all empty when found.

Where, then, did the reference to Lady Gomm come from? 'Cerne' did not mention either the Governor or his wife. Moens, writing in 1899, two years after Cerne's anecdote was published, said that the ball was given by the Governor. In a continuation of his account some months after this, Moens responded to doubts apparently expressed to him as to the purpose of the invitation. The nephew of Madame Duvivier (Aimé presumably) had written to Moens: 'The envelope had contained an invitation to a ball given by Lady Gomm, the wife of the Governor.' This appears to be how the connections between Lady Gomm, the ball, the stamps and the envelopes were made. The oral tradition was sound, for Aimé had it directly from his aunt, who would have attended the ball herself.

The Duvivier envelope was first offered for a large sum (reportedly £1,500) to the firm of Stanley Gibbons, but it ended up in the hands of dealer W. H. Peckitt in London for 'over £1000'. The sale commanded attention in the press and was noted as 'the highest price ever paid for a single stamp'. Comparisons with the estimated cost to Tapling of the Marquay envelope in the 1880s were gleefully drawn: Tapling had paid the equivalent of around £65 to £85.

How much Peckitt really paid for the envelope is not certain, and that is precisely the air of mystery about his business the dealer wished to create. While it was reported in the press at the time as 'over £1000', it seems that he paid only £600. (Moens, in *Le Timbre-Poste* of June 1898, originally gave the £600 figure, and later noted the £1,000 figure with some scepticism; one T. A. Pope, in a lecture published in 1906, said that he was in the island when Madame Duvivier found the envelope, and Peckitt, soon hearing of the find, 'telegraphed out £600 for it'.) Peckitt was apt to keep his prices close to his chest – having paid the 'highest price' ever for a stamp was good for business – and even went so far as to give out false information to Moens, who was putting together his biographies of the 'Post Office' stamps known to date.

Whatever the amount paid, it was a large sum, and it sent a ripple effect through certain quarters of the population in Mauritius. As a solicitor, Edmond Duvivier was probably by nature and profession a good record-keeper, but had he and Alcide Marquay been the only good record-keepers of the hundreds who had attended Lady Gomm's ball?

A retired gentleman in his seventieth year, Charles Félix Henry Adam, known as Henry Adam, recalled that he too had attended that fancy-dress ball more than fifty years ago. Thus inspired, he began to search through the wealth of papers he had accumulated in his long business life. Adam belonged to a well-known Franco-Mauritian family. His father, Joachim Henri Adam, had left France for Mauritius in 1817 and set up in Port Louis as a merchant. Henry Adam followed his father into business, before eventually moving into politics. He held numerous directorships, including that of the Commercial Bank (now the Mauritius Commercial Bank).

Adam had been only eighteen at the time of the ball, not generally an age when a pretty little envelope might be expected to mean much to a young man, so the search was a long shot – but one that paid off. Among his papers Adam found a small buff-coloured envelope, addressed to his younger self – H. Adam Esq Junr. – and bearing in the upper right-hand corner an orange-red one penny 'Post Office' stamp.

Unlike the Marquay and Duvivier envelopes, both postmarked 21 September 1847, curiously Adam's had been sent on 27 September, only three days before the ball. Perhaps, as a later commentator has speculated, a last-minute invitation was acceptable to a junior. His parents, the Adams senior, must also have been invited, but Joachim Henri Adam was now long dead, succumbing to the island's cholera epidemic in 1856, and no one at that time would have thought to check the family papers for something as ephemeral as an envelope.

Adam apparently felt some embarrassment at selling off something personal for profit, so when he sold the envelope to the French dealer Théophile Lemaire in 1899, he requested that the price be kept secret. He also requested that his name be erased from the envelope and some attempts were made to do so. The 'Adam' was scraped away, but the ghost of an outline remains and is clearly discernible. Despite these efforts, Henry Adam's name lived on in philatelic circles worldwide and in Mauritius in a way he could never have foreseen.

W. H. Peckitt was particularly acquisitive when it came to these specimens of the 'Post Office' on cover. 'I have a great opinion of rare stamps, which are constantly getting rarer,' he said with a notable smile in an interview early in 1899. Although more profit was to be made on the commoner stamps, he preferred the larger turnover and greater sums of money associated with rare stamps – 'old Continentals, old Colonials, old anything,' he once said with measured glee. Like many other stamp dealers in London, he worked from premises on the Strand. It was coincidence perhaps – although with Peckitt there was always the chance that it was showmanship too – that his rooms were above those of a jeweller's. A small glass showcase, containing a few choice stamps and a card, 'W. H. Peckitt, Dealer in Rare Stamps, First Floor', glittered among the jeweller's window display of gold and silver, beckoning philatelists up the nearby winding staircase. 'There,' wrote one visitor, 'are gems brighter in the eyes of the philatelist than any that his neighbour the jeweller can supply.' Peckitt acquired the nick-name 'The Panther of the Strand' for his quickness to close deals and beat rivals to the prize. He was able to retire on his profits at the age of forty.

Peckitt acquired the Adam ball envelope from Lemaire in 1899 for £800 – a figure given in the journal *Postage Stamp*. Although some in the philatelic world were sure that Peckitt had paid £1,000 for Madame Duvivier's envelope the previous year, Lemaire must have known that he hadn't.

What is clear from these transactions is that, in the space of a year, the value to the dealers of a one penny 'Post Office' on cover had risen at least 30 per cent, from £600 to £800. From the collectors' point of view the price had risen from £850 to £1,080: the Earl of Kintore bought the Duvivier envelope from Peckitt for £850 in 1898, and Henry Duveen bought the Adam envelope from Peckitt for £1,080 in 1899. When the discovery of the Jerrom letter became known, Moens thought that this might 'arrest the upward movement in the price of these stamps', but it did not have that effect.

The value of the two pence 'Post Office' was another story. Henry Duveen, the purchaser of the Adam envelope, had previously paid £1,200 for Legrand's unused ex-Borchard two pence in 1898, more in fact than he paid Peckitt a year later for the Adam envelope (£1,080). This perhaps reflected a higher value placed on unused specimens and the beginning of a slight bias in favour of the two pence blue over the one penny orange-red.

'Post Office Mauritius' prices were escalating. So too was the interest of the daily press in the sale of postage stamps and stamp collections generally. From little or no interest in stamps as objects of curiosity and commodity in 1893–4 (of more note in these years, according to the indexers of *The Times*, were sales of exotic lepidoptera, the Queen's Jersey cattle, violins, autographs and orchids) newspapers began to report their sale at auction more regularly from the mid-1890s, often under the heading 'High Prices for Postage Stamps'. At one of these, in October 1895, the firm of Ventom, Bull and Cooper realized the highest price to date paid for a stamp at auction: £140 for an unused two pence blue 'Post Paid' stamp of Mauritius. It wasn't a 'Post Office', but it *was* a Mauritian stamp, confirming the rarity and desirability of all the early issues. The sums were less than what was being made by dealers through private sales, but they were enough to catch the attention of the general public. Stamp collecting was fast becoming 'the spoilt darling of the drawing rooms'. Critics of stamp collecting began to focus on the high prices paid for rarities – those 'dirty little scraps of paper' – and on their relative intrinsic value.

'Intrinsic' means 'belonging to a thing by its very nature'. Used in relation to stamps, the phrases 'intrinsic value' or 'intrinsic merit' were commonly used to mean the base value of stamps – the sum for which they could have been bought when first issued, available to any purchaser over the counter in a post office. The intrinsic value of stamps was acknowledged to be small. A one penny stamp had an intrinsic value of one penny. In reminiscences published in the *Stamp Collectors' Fortnightly* in 1900, philatelist Walter Nathan described the development of the free market and the rise of philatelic auctions. Before the days of auctions, he stated, it had been difficult to quickly realize the financial value of stamps: that is, convert them into cash. By the late 1890s auctioneers were more inclined to offer cash advances to philatelic clients wishing to sell, indicating that 'from a merely fancy value' they had become a 'pawnable commodity'. Stamps had attained an acknowledged base value beyond the original face value – a value improved by stable supply and demand.

In the eyes of many nineteenth- and early twentieth-century observers, when it came to intrinsic beauty, sibling to intrinsic value, the stamp was deemed a failure. Beauty was a serious business in the *fin-de-siècle* years of 1890s Britain. Many found the early colonial stamps profoundly ugly (and a great insult to the Queen). In 1891 London's *Evening Standard* declared, 'We can understand a new or unique orchid fetching a large price, for a flower is in itself a thing of beauty. But what is there in an old postage stamp, which has been used, or has ceased to be issued, that men should be willing to give hundreds of pounds for it?' Philatelists, of course, took issue with such a view. The editors of the *Philatelic Record* countered with 'A unique orchid would probably not long remain so, and it might be nipped in the bud.' Unlike an orchid, a rare stamp could not be propagated, and the gentleman of the *Philatelic Record* felt that if it was mad to pay £100 for an old postage stamp, it was equally mad to give greater sums for orchids, Dutch bulbs, fox terriers, marqueterie or china vases. While some commentators saw high prices as directly proportional to the intrinsic beauty of the items being offered, some philatelists at least were prepared to state the real reason: 'These values do not represent the intrinsic beauty of the several articles except to a very limited extent, the balance being paid for the privilege of owning something that is either rare or unattainable.'

There was more to the collector's passion than this, however. Another philatelic detractor harrumphed at the price of the two 'Post Office Mauritius' sold for more than £1,600 in 1896, 'simply because they bore the misprint "Office" instead of "Paid", and because only a very limited number were issued in that way'. Between 1895 and 1908 a number of stamps were put up as 'rarer than the Post Office Mauritius', such as a 20¢ stamp of St Louis, a 10¢ stamp of Baltimore and a 4½ on 40 reis stamp of Portuguese India dated 1882.

'Rarer than the Post Office Mauritius' became a catch cry, yet no guarantee of commensurate fame and fortune. There was only one stamp – a single specimen of the 1¢ 1856 stamp of British Guiana, discovered in the late 1870s and bought immediately by Ferrary, of course – which did eventually garner the honour of being the most expensive and the rarest stamp in the world. This was in 1980 and the record has been eclipsed many times since by other stamps, including the 'Post Office'. By the early 1930s Charles J. Phillips acknowledged that there were numbers of nineteenth-century stamps rarer than the 'Post Office Mauritius'. They were indeed desirable, but, Phillips noted, 'Do not for a moment think that they should be priced as high. Many of these varieties are of minor importance.'

What, then, were the attributes of the kind of rarity that, as one

British philatelist expressed it in 1895, nourished covetousness, materialism and even 'filthy stinginess'?

Rarities could not be purposefully engineered just by limiting the issue. A stamp was usually deemed more desirable if it had been used for its intended purpose, or had been issued with a genuine purpose, not with an eye to the collecting market. The tendencies of governments to increase the number of stamp issues grew in proportion to the stamp-collecting market, so much so that by the 1890s a group of concerned philatelists in Britain had set themselves up as the SSSS – the Society for the Suppression of Speculative Stamps. Members of the SSSS refused to play into the hands of such speculation. (Not everybody was averse to such stamps, and a tongue-in-cheek plea for an SSSSSS – Society for the Suppression of the Society for the Suppression of Speculative Stamps – was also made at this time.) In a curious reversal of all this, Leonard Sherman, an American collector of new issues, discovered a genuine error on a sheet of US 4¢ Dag Hammarskjöld commemorative stamps he purchased in 1962 (an inverted centre, where the central part of the design was printed upside down in relation to the frame). His discovery was made widely known and the stamps were estimated to be worth up to $500,000. However, on learning of this, the US Postmaster General ordered the further printing of 400,000 copies of the Hammarskjöld stamp with the inverted error... so that all collectors could enjoy them. They proved so popular that ten million of the stamps were ultimately issued and Sherman's dreams of being able to fund his children's college education were sunk, his stamps worth little more than the paper they were printed on.

For a stamp to be worth something it obviously had to be scarce, but more importantly it had to have been available for sale through a post office 'at face value to all comers'. While the 'Post Office

Mauritius' stamps may have ended up the prizes of millionaires, they began life as more democratic, everyday objects in the island colony, available to men of business, the Governor's wife and immigrant workers alike. They could have ended up anywhere and they did, from schoolboy collections and business archives to an exotic Indian bazaar. In such circumstances there was always the chance that another specimen might be discovered – by anybody. Romantic tales of such discoveries enhanced the desirability and reputation of rare stamps. Finding a large cache of a certain rarity might ultimately diminish a stamp's rare status and affect its value, but small clusters of discovery, such as those of the 'Post Office Mauritius' around 1897–9 and later in 1902–3, did nothing but fan the flame.

A stamp's scarceness was partly determined by how many were known in collections and was judged by its past and present availability through dealers. Stamps of great rarity were always heavily researched – particularly the circumstances of their production and initial sale. Major Evans's detailed research in Mauritius in the 1870s (described by one philatelic wag as his 'Parliamentary Blue Book on the exact number of stamps used by each man, woman, and child in Mauritius since the creation of the world') pioneered this kind of philatelic study and proved that the 'Post Office Mauritius' was a separate, genuine and unique issue of no more than the very small number of 1,000 stamps.

It was not only rarity that made stamps favourites. Historic and romantic associations concerning a stamp's circumstances of production, sale or subsequent travels through the collecting world, combined with rarity, elevated certain stamps to superstar status. A 2¢ Hawaiian 'Missionary' stamp of 1851 became known as the 'murder' stamp when Gaston Leroux was murdered for possession of the stamp by his friend Hector Giroux in the 1890s.

Stamps, like other collectables, also acquired value (as well as legitimacy) through their provenance. The 'murder' stamp was owned by both Philipp von Ferrary and a later 'Post Office' owner, Maurice Burrus.

Sometimes there is simply no accounting for taste and as one writer put it in 1924, 'In rare stamps, as in other things in life, "kissing goes by favour".'

THE SCHOOLBOY AND THE
BORDEAUX LETTERS

If… an Elizabethan coin is put in my hand
I can't help feeling thrilled by the contact, even so
slight, with past generations… And so with stamps…
Is there no romance in those little boxes of stamps
found in attics? They always seemed to contain
a rarity which brought comfort after penury
to dear old maiden aunts.

W. Bernard Livermore, 'There *is* romance in stamps',
Stamp Collecting, 1933

Like his British counterpart Peckitt, Théophile Lemaire was already a veteran of the stamp-collecting and -dealing world. By 1899, at the age of thirty-four, he was well established in premises on one of Paris's better streets, the Avenue de l'Opéra, and employed almost thirty people in his stamp business. Along the way the French dealer, 'a typical French gentleman… always smiling', had exhibited at numerous philatelic exhibitions, been regularly rewarded with medals and published his own stamp catalogues, albums and magazine. His fame was assured – and perhaps his taste for the 'Post Office' acquired – with the purchase of Legrand's great collection in 1897.

Lemaire had done well out of the first Mauritius issue. He made a substantial profit on Legrand's one penny and two pence pair, valuing them at 30,000 francs, or around £1,200, selling them not long after purchase to Jules Bernichon for 46,500 francs, or around £1,860. Lemaire was also the first purchaser of the Adam ball envelope. After allowing himself the pleasure of exhibiting it at a philatelic exhibition in Manchester, he made a reasonable profit from its sale to Peckitt in 1899. Moens, describing this transaction with assured irony, said that it was with a heavy heart Lemaire had forced himself to part with his 'Post Office' for hard cash.

Capitalizing on this sale and the growing interest in the 'Post Office' stamps, the French dealer followed Moens into print, quite literally. He reproduced the Belgian dealer's June 1899 biography of the stamps in his own journal, *Le Philatéliste Français*, in a series of articles from December 1899 to February 1900. Information was allowed free passage from one journal to another as long as due acknowledgement was given. This practice (in the philatelic field at least) makes it easier to trace the origins of some of the myths which proliferated about the 'Post Office' stamps. (Each time a new stamp magazine started up, the 'Post Office' story soon graced its pages, presented as the pinnacle of philatelic delight, the error and essay theories again in evidence. By 1890, the *Monthly Journal* was already bemoaning the tendency among 'philatelic Rip Van Winkles' – let alone the layman – to ignore Major Evans's research and rehash ancient theories in relation to the 'Post Office'.)

In 1898 a German philatelic magazine, the *Illustrierte Briefmarken Journal*, published its own summary, precise and correct, of the literature and research on the 'Post Office Mauritius' to date (making no connections with Lady Gomm's ball). The editors observed, 'Within the past few years these two rarities have been repeatedly touched upon in the daily press as well as in our philatelic papers, either for the reason that one or the other was sold at exorbitant prices, or because to those few specimens known another copy was added several months ago.' The Duvivier ball envelope had been reproduced in the *Stamp Collectors' Fortnightly* in 1898, under the heading 'Mr Peckitt's Thousand-pounder'. The journal's editors advised, 'readers of the *Fortnightly* who have not yet acquired the Penny "Post Office" Mauritius may derive some little consolation from this excellent picture'. Five 'Post Office' stamps – both the Adam and Duvivier envelopes, two unused two pence and an unused one penny – were exhibited in London late in December 1902, a surfeit of philatelic richness. Knowledge of the stamps and their desirability was seeping through into the public consciousness.

Around this time, with interest growing in the value of rare stamps, a schoolboy in Bordeaux began wondering what he could do to join the ranks of those lucky stamp hunters. His imagination had been fired by the stories of the ball envelopes and the Jerrom letter found in the bazaar in Bombay. It was 1902, three years since any new discoveries of the 'Post Office' stamps. But Mauritius? What connection had he with that small island so far away?

One version of his story was told by British philatelic writers the Williams brothers in their *Famous Stamps* (1940). According to them, the schoolboy had told his mother what he had been reading about the Mauritian rarities. She, 'her interest kindled by her son's enthusiasm, recalled some of her late husband's early dealings with Mauritius, and told the boy that there might be some old letters from Mauritius in the correspondence files of the firm'. The story continued, in classic fairy-tale fashion:

> Many weary and dusty days the boy spent in turning over piles of musty papers, until his youthful enthusiasm began to wane. It is true that for his labours he was rewarded with finding some old stamps, but there were none among them

of notable rarity, and he almost despaired of making any worth-while discovery. The spark of enthusiasm, although dimmed, continued to burn, and as he came to the last few bundles of letters...

It was natural, of course, to think of correspondence in relation to stamps. Would he be as lucky as Monsieur Adam so recently and find that his father's business correspondence had survived intact after more than fifty years? What if only the letters had been preserved and not the envelopes? Monsieur Adam was fortunate that at the tender age of eighteen he had enjoyed the ball enough to preserve the envelope, along with the memories of that grand occasion.

The French schoolboy *was* lucky, for he found two gems among the old correspondence of the firm of Messieurs Ducau and Lurguie, wine merchants of Bordeaux. Although at first glance they appeared to be envelopes, they were in fact letter sheets. (Had the letters been sent in envelopes, it is unlikely that either envelopes or stamps would have survived.) Both letters were addressed in the same beautiful flowing script, characterized by large, looping capitals, with particularly delightful Ms, Ls and Bs (the ball envelopes were a scrawl in comparison). Most importantly, between them they bore three of the 'Post Office Mauritius' rarities. One letter bore a single two pence blue stamp, a small piece torn out of the left-hand side, which sliced off the top of the O in 'Office'. The other letter was an outstanding find, the first entire to be discovered bearing both a two pence and a one penny 'Post Office' side by side.

Here were superb examples of all any stamp collector could ever ask of the hobby – brilliant stamps on cover, tied to the cover by hand stamps which clearly dated their use, bearing an array of hand stamps which tracked the story of the travels of the letters on their voyage halfway around the world, their purpose clear from the intact contents, and the sender and recipient knowable, alive in spirit if not in fact.

Both letters were addressed to Messieurs Ducau et Lurguie, Bordeaux (Lurguie spelt Lurguy on the single two pence letter). Neither letter bore a street address, but local directories for 1847 reveal that the two Messieurs could be found at number 26, Quai des Chartrons, a large pale stone building of several storeys directly overlooking the port. Close to the hub of Bordeaux commerce, it was a good 'Post Office' address. Adolphe Borchard at this time lived a block back from the quay on the rue Notre-Dame, and his fellow ship brokers, Serizier and Laffitte, were also situated at the Quai des Chartrons, at numbers 2 and 44 respectively.

The letter bearing both stamps, which came to be known as the Bordeaux letter, was inscribed 'via England' in the upper left-hand corner, while the second letter was inscribed 'p. Mischief via

The Bordeaux letter, bearing both one penny and two pence 'Post Office' stamps, found by the mysterious schoolboy in 1902.

England' in the same position. The Bordeaux letter was written by Edward Francis & Co., merchants who were based down at the bustling Port Louis wharf, not too far from the post office. Written on 4 October 1847, the letter was taken to the post office the same day, a Monday, where it was stamped on the back with a neat, crisp impression of the large round MAURITIUS POST OFFICE hand stamp (OC 04 1847) – also used on the ball envelopes. The stamps themselves were tied together by an upside-down PENNY POST hand stamp. The next ship for England, the *John King*, set sail on 7 October. (The next ship to depart Port Louis direct for Bordeaux, the *Equateur*, was not due to leave until 15 October.) Some two months later the *John King* arrived at Plymouth. The mail was there received and stamped on the back SHIP LETTER PLYMOUTH. While in England it was also stamped on the front COLONIES & C. ART.13, as required by the Anglo-French Postal Convention. From England the letter went to Boulogne-sur-Mer on the French coast, not far from Calais, where the two stamps were cancelled again, tied to the envelope with a red hand stamp, BOULOGNE 26 DEC 47. From Boulogne it made haste inland to Paris, where it was received the same day (PARIS 26 DEC 47) and sent on to Bordeaux, arriving two days later (BORDEAUX 28 DEC 47). Once in Bordeaux, Messieurs Ducau and Lurguie paid ninety centimes' delivery charge, eighty-five days after it had been sent from Mauritius.

The content of the letter was typical merchant's correspondence about the sale of thirty barrels of red wine on consignment from Montferrand in France. (Montferrand was not far from Bordeaux, 'a small village hid by poplars'.) The second letter, bearing the single two pence blue stamp, was an exact copy of the first, except for a note at the bottom of the contents, 'Dup. a. p. John King', meaning a duplicate had been forwarded by the ship *John King*. (The long-standing practice of sending duplicates insured against unforeseen mishaps to ships.) The 'p. Mischief' on the cover of this second letter indicated that it had been sent to England via the ship *Mischief*, which left Mauritius a week after the *John King*, on 14 October. It arrived at Boulogne only a day after the first letter (ANGL/BOULOGNE 26 DEC 47). Both letters were carefully filed away by the recipients, evidence of a simple business transaction which long survived any of the parties to it.

In his research on the Bordeaux letters and the postal rates of Mauritius, postal historian Peter Ibbotson pointed out the difference in rates on the identical letters, three pence for the Bordeaux letter and two pence for the letter which followed. He found that there was no such rate as three pence for overseas letters. Two pence was the correct rate for a letter weighing half an ounce and the figure doubled for anything over that. Ibbotson speculated that perhaps Edward Francis & Co. mistakenly thought they had to pay the extra penny to cover the 'inland' delivery of their letter from the post office out to the *John King* in the harbour. Perhaps. A week later, they prepaid the second letter at the correct rate.

As is philately's wont, the postal rates of the two Bordeaux letters have been examined, the letters' voyages documented, even the interpretation of the handwriting has been picked over and local directories in Bordeaux cursorily consulted to correct the spelling of the recipients' names, long accepted unchallenged as Ducan and Lurgney. But the identity of the 'French schoolboy' remains a mystery. From the very beginning his name is missing from the record, which leaves a very cold trail indeed. How and when did he find his way into the literature?

There is little in the way of original documentation recording his discoveries; in Georges Brunel's biographies of the stamps, published in 1916, the schoolboy is listed enigmatically as M. X.

(Monsieur X), identity unknown. Brunel also used a question mark in his listing's price paid column, rather then a zero, indicating that he thought M. X. may not have been the original finder of the stamps in question, but had himself purchased them for an unknown amount.

Early in 1903, the finder of the Bordeaux letters offered them to Théophile Lemaire. The dealer purchased them on 17 January 1903, and two weeks later announced the discovery – of the letter bearing both values of the 'Post Office' stamps only – in his new journal for philatelists, *La Cote Réelle des Timbres-Poste.* Lemaire reminded his readers that only two issues before he had invited any collectors possessing specimens of the 'Post Office' or other rare stamps in good condition to bring them to the house of Lemaire for the best price. The ink had barely dried, he continued, when a collector came forward with the Bordeaux letter, found among some old correspondence. Lemaire used the word 'amateur' to describe the finder of the letter, by which he may have meant to indicate a less serious stamp collector, rather than a philatelist. It was a phrase he used generally in his journal – subtitled *Journal des Philatélistes* – to describe his readers: 'Les amateurs trouveront également le plus bel assortiment à la Maison.' Perhaps he just meant lovers of stamps. There was no mention of a schoolboy.

Lemaire may not yet have known the full details of the find, although as a smart businessman he would surely have gathered what information he could about the circumstances of the discovery. Perhaps the finder, like Henry Adam, had requested anonymity – not that Adam's anonymity had lasted long. Moens, reporting the discovery of the third ball envelope in 1899, noted the addressee's wish that his name be suppressed, but as it was easy to determine from a photograph of the envelope, the old Belgian dealer published Adam's name without a moment's hesitation. Lemaire subsequently proclaimed Adam's identity too.

News of the latest discovery appeared in a short note in the *London Philatelist* in February 1903, courtesy of respected British philatelist Edward Bacon, noting that Lemaire had purchased the one penny and two pence 'Post Office' together on cover. A longer note followed in the March number, the information supplied by Lemaire himself. The discovery was said to have been made by a schoolboy in Marseilles 'among his late father's papers'. The note continued:

> Having heard that some stamps were valuable, the sapient lad procured a catalogue [Lemaire's naturally?] and was able to identify his discovery; to confirm his hopes he took counsel of a collector in Marseilles, who promptly assured him of the value of his stamps, and advised his taking them to Paris. Arrived in the metropolis, the fortunate lad had no difficulty in disposing of them to M. Lemaire for about £1,600, and we trust, in gratitude for his good fortune, will remain a steadfast Philatelist for the remainder of his life!

Marseilles? There was no mention of Marseilles in *La Cote Réelle*. Was Marseilles an inadvertent error introduced by the *London Philatelist*? The early editorial correspondence of the journal cannot now be found in the archives of the Royal Philatelic Society London to check. It is possible that Lemaire might have been laying a false trail about the owner's identity, but he had himself earlier written of the discovery in *La Cote Réelle*, 'Found among old correspondence. Where? But in Bordeaux, good Lord!'

The suggestion that the schoolboy's mother remembered 'some of her late husband's early dealings with Mauritius' appeared nowhere in the information circulated in the British philatelic press or published by Lemaire, the source closest to the find. It appears to be a fiction of the Williams brothers dating back to *Famous Stamps* of 1940 – a fiction apparently deemed appropriate given the popularizing nature of that work.

Because great sums of money were involved, the finder's wish to remain anonymous was understandable. But could there have been other reasons underlying the desire to protect his identity, such as concern about his title to the letters? Who really owned the cache of correspondence uncovered by the 'schoolboy'?

As more than half the known 'Post Office' stamps were found among the correspondence collections of the original receivers – Borchard, Duvivier and Adam – it seems logical that a member of the Ducau or Lurguie families found the Bordeaux letters. The term 'schoolboy' suggests an age of around twelve to eighteen, which would make the schoolboy's birth year anywhere between 1883 and 1890. Even if his mother were as old as forty-five when she bore him, that would still make her younger than ten in 1847, when her 'husband' received the letters. The Williams brothers' notion of a direct father–son relationship between the recipient and the later owner of the letter seems out in its reckoning.

If there was a family connection, it was likely to have been several generations removed. Business listings in the Bordeaux *Annuaire* reveal Messieurs Ducau and Lurguie ensconced at number 26, Quai des Chartrons, and a Ducau nephew just around the corner in the rue du Couvent in 1847. By 1855 Lurguie was still listed at number 26, Quai des Chartrons, and a Ducau Junior (the son presumably of Lurguie's former partner) was listed next door at number 27. By 1864 the Lurguies had disappeared from the directory listings in the Bordeaux *Annuaire*. Ducau Junior still traded in wine from numbers 26 and 27, Quai des Chartrons, and lived at the rue de la Course, further away from the port, situated alongside the beautiful public gardens. By 1866 he was listed only at the rue de la Course. This Ducau, Jean, was noted as aged forty-two and married in the 1866 census, though only a domestic and a cook are recorded as living with him. Moving forward to 1902, when the 'schoolboy' made his discovery, only two Ducaus are listed in the Bordeaux *Annuaire*: Mademoiselle Ducau, a grocer, at the Quai de la Monnaie, and another Jean Ducau, a shoe repairer, at the rue Borie.

Might the shoe repairer's family be related to the wine merchants from the 1840s? If anything can be derived from the proximity of these Ducaus' domiciles to those of their possible forefathers – the lucky recipients of the letters from Mauritius – then the Ducaus at rue Borie are a possible candidate. The rue Borie ran on to the Quai des Chartrons and was only a stone's throw from number 26. The head of the household was called Jean, a common name, but it is at least a link to that Ducau Junior, also Jean, who was probably the son of *the* Ducau. It is not impossible that a relative of presumably well-to-do nineteenth-century merchants ended up as a shoe repairer. A family of Ducaus, wine makers, based not far from Bordeaux at Loupiac, further inland on the Garonne, now own and run the vineyard Marc Ducau. Although their present profession is closely allied to that of the original Ducaus of the Quai des Chartrons, they know nothing of the Bordeaux merchants or the Bordeaux letters.

The shoe repairer did have a child of the right age. He had three sons: Charles, a baker, aged twenty-seven in 1903; Jacques, a waiter, aged twenty-two; and the youngest, André, who at eighteen might be deemed of schoolboy age and would certainly have seemed so in stature, being a jockey by profession.

Might the cache of old business correspondence have survived all the removals it must have been through to be still in the possession of André's father, Jean, in late 1902? The experience of the widows Borchard and Duvivier suggests not, yet fragments of their correspondence survived. Perhaps, like the remainder of the Borchard correspondence, the papers of the firm of Ducau and Lurguie ended up at a waste-paper merchant's, and it was the merchant, an employee or even a later purchaser of the waste-paper who profited from a closer perusal of the papers. Or perhaps the correspondence was simply left behind in numbers 26 and 27, Quai des Chartrons, or at one of the Ducau's later addresses, and the new tenants of the building claimed the correspondence as their rightful property.

News of the find filtered out via Théophile Lemaire's journal, *La Cote Réelle*. The story – or what Lemaire knew or was prepared to say about it – was soon widely known in philatelic circles within and outside of France. Whatever the truth, it seemed calculated on all points to foster an interest in stamp collecting and hunting for rarities. It must have brought back memories for Madame Desbois, never far from the Chartrons area (the family business in old books and rare stamps still prospered at the Cours du Jardin Public), when she heard the news.

With Lemaire, as with Peckitt, it was always difficult to know precisely how much the 'Post Office' stamps had cost him. In 1897 Lemaire had valued the heavily obliterated one penny and unused two pence 'Post Office' pair in Legrand's collection at 30,000 francs. However, this seems a low valuation, given that 42,000 francs had been paid for used one penny and two pence specimens six years earlier. Perhaps Lemaire had valued Legrand's two 'Post Office' at a lower price in order to create the impression of having made a greater profit. The French dealer said he paid 30,000 francs

Artful Monsieur Théophile Lemaire, the French dealer who bought
Legrand's collection and both Bordeaux letters.

(around £1,200) for the single two pence 'Post Office' on the
second Bordeaux letter and 40,000 francs (around £1,600) for the
Bordeaux letter bearing both the one penny and two pence. The
latter sum was noted at the time in journals. Lemaire himself
proudly compared the price with the 100 francs paid for a 'Post
Office' back in 1872 (a reference to the stamp Moens purchased
that year and passed on to Rothschild). Together, the amount paid
for both letters was an extraordinary sum for a schoolboy (for
anybody) to receive from an inspired piece of rummaging through
a load of old letters.

But why was *the* Bordeaux letter worth only a third more than
the price of the other letter bearing the single two pence 'Post
Office'? Why not twice the price or at least half as much again? In
1899 Lemaire had purchased the Adam envelope for around the
same amount as Peckitt paid for the Duvivier envelope – £600. So,
a few years on, from a dealer's point of view, to pay around £1,800
for a 'Post Office' pair on cover might still be reckoned a good

price. The philatelic journals were beginning to focus on the ratio of one penny to two pence, twelve to eight before the Bordeaux discoveries in 1903, which may explain the market's valuation. But there was also value in uniqueness. The *London Philatelist* described the Bordeaux letter as a 'novel and highly interesting discovery, and we can but hope that some other schoolboy may now find two twopennies side by side, and thus complete all the possible combinations of these popular rarities'. The relatively low price paid for the Bordeaux letter bearing both values of the 'Post Office' stamps would become an anomaly, for it was destined to be philately's ultimate prize and is unlikely now to be eclipsed as the most expensive philatelic item in existence.

Lemaire did not hold on to either of the Bordeaux letters long. In their year of discovery he sold the letter bearing the one penny and two pence 'Post Office' to Brunet de l'Argentière for £1,800 – £60 less in fact than he had received in 1897 for Legrand's one penny and two pence, neither tied together on cover. A few months after announcing the discovery of the letter bearing both values of the 'Post Office' stamps, Lemaire sent the second, single-stamped letter to a philatelic exhibition in Mulhausen in France. The gentlemen of the *Stamp Collectors' Fortnightly* admonished the French dealer ('Artful Monsieur T. H. Lemaire!') for holding back news of the discovery of the twenty-third 'Post Office Mauritius', 'just by way of producing an effect and driving all the other dealers green with envy'.

Since 1872 Berlin had been the proud possessor of a museum dedicated to all things postal, the Reichspostmuseum. The vision of its founder, a man called Stephan, was summed up by the editors of *Stamp Collecting* in 1922: he regarded the post office 'as the Institute of Culture... it was the nation's friend, the bringer of Peace, the promoter of well-being and intelligence, and an element of power for the Fatherland'. The museum had both a technical and an illustrative purpose, containing 'objects and apparatus required for transport and forwarding purposes' and 'whatever was calculated to illustrate the systems of carrying and imparting news among all peoples and in all times'. As well as letter boxes and postmen's pouches and, even in 1878, two novelties which drew great crowds – the Pneumatic Tube and the Bell Telephone – there was a growing collection of the world's stamps. Still, the British press enjoyed taunting the nation as a whole for not possessing a 'Post Office'. ('How many of the "Post Office" stamps of the world can Germany claim to possess?' asked the *London Philatelist* in 1898, and 'Cannot Germany or the United States "pluck up" and buy one while they remain cheap?')

Back in 1897, Théophile Lemaire had offered Legrand's one penny and two pence specimens to the Reichspostmuseum for £2,000 but they had declined to buy them. However, an opportunity too good to miss, the stamps were faithfully copied on to an engraving plate while in the hands of the museum on approval. Samples were printed by the German State Printing Office as reproductions for display in the museum, much to the amazement and indignation of Lemaire and other philatelists. The *Stamp Collectors' Fortnightly* gleefully noted that, 'while a merchant in Paris can hold the original gems the Imperial Philatelic Museum of the Fatherland must rest content with paste!' In 1901 the museum obtained their first 'Post Office', Legrand's heavily obliterated one penny 'Post Office', by exchange, through the agency of German dealer Philipp Kosack. The reproductions were removed from display as soon as the museum obtained its genuine specimen.

Keen to complete the pair, the curator of the museum contacted Lemaire early in March 1903 about the second Bordeaux letter, but again quibbled over the asking price of 50,000 francs (around £2,000). Hennecke, the museum's curator, couldn't reconcile the French dealer's description of the stamp's condition as 'excellent' with the obvious cut in the left-hand side. The German was concerned that Lemaire hadn't mentioned the second letter in the January 1903 announcement in *La Cote Réelle*, was suspicious about the apparent lack of cancellation (he had a photograph of the front of the letter, sent by Lemaire) and even thought the inscription 'p. Mischief via England' indicated Lemaire or somebody else might be up to just that. Hennecke was prepared to pay 40,000 francs upon authentication of the stamp.

Lemaire immediately replied that by 'excellent' he was referring to the quality of the printing and depth of colour in the stamp – superior in that respect to the two stamps on the other Bordeaux letter. He correctly pointed out that a number of the 'Post Office' stamps found in Bordeaux by Madame Borchard bore no trace – or only the slightest hint – of a cancellation from their point of issue in Mauritius, and noted with irritation that he had not been born when the *Mischief* left Mauritius for England and wasn't in a position to speculate on its existence. (There was no reason to worry – the *Mischief* had existed.) His reason for not announcing the existence of the second letter at the same time as the first was that he had wished to keep the stamp for himself and not to disappoint other keen collectors of Mauritius. (Although it is more likely that, as the *Stamp Collectors' Fortnightly* thought, Lemaire was being artful. Keeping back the second letter *was* an act of showmanship and probably an attempt to control the perceived value.) The French dealer naturally thought that the price wasn't excessive and pointed out the greater comparative rarity of the two pence blue.

While this correspondence was taking place, an article in a local

Berlin newspaper described the 'Post Office' stamps as the dream and quiet desire of philatelists everywhere, and noted the regret of German collectors that the Bordeaux letter bearing both specimens had gone elsewhere. A few weeks later, Hennecke closed his correspondence with Lemaire, refusing to purchase the cover. For reasons not known, the museum subsequently acquired the second Bordeaux letter that same year in an exchange for other German colonial stamps, again through the agency of Philipp Kosack. (Records relating to both transactions with Kosack were destroyed by the German government in an act of anti-Semitism in 1916.) The stamps were displayed in a purpose-built case vertically mounted on a wall of the museum, shielded from the light by a metal cover, alongside other precious rare stamps of British Guiana and Hawaii. The enduring German fascination with the 'Post Office Mauritius' had begun.

THE BLUE MAURITIUS

Diamonds are beautiful, but they are no more useful
than a cancelled stamp.

Bill Bloss, 'The Dealer and his Stock',
Stamp Collecting, 1916

The second of the great 'schoolboy' discoveries occurred as 1903 was drawing to a close, only in this case the schoolboy was a grandfather. James Bonar, of Scots descent, was a civil servant living in Hampstead, London. Some time late in 1903 he came across a long-forgotten pocket book album in which, as a schoolboy in Scotland back in the 1860s, he had pasted the stamps which happened to come his way. Did the pages of the makeshift album, light in his hand, take his mind back to his childhood? Stamp collecting now seemed a much more legitimate hobby than it had then, and a most beneficial one for children. Perhaps his own grandchildren would find them interesting.

The young Bonar's collecting activities had coincided with the rise of serious interest in the hobby in Scotland. One of the classics of early philatelic literature hailed from Edinburgh in 1863 – Lewes and Pemberton's *Forged Stamps: How to Detect Them*, indicating a ready market for both genuine stamps and the forged variety. A number of men who dealt in stamps in Glasgow and Edinburgh produced price lists of foreign stamps for sale and advertised them in Beeton's *Boy's Own Magazine* from 1862 onwards, again suggesting a ready, and *youthful*, market. Perhaps Bonar had read the *Boy's Own Magazine*, spotted the early dealers' advertisements of price lists and ventured out to purchase a few extra stamps for his pocket book album, or had seen similar in the *Stamp Collector's Herald and Advertiser* or the *New Stamp Magazine*, published in 1863 and 1864 in Glasgow.

Bonar's interest failed to survive beyond his schooldays, but luckily for him the album did. Not long after rediscovering it, he brought it out one evening to entertain a guest. This lady seemed more knowledgeable in matters philatelic than her host. By 1903 anyone who called themselves a stamp collector knew of the 'Post Office Mauritius' – five specimens of the stamp were the highlight of an exhibition of South African Colonies held in London only the year before. Bonar's guest was quite sure the little blue stamp from Mauritius was valuable and suggested her host contact a specialist. Bonar chose to contact Nevile Lacy Stocken of the firm Puttick and Simpson. Stocken called upon Bonar, examined the stamp, thought it genuine and (with some glee, one imagines) cut it out of the pocket book to take away with him.

Bonar's lady friend turned out to be a Miss D. Thomas. Three decades on she recalled her brush with the famous stamp for readers of the *Daily Mail*. Then Miss Thomas claimed that she had taken the album to a dealer herself. Offered only a token sum, she was suspicious of the dealer's interest and took the album back. Reluctant to see his prize slip away, the dealer followed her to Bonar's. Miss Thomas and her host picked up the pocket book again and when the page fell open at the Mauritius stamp, they determined to find a philatelic auctioneer. A contemporary account in *Stanley Gibbons Monthly Journal* in December 1903 gives credence to Miss Thomas's later version. A rumour was already circulating in November 1903 that a ridiculously low offer had been made for the stamp, causing the owner to seek out Puttick and Simpson instead. The rumour proved true and the unfortunate dealers to whom the pocket book was first shown contacted the *Monthly Journal* to correct the 'false impression'. A lady had definitely brought a collection to them and they had offered her £24 (£24!) because she had stated that 'she thought the owner would be glad to part with it for £20' – suggesting that Miss Thomas had only slightly more philatelic knowledge than Bonar. The unnamed firm of dealers followed up the next day with an offer of £600 to £700, but Bonar was not prepared to negotiate.

Mr Simpson recalled, some fifteen years later, that the firm had assured Bonar 'it would realize a large sum if put up to auction, and a sufficient time allowed to advertise it throughout the world'. Puttick and Simpson began to let the philatelic world know that the finest specimen in existence of the famous two pence blue 'Post Office Mauritius' had been discovered in London – the first discovery in Britain itself.

And what a fine specimen it was. There were no marks of any kind on the stamp. (It has always been described as 'unused'.) Stocken, of Puttick and Simpson, soaked the gummed stamp in water and carefully, using tweezers, loosened and removed it from the pocket book paper it was pasted on. Whoever had taken the scissors to the printed stamp all those years ago had left several millimetres of plain paper around it, considered a large and excellent margin by philatelists. A number of dealers and philatelists (or their agents) planned to attend the auction early in the new year. Bonar, however, received a private offer of £1,200 and attempted to retrieve the stamp from Puttick and Simpson, but they convinced him that to accept the offer would be a breach of faith and putting the stamp on the open market would be in his best interests.

Puttick and Simpson had come a long way, philatelically at least, since the firm opened its doors in 1794. With a name for themselves already as literary and fine art auctioneers, Mr Simpson Junior had had a hard time convincing Mr Simpson Senior that there was money to be made in stamps. 'Philately', went the view, 'was merely an ephemeral pursuit, and, in the nature of things, could never last.' But the younger Mr Simpson had his way and the firm began holding stamp auctions, engaging the philatelic specialist Nevile Lacy Stocken. The projected auction of Bonar's 'Post Office' would be the first time that any 'Post Office' was put up to the highest bidder in the open market, or so *The Times* reported the day after the auction finally took place on 3 January 1904.

Bonar, according to Puttick and Simpson, had put together his little collection at the same time as the first documented discoveries by Madame Borchard across the Channel in Bordeaux. How had he come across the stamp? The 'Post Office Mauritius' stamps were still unknown at this time, although quite possibly – and surely given the relationship between the mother country and Mauritius, a colonial possession of Britain – any number of missives to business houses who traded with the island bore specimens of them. The house of Robert Hastie & Co., for example, had a business in Glasgow, with an arm of the business established in Mauritius. Alex Hastie, a partner, was one of the many former Port Louis merchants who supported the former Colonial Postmaster of Mauritius, James Stuart Brownrigg, during his troubles in the 1850s. Hastie's partner's son was also Brownrigg's son-in-law. The house of Hastie may well have had a swag of 'Post Office Mauritius' and other early stamps from the island among its business correspondence; alas, records from that period no longer exist.

Perhaps such an example found its way to young James Bonar via a family friend. Possibly, on the closure of a business its correspondence avoided the usual fate of the waste-paper basket and ended up with a local dealer who, in those early days of collecting, was unaware of the rarity of the issue. Although the stamp has been described as unused it may be that Moutoussamy or another underzealous postal employee failed to cancel the stamp in Port Louis, and the plethora of postmarks which letters attracted on their travels all somehow avoided the brilliant blue specimen of Bonar's 'Post Office'. One of Madame Borchard's two pence 'Post Office' finds, now in the Swedish Postal Museum, bears only part of a faint red postmark in the lower left corner, as does the single two pence blue on the second Bordeaux letter (as Lemaire was obliged to point out to the Reichspostmuseum's curator in 1903). A friend or relative of the Bonars, returned from residence in the island, may have kept a copy of the stamp and no longer had any use for it. Or in similar circumstances an unused specimen found its way into a dealer's hands.

Forty years was too far back for Bonar to stretch his memory, but his experience might have been similar to that of Captain R. S. Chambers, recalling for readers of *Stamp Collecting* his own youthful days in pursuit of the hobby in Scotland around the turn of the century:

> I remember that, as a very small boy, I used to go to tea with an old lady – a distant relation – in a small house in Portobello, near Edinburgh. Every time I went I got a present of a few postage stamps. If I didn't get them I used to ask for them! I am afraid expectation of getting a few stamps, rather than affection for my old relative, was what brought me at fairly regular intervals to her house. I remember these stamps were chiefly African, and what became of those I had not succeeded in appropriating I do not know.

*

Scotland, probably because of its connection with the Bonar find in 1903, was in later years viewed as an ideal place for the stamp hunter. Scots-born Captain Chambers was sure of it, commenting in an article on 'interesting finds' in 1919 that 'Certain of the older business firms and country houses probably have letters and papers lying in their vaults which have not been looked at for thirty or forty years'. He described his own experiences in the family business:

> ... various old stamps had been turning up in our offices in Edinburgh whilst hunting up old records. These stamps my father always carefully preserved, but I am afraid a great many were destroyed before his day, when many old letters and papers were burnt as being of no further use. However, I determined when I entered the business that I would make a very thorough investigation of all our old papers and records... of the later day stamps I found very few, owing to the fact that envelopes were then used, and these had been destroyed with the stamps.

Captain Chambers's experience is probably typical of the time. As the years passed, certain types of records lost their relevance to businesses and as this happened they were taken off to waste-paper merchants or disposed of by other means. There were no regulations as there are now for minimum periods of retention of certain types of business records – and had there been there is even less likelihood that nineteenth-century business records would have survived at all. Those that survived did so by chance and oversight – sometimes even foresight. A 1918 treatise on the recovery and remanufacture of waste-paper, published in Aberdeen, makes painful reading for historians, archivists and philatelists alike. Among important sources of waste-paper supply are listed all types of correspondence, notebooks, account books and ledgers from advertising agencies, architects, banks, educational institutions, government offices, lawyers' offices, libraries, municipal authorities, post offices, shipping offices and unions – from offices and businesses of all kinds. Nor was the private sphere immune.

In 1920 philatelic journalist Fred Melville travelled up to Scotland to give a lecture to the Aberdeen and North of Scotland Philatelic Society on the fascination of stamp collecting. The *Aberdeen Daily Journal* reported on his talk:

> Mr Melville said Scotland ought to be a happy hunting ground for collectors of old stamps. He had been in Aberdeen since Tuesday morning, and had noticed many legal gentlemen. A large number of these must be in possession of old correspondence and letters which had accumulated since 1840, with stamps of that period. In those days there were no such things as envelopes. People simply folded their letters and affixed the stamps to the sheets, so that where old letters had been kept the stamps too would have been preserved.

But the caches of old, rare stamps in Britain were thought to have been played out long before the depredations of Captain Chambers and the encouragement of Mr Melville.

The optimism of the gentlemen of Messrs Puttick and Simpson was not misplaced. In 1898 the collector Henry Duveen had paid £1,200 for an ex-Borchard two pence blue 'Post Office', deemed unused (like the Bonar specimen), but with almost no margins and cut into in the lower right corner, with a blue smudge over the AU of MAURITIUS. The second Bordeaux letter bearing the singular example of the two pence blue 'Post Office', also cut into, had been purchased by Lemaire for £1,200, sold and then exchanged for an undisclosed sum, all in 1903, its year of discovery. It came as no surprise, then, that in the hushed silence of the crammed auction rooms of Puttick and Simpson in Leicester Square that cold Wednesday in January, when lot 301 was called, the bids soon exceeded the sum for which Bonar had been prepared to part with the little scrap of paper. At £1,400 the Stanley Gibbons dealer Charles J. Phillips, bidding for the Reichspostmuseum in Berlin, had declared himself out. Hugo Griebert, bidding for German dealer Philipp Kosack (who the year previously had bought and exchanged the second Bordeaux letter with the Reichspost-museum) also dropped out as the bid rose to £1,450.

Simpson (the younger) was never to forget the sale which put them on the philatelic map. In an interview years later he recalled the excitement of the day and the crowded room: 'When the lot was knocked down the audience broke into hearty cheers. Their curiosity, however, was sadly exercised as the buyer was unknown. The Prince's agent "simply called out money and planked down Bank notes, taking the stamp away with him".' The prince was the Prince of Wales, and the person who walked away with the stamp, purchasing on secret behalf of royalty, was a Mr J. Crawford. The schoolboy's stamp had progressed to the royal collection.

Born in 1865, the Prince of Wales, second son of Edward VII, was a keen philatelist. He joined the Philatelic Society of London in 1893, becoming the society's honorary vice-president. During this period the serious side of philately was duly recognized when his father, Edward VII, granted the society permission to use the prefix 'Royal' in 1906. Before he became King, the Prince occasionally presided over meetings of the society, showed his collection to the members and read a paper in 1904 entitled 'Notes on the Postal Issues of the United Kingdom during the Present Reign'. Understandably, he specialized in the stamps of the British colonies, bearing his father's and grandmother's likenesses. Elected president in 1896, the Prince remained so until his accession to the throne as George V in 1910.

The British royals weren't alone in their passion for the hobby of kings and prince of pastimes (philatelists were fond of royal associations). In the 1920s Queen Elena of Italy, Humbert the Prince of Piedmont, Gustavus Adolphus the Crown Prince of Sweden, King Alfonso of Spain, King Alexander of Yugoslavia, Princess Charlotte of Monaco, the royal family of Belgium, King Ahmed Fuad of Egypt, Prince Hiroyasu of Japan and the Nawab of Sachim were all listed in *Who's Who in Philately*.

George, however, was particularly enthusiastic. He loved stamps and appreciated quality. Unable yet to count himself among the possessors of the 'Post Office', the Prince's interest, like that of many others, was piqued by Puttick and Simpson's announcement late in 1903 of the discovery of Bonar's perfect two pence specimen. Determined to have the stamp, it was George who had tried to circumvent the auction process and had sent J. A. Tilleard, the curator of his collection, to see Bonar with the private offer of £1,200, two days before Christmas 1903. With his offer refused, the Prince had to wait like everybody else.

Correspondence between the Prince and Tilleard in the letter book of the Royal Philatelic Collection reveals an anxious wait. The Prince was prepared to pay up to £1,550 for the 'Post Office', inclusive of the expected agent's fee. Crawford was engaged to do the job, undoubtedly to protect his employer's anonymity, as Tilleard was known to the philatelic world as his curator. The Prince was also keen to keep the amount paid secret from gossiping tongues in the royal household. 'Better say merely

"Stamp is yours" & write later full particulars' ran his instructions to Tilleard on how to convey news of the auction's outcome. He was worried that it was such 'a great deal of money'.

On the day of the sale the Prince was shooting at Sandringham, but unable to perform to his usual ability on the field. By the end of the day he was the happy possessor of his first 'Post Office', as yet unseen and safely locked away in Tilleard's safe. Writing to Tilleard the next day, he stated his pleasure at having the stamp in his collection, 'as I believe it is such a fine copy', adding in true British philatelic spirit, 'I am also very glad that I have kept it in England & prevented it going to Germany.' His mind immediately turned to the question of finding a one penny to match and he directed Tilleard to 'ascertain quietly' the price of the Duvivier envelope in the Earl of Kintore's possession. By the end of 1904 it too had been captured for the royal collection.

The price realized at auction for Bonar's two pence 'Post Office' was the highest yet paid for a single stamp, acknowledged as the finest copy yet known of the issue. The sale 'has been on everyone's lips in club and home alike, and has been practically the sensation of the week', noted the *London Philatelist*. Bonar pocketed a tidy sum. That and the final resting place of the stamp, in the collection of the future King no less, ensured that his name and the story of his good fortune long survived him.

In philatelic circles Bonar's specimen was sometimes called 'the £1,450 Mauritius'. The 'Post Office' stamps had acquired a fame beyond philatelic circles – so much so that by the early 1920s they were popping up regularly in fiction. Along the way, a few philatelists were moved to light-hearted balladry celebrating their fame. But the earliest appearance of the stamps in fiction dates back to 1896.

A few years after the very active period of 'Post Office' sales in 1893, in which three specimens of each value changed hands several times, the stamps – specifically the two pence value – made what was probably their first appearance in general fiction:

Hope apparently had nothing to desire. True, he hadn't a tortoiseshell brown cat, or a blue Mauritius postage stamp; but these were spots on the sun, and besides, he didn't want them.

A reader of the *Stamp Collectors' Fortnightly* with doubtful taste in fiction found this reference in a recently published novel by one F. M. White called *The Robe of Lucifer*, the extract appearing in the *Fortnightly* on 5 September 1896. Earlier in the year the *Philatelic Journal of Great Britain* published a poem by C. E. Johnstone, 'Ballade of the Stamp-Collector's Paradise', in which the author dreams of a paradise whose paths are strewn with 'manifold Mulreadys' (highly desirable postal stationery of Great Britain, featuring a design engraved by William Mulready), and where:

I chortled joyfully 'Calloo!
　　Callay!' The object of my chase –
The Twopenny Mauritius Blue –
　　Is safe at last in my embrace.
Of philatelic trumps the ace!
　　Pearl of incalculable price!
On thee is founded, as its base,
　　The Stamp-Collector's Paradise!

Since the late 1890s, with the discovery of five one penny orange-reds to three two pence blues, the blue 'Post Office' had been rated higher in the rarity stakes than its orange-red sibling. Of the twenty-four specimens known by 1904 there were thirteen of the one penny value and eleven of the two pence. However, there is no obvious reason why, back in 1896, the two pence should have caught the public's attention over the one penny – it was no rarer. Eight specimens of each value were known then and the one penny was actually *rarer* in unused condition than the two pence, and remains so. Perhaps it was merely a preference for the colour blue, long associated with royalty and considered a costly pigment, together with the higher intrinsic value of two pennies over one. The sale of Bonar's '£1,450 Mauritius' in 1904 set the two pence's star firmly in the ascendancy.

The 'Post Office Mauritius' must have featured in other stories as well, for *Stamp Collecting*, discussing a Neapolitan provisional government stamp of 1860 dubbed 'the Blue Trinacria', stated in 1919, 'its fame is such that it has even been discussed in fiction, like the Post Office Mauritius', which suggests familiarity with more than the one reference in a twenty-year-old novel.

The editors of *Stamp Collecting* in the 1920s always included a balance of more scientific articles on philately with excerpts from the popular general press. In April 1921 they reported the following under the heading 'Triangular Mauritius':

> A popular weekly periodical publishes a story – more or less exciting – in which the author refers to the 'triangular shape of the Blue Mauritius' stamps. We believe they are as rare as the sexagonal Green Utopians!

The editors were making the point that the author of this story was in error and had made a rather silly error at that, confusing the distinctive triangular shape of the well-known Cape of Good Hope stamps with the famous 'Post Office' stamps. However, what is interesting about this briefest of extracts is the use of the phrase 'Blue Mauritius'. Mr 'Robe of Lucifer' back in 1896 had described the stamp as 'a blue Mauritius stamp', but the unknown author writing in 1921 shortened the description and used it as a phrase – the 'Blue Mauritius'. Its use as a phrase by a popular weekly meant that it was probably already part of the vernacular for the rarest and most famous of stamps.

This is confirmed by the appearance of another poem about the two pence blue, reproduced in *Stamp Collecting* in April 1922, having previously appeared in a non-philatelic journal called *Great Thoughts*. Originally entitled 'Tuppenny Blues: A Tale for Philatelists' by P. R. Chalmers, the editors of *Stamp Collecting* published it as 'A Lay of the Blue Mauritius'. It tells the tale of the author's great-aunt Prue, who, in 1847 ('a year of philatelic fame'), received a letter from her beloved cousin Tom in Mauritius. She exclaims at the stamps:

> 'What pretty blue! – the dear Queen's head!
>   Why, anyone might crave them!
> How kind of Tom!' (I'm sure she said)
>   'I certainly shall save them.'

Alas, cousin Tom has married a sugar planter's daughter and Prue burns the letter with the pretty stamps ('Tom was always horrid'):

> And now, whene'er I hear my friends
>   Their grand relations naming,
> Who burnt their candles at both ends,
>   And lost a fortune gaming;

Or saying how Sir George went strong
   (Their tales are long and many)
And sold the Romneys for a song
   And didn't leave a penny.

Then – as I say – when thus they do –
   Though pride is meretricious –
I always counter with Aunt Prue
   Who burnt the Blue Mauritius!

But the one penny 'Post Office' was not forgotten, nor the value of a pair. *Stamp Collecting* reported a story with a philatelic sub-plot, which had appeared in *Lloyd's Magazine* of April 1921, by A. M. Burrage, entitled 'A Gamble in Unknown Stock', extracting the following:

> It was the envelope which had contained the Mauritius letter. He discovered that an hour later by the light of a street lamp. He knew because there were four old Mauritius stamps on it, two red and two blue.
>
>   'Of course,' said Fewgin next day, 'it was the stamps I was after. The period when the letter was written set me thinking. The last 2d. blue Post Office Mauritius fetched over £1,500 at auction. A pair is almost priceless. The 1d. red is just as valuable. These two pairs simply can't fetch less than £10,000.'

The editors of *Stamp Collecting* made no allowances for the leeway of fiction, chiding Fewgin because 'of course, there is no envelope in existence bearing *two* pairs of the Post Office Mauritius'. Fewgin, the journal continued, was also sadly out of date, the editors citing the real-life example of a recent purchase of the Bordeaux letter: 'The unique envelope with one example of each value has just come into the possession of Mr. Arthur Hind, the American Philatelic Mogul, who paid more than £11,000 for it!' However, although flying in the face of the popularity of the 'Blue Mauritius', the author of the story, Mr Burrage, wasn't far wrong in his statement that the one penny red was equally valuable.

In 1922 the *Scout* magazine published a story by John Margerison called 'The Red Mauritius': 'It tells of a rogue who pilfered a "fifteen thousand pound stamp" but found a Scout "one too many" for him.' The reference to the nice round figure of £15,000 is excessive for a one penny 'Post Office' at this time, and perhaps the author, confused, had the £1,450 sum of Bonar's two pence blue in mind (as had Mr Burrage in his 1921 story). Bonar's 'Post Office' still came up in quizzes and discussions on fame, rarity and great price in the philatelic world, particularly in the schoolboy context. Perhaps by entitling his story 'The Red Mauritius' at this time, Margerison was trying to stand out in a crowd.

'Rarities,' stated the *Philatelic Record*, 'and especially in fine condition, always command a ready sale, and it is our opinion that they will continue to do so at increasing prices, except, perhaps, in the case of the Mauritius, where it would really seem probable that the high water mark had been reached.' With the Bonar sale and purchase for the Prince of Wales, stamp collecting did seem to have reached its zenith. Certainly, the brilliant blue two pence 'Post Office' had staked its claim to fame in the minds of stamp collectors of all means and persuasions.

In the immediate years following the sale of the Bonar two pence it is difficult to gauge whether those urging caution were correct. The dealer W. H. Peckitt bought the Jerrom letter for the second time in 1905 for the sum of £2,000, meaning the one penny 'Post Office' was valued at £1,000 apiece. He sold it the following year for £2,200 to George Worthington (1850–1924), apparently the first American-based collector to own the 'Post Office' issue. In 1907 the firm of Stanley Gibbons bought the entire philatelic holdings of the Russian collector Frederick Breitfuss (1851–1911), which contained an ex-Borchard one penny 'Post Office'. The dealers extracted the 'Post Office' from the collection and sold it in 1908 to the German dealer Philipp Kosack for only £450 (it was one of the most heavily obliterated specimens, the Queen's head almost totally obscured and the stamp cut into at the side, with poor margins).

Then the following year four of the stamps changed hands several times, as a result of the death of collector William Avery, involving buying, selling, swapping and exchanging between the dealer Peckitt and the collectors Henry Duveen and Henry Manus. Due to the nature of the acquisitions, it is difficult to put a market value on the stamps; the prices had settled, as some had speculated. That said, the stamp was still only affordable for wealthy men.

One more piece of the puzzle, a puzzle long thought to have been solved, was unexpectedly put in place with the extraordinary and somewhat mysterious discovery in a London bank vault in 1912 of the original plate (singular) from which the 'Post Office' stamps were printed. Major Evans, it will be remembered, during his researches in Mauritius, had found a letter from Colonial Postmaster Brownrigg explaining the delay in the issue subsequent to the 'Post Office'. In so doing, the postmaster had referred to the 'Post Office' plates in the plural – 'had I been permitted to use in the meantime the original plates'. It was a logical presumption that two separate plates for the 'Post Office' issue had existed. But this proved not to be the case. The single piece of copper uncovered in 1912 was the size of a typical ladies' visiting card, little bigger than a standard business card today. The one penny 'Post Office' was engraved in the upper left-hand corner and the two pence was engraved in the upper right.

But where had it come from and how had it ended up in the dark recesses of a London bank vault? The story of its discovery was proudly announced in a scoop to the philatelic world through the pages of the London journal the *West-End Philatelist*, whose publisher, Mr D. Field, had briefly owned the plate before selling it to a well-known philatelist, Sydney Loder. Under the heading 'Discovery of what is undoubtedly the Greatest Philatelic Treasure existing', Alexander Séfi speculated that the financial value of the plate was inestimable, certainly more than the combined value of unused specimens of the two great rarities themselves, perhaps even £5,000. The provenance of the plate seemed quite prosaic:

> The history of this plate, since it was used for printing, has been a very uneventful one. In it's [*sic*] early days it had been kept by a high Official in Mauritius as an interesting souvenir of the first stamp of the country. In due course it passed to his son, who handed it over to the safe-keeping of his bankers, from whose custody it has only just been removed...

Nevile Lacy Stocken, involved in the Bonar find and sale in 1903–4, had again been fortuitously contacted in relation to this 'Post Office' find. He was the initial purchaser of the plate, before selling it to Field. Many years later, in 1930, in the pages of *Stamp Collecting*, he recalled, 'How I found the most valuable piece of copper in the world'. While seated in his office one fine summer's

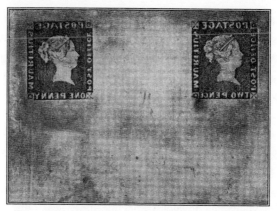

The original copper plate (perhaps) used to print the
'Post Office' stamps.

morning in 1912, his thoughts happily far from philately and
floating down a river somewhere, Stocken was startled out of his
reverie by a solemn-faced colleague who announced that by
chance he had discovered the whereabouts of the original plate of
the 'Post Office Mauritius'. Informing his interlocutor that 'at this
early hour of the day it was always advisable to increase the
proportion of soda taken with it', Stocken nevertheless hastened off
in a taxi to Drummond's Bank in Charing Cross to meet with the
possessor of this great treasure. The plate, according to Stocken:

> had been reposing all unknown and undiscovered amongst
> the papers of the late Governor until his grandson unearth-
> ing it had, not being himself a philatelist, wondered what it
> was. He had taken it to the Army and Navy Stores to seek
> some information upon the subject, and my friend, being
> also a member of that institution, had thus heard of it and
> brought the astounding news to me.

*

The supposed grandson of the Mauritius Governor identified by Stocken was one Colonel Dominic Henry Colnaghi, of the Royal Engineers, and this statement was accepted as truth for many years. It wasn't until some forty years after Stocken's article that postal historian Peter Ibbotson, attempting to extract the strands of truth from the myths and mysteries surrounding the 'Post Office' issue, realized that the sums didn't add up. Sir William Gomm had died, childless, in 1875 at the age of ninety. Neither his first wife nor Lady Elizabeth had borne him children.

Much closer to the actual date of the finding of the plate, Albert Rae, the Mauritian philatelist and one-time 'Post Office' owner, was more circumspect. In an article on the island's early stamps for *Mauritius Illustrated* (1914) he merely stated that Field 'had bought them from the son of a gentleman who had resided in Mauritius, but whose name, unfortunately, has not been ascertained'.

The Drummond's Bank connection also seems an inaccurate memory on Stocken's part. Peter Ibbotson investigated this assertion in the 1980s, and the bank's records show no withdrawals from Colonel Colnaghi's strong box in 1912.

By October 1912 the original 'Post Office' plate was on display at the International Jubilee Philatelic Exhibition in London. A year earlier the two 'Post Paid' plates, re-engraved in the late 1850s, had been discovered in a cellar in a government building in Mauritius and, on the point of being destroyed, were rescued by the then Governor, Sir Cavendish Boyle, who thought George V might like them. The King ordered that they be defaced to prevent fraudulent misuse (fine lines were drawn through them) and that they be presented to the Royal Philatelic Society, where they remain on display today. Before selling the 'Post Office' plate to Field, Stocken claimed he had tried to sell it to Henry Duveen, owner of two 'Post Office' stamps, and to the Earl of Crawford, then president of the

Royal Philatelic Society. Both declined to buy. Stocken requested the Earl to show the plate to the King, out of interest, but curiously little interest was forthcoming. (Correspondence relating to this in the Royal Archives was destroyed at some point, deemed of no enduring value.) As he had with the 'Post Paid' plates, the King could surely have demanded that the 'Post Office' plate be similarly defaced and handed back to the Mauritius government or to the Royal Philatelic Society. It seems he did not. The Reichspost-museum in Berlin offered £2,500 for the plate, but Stocken eventually sold it to Field. (Some time during 1912 a small mark was added to each engraving on the plate, so that any reprints would be distinguishable from the original stamps printed in 1847. Reprints were made, and the mark is relatively easy to find in the one penny, but few people even now know what to look for in the two pence.)

Major Evans, who wrote most of the editorial material in *Stanley Gibbons Monthly Journal* at this time, concurred with Alexander Séfi's account of the find, which was probably the essence of that given out by Stocken at the time too (the man just had an execrable memory, or was apt to muddle facts in his later years): a high official in Mauritius had passed the plate to his son, who kept it in a bank vault in London. Evans, however, queried the dubious nature of the said son's title to the plate, which was government property. Stocken later wrote that the Colonial Office had sent him 'a portentous and peremptory mandate' requesting the plate's immediate return. 'Of course,' he said, 'I did no such thing.' But it *was* the property of the colonial government of Mauritius.

In 1914–15, following the discovery of the 'Post Office' plate, a commission was set up to inquire into the whys, where-fores and wrongdoings of its reappearance. It transpired that Colonel Colnaghi *was* the person who discovered the plate. In correspondence to the commission, he stated that he had been given the plate as one of a number of curios found among a box of clothes belonging to his great-aunt. The plate was bent and he had tried to straighten it, having no idea what it was. This was some time in the 1880s. It wasn't until around 1909-10 that he looked through an old case and discovered the plate again. While buying some stamps at the Army and Navy Stores in Victoria Street, London, the assistant mentioned the recently discovered 'Post Paid' plates, which jogged the Colonel's memory. He brought the plate in to the Army and Navy Stores to show the assistant, which is how Stocken's friend came to hear of it.

The commission also interviewed past and present employees in the Mauritius postal service. A former Assistant Colonial Postmaster of Mauritius, Samuel Standley, who joined the postal service around 1866, stated to the commission that he had never seen a 'Post Office' stamp or the 'Post Office' plate, but had always believed it was held in the vault of the Mauritius Treasury. Evidence from other witnesses showed that in the 1870s some plates were known to have been kept at the Port Louis post office and were even reprinted. But these, it seems, were the 'Post Paid' plates. Major Evans and Colonial Postmaster Thompson had organized the reprinting, with the Governor's permission. Evans had recorded this in the *Philatelic Record* in 1880 and noted it again in 1911 when reflecting on the presentation of the 'Post Paid' plates to the Royal Philatelic Society.

However, other witnesses claimed that reprints had been taken from the 'Post Office' plate, but all varied in their testimony as to when this had occurred – 1892-4, 1897-8 or 1904. Most of the evidence was contradictory.

William Rae, brother of Albert and Colonial Postmaster at the time of the inquiry, said he knew 'absolutely nothing' about the plate. Bernard Morel's testimony was altogether more startling. One morning in 1897 or 1898, the proprietor of the Port Louis newspaper he worked on, Leopold Roussel, produced a parcel containing the 'Post Office' plate, the original paper it had been printed on (after all these years, when the paper stock would have been held by Barnard, long deceased?) and one of the obliterating stamps used by the post office in 1847. He had, he said, been made a generous offer by a clerk in the post office to secretly print a few copies from the plate. Roussel apparently consulted a lawyer and declined the offer. He was never interviewed for the inquiry, presumably because he had gone to pastures greener. Henri Robert, chief clerk of the Mauritius Agricultural Department, corroborated Morel's story about Roussel, but remembered the events taking place around 1892-4. Edouard de Robillard, a public notary, thought Roussel had told him about the plate in 1904, but 'I cannot be precise as to the date and even as to what Roussel told me.' Neither Morel nor Robert nor de Robillard mentioned what happened to the plate after this.

François Bayeroux, deputy postmaster at Mapou in Mauritius, who had spent a few months at the post office in Port Louis in 1893, had heard there was a plate 'from which the 'Post Office' stamps could be made, but that there was no paper available similar to that used in printing the genuine 'Post Office' stamps'. Pierre Robert, until 1906 a clerk in the Port Louis post office, only saw the 'Post Paid' plates in the post office safe and faintly recalled being told that the 'Post Office' plate had been destroyed. Leon Philippe, also a former clerk at the Port Louis post office (1894–1904) claimed not to have heard anything about it. He had formerly been postmaster at the Mahebourg post office and remembers contacting Colonial Postmaster Thompson about the 'Post Office' plate back in 1878, wishing to see it on his next visit to Port Louis, as he had often heard of the stamps. Thompson apparently wrote back that he could not comply with the request and that it was a question of 'sending the plate to the Treasury where I might apply later on to see it'. But Philippe never bothered. Another post office clerk (from 1877 to 1910, in the Port Louis post office only from 1892), Alfred Beaupré, said he had often heard gossip about the plate but had never seen it. A certain Dupré (not to be confused with Beaupré) claimed that the clerk Pierre Robert had given the 'Post Office' plate to the then Procureur General, Francis Piggott, but Robert himself denied this, and Beaupré supported Robert. Both Beaupré and Pierre Robert had ultimately been dismissed from their positions in the post office, as much home to dissension and accounting anomalies in the 1900s, it seems, as it had been in the 1850s.

Did anybody know what they were talking about?

If the 'Post Office' plate had existed at the Port Louis post office in 1878, as Thompson's alleged correspondence with Leon Philippe intimated, then surely the obliging Thompson would have shown it to Major Evans. Together they had gone to get reprints made from the 'Post Paid' plates. Evans must surely have sniffed out the 'Post Office' plate had it been available.

Gossip was flying around the island about the existence and whereabouts of the 'Post Office' plate before it eventually turned up. The commission, consisting of the current Procureur General, Receiver General and Colonial Postmaster of Mauritius, decided in 1915 that 'There being no prospect of any further information being obtained... the enquiry may now be closed.' Closed it was. The interested were left only to wonder and the Mauritius government never retrieved its property.

Rumours were rife in the philatelic press that Sydney Loder, the philatelist who had purchased the plate from Mr Field, was going to give it to the British Museum, but this doesn't seem to have happened. In September 1930 *The Times* reported that the 'Post Office' plate was sent by air from London to Germany for the International Stamp Exhibition being held in Berlin, in the charge of H. R. Harmer, a philatelic dealer and auctioneer. At the same time, Stocken, who is difficult to trust, said Loder had disposed of the plate about two years previously (1928) to 'the present mysterious owner'. Who that owner was has been much speculated upon. The little plate surfaced one last time, at an exhibition in London in 1935; its whereabouts are now unknown.

In the months leading up to the First World War, rumours of further finds of the stamps surfaced around the world. New specimens of both values were reportedly discovered in Paris late in 1913, 'for which no less a sum than £4,000 is being asked'. A week after *Stamp Collecting* reported this find, they announced further ones:

> It looks as though 'Post Office' Mauritius will soon be as plentiful as blackberries in August if copies continue to turn up at the rate they have been doing during the past few weeks. Following on the rumoured discovery of two copies in Paris last week, we have recently heard of a third that has been offered for sale in London. And now the *Australian Stamp Journal*, just to hand, reports the finding in Perth, W.A., of a heavily obliterated copy of the one penny 'Post Office', belonging to an old lady who formerly resided in Mauritius. The stamp is being submitted to experts for examination, but there appears to be little reason to doubt its authenticity.

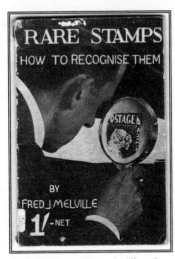

Fred Melville's *Rare Stamps: How to Recognise Them*, London, 1922, featuring, undoubtedly, a 'Post Office Mauritius' on the cover.

The *Australian Stamp Journal* had been told that a woman in Perth, Western Australia, claimed 'she had originally lived in Mauritius, and many years ago had the stamp given to her with an injunction to take care of it as it might prove of value'. A respected Perth philatelist, contacted about the poor specimen (the word OFFICE was heavily obscured), had the stamp photographed and sent both stamp and photograph to London. Major Evans was the expert consulted. He was sure, even from an examination of the photograph, that it was not a 'Post Office', but a later impression of the 'Post Paid', wondering in his musings in *Stanley Gibbons Monthly Journal* why the leading philatelists of Perth had not consulted a copy of the Royal Philatelic Society's book on British Colonial stamps, which would have sorted out the matter easily. They cannot have owned the book, which invoked the dry rider from the Major, 'This of course is another matter.'

While none of these rumoured finds ultimately proved to be

genuine, they demonstrated the grip on the public imagination that such stories as the schoolboy finds earlier in the century – and the pecuniary rewards attached to them – had attained. Philatelic journalist Fred Melville, writing in 1911, noted that a collector would 'have to loosen wide the strings of a bounteously filled purse' to possess the earliest issues of Mauritius (both the 'Post Office' and the 'Post Paid') and other rare stamps, such as the first issue of British Guiana and the Hawaiian 'Missionaries'.

Although it was now acknowledged that there were rarer stamps than the 'Post Office', the Mauritian stamps were deemed to possess a certain rare quality – 'as examples of a genuinely necessary issue, small in quantity' – and to Melville and most of the world's philatelic community, they would 'always be looked upon as the ultimate, even if seldom attained, goal of the Philatelist'. Or, as Melville put it another way, summing up the position the 'Post Office' stamps had attained in the pre-war years, 'Incomparable as regards romantic interest and actual value, the first two stamps of Mauritius have been, ever since their discovery in the 'sixties, the *desiderata* of every collector.'

Apart from the rumoured finds in 1913, there were no fresh discoveries of genuine 'Post Office' stamps and no specimens changed hands for another five years. The best of them had already been locked away by long-term specialist collectors, their desires well satisfied: Ferrary now had four, Duveen and Manus each had two, Worthington in America had three and King George V was content with specimens of both values.

Stories of finds, even the possibilities of finds, and musings on stamp hunting would always fill the columns of the philatelic press, but they were very common in these lean 'Post Office' years. Bonar's find and the subsequent price fetched were usually trotted out as an encouragement. Some felt that finds of rarities were a thing of the past: 'All the old grandmothers' trunks and grand-fathers' bureaux have been ransacked; all the old stacks of correspondence have been overhauled' – the choice of verbs indicating the proactive and voracious nature of stamp collectors.

However, although admitting the problem, Percy Bishop, the philatelic journalist who founded the *Stamp Collectors' Fortnightly*, begged to differ. In a 1913 article, entitled 'Where to Hunt for Rare Stamps', he rallied his brother collectors to arms and detailed the places to search:

> Don't tell me all the old correspondence has been over-hauled, for I know it is not so. There are ancient houses of business in the City of London wherein, to my certain knowledge, the correspondence of a hundred years is still retained; and, remember, it was formerly the custom of these old business houses to retain both letter and envelope. In a publishing house with which I was connected when a boy, every envelope received was religiously preserved, and it was not until 1890, or thereabouts, that this practice was abandoned.

He also recommended 'drowsy rural districts' and 'ultra conservative homes', where 'letters and documents that have been hoarded as keepsakes or for family reasons may remain hidden for decades before a household removal or a fit of "clearing up" brings them to light'. It was such a removal that potentially saw many 'Post Office' specimens from the Borchard firm pulped by a Bordeaux waste-paper merchant in the late 1860s, and which saw one of Lady Gomm's ball envelopes rescued from a similar fate in Mauritius in 1898. How one was to penetrate the dark and cluttered recesses of these homes without a familial entrée was not addressed, calling to mind visions of a parade of besuited philatelists armed with scissors roaming the backwaters of Britain. Philatelic treasures might be looked for in bookcases between the leaves of old tomes, or in 'old deed boxes, in abandoned writing cases and blotters, and even in the quaint old "needlework boxes" favoured by our mothers and grandmothers'. And with the obligatory reference to Bonar's 'schoolboy hoard' and the £1,450 sum, Bishop posed the question, 'How many of us have boxes containing miscellaneous hoards of odds and ends that date back to our schooldays?'

'Stamp hunting' was a phrase in use in the philatelic press by at least the 1920s, referring to the seeking out of philatelic rarities, gems and treasures, the latter resting very much in the eye of the beholder. The joys of the hunt, as expressed in 1924 in the pages of *Stamp Collecting* by a Mr J. Franklin (an 'enthusiastic collector in a humble way'), lay in the true meaning of the word 'collect'. Procuring stamps through a new issue service or spending one's time and money haunting dealers were behaviours too passive to mark a true collector. 'Half the interest, or more,' wrote Franklin, 'is gained by worrying and searching after stamps, and to buy automatically, as numbers do, each stamp as it is issued is to forgo all the excitement of the game.'

Mr Franklin was a little harsh in his definitions, but he typified the collector who was patient and took years and decades to gather their accumulation of stamps through acquisition, exchange and chance discovery. This type, if they travelled for business or recreation, might seek out local dealers or philatelic societies in their spare moments. (Remember Major Evans, who used his numerous military postings to foreign climes to further his philatelic knowledge and fill the pages of his stamp album.) Or they might politely badger friends and relations for old corres- pondence. The much-travelled and anonymous author of *People and Places*, published in 1922, suffered such a harassment: he was 'not apparently addicted to stamps, yet his residence in distant lands led to his persecution by those who were' – so much so that he felt driven to include a chapter on stamps in his book. Travel and travelling friends were a great boon to collectors.

Then there were the stamp hunters who specifically targeted locations in search of stamps of worth. In 1934 London's *Daily Mail* reported that a group of American collectors and dealers, bound on a modern treasure hunt, had chartered a cruise ship to visit Caribbean ports, looking for copies of rare British Guiana stamps.

Mauritius, naturally, and places likely to have received correspondence from Mauritius came in for this kind of attention too. An anecdote related by the Williams brothers tells the story of two such gentlemen hunters, an Anglo-Indian tea planter named Walker and an American tourist named Bratt. Holidaying together in India, Walker and Bratt purposefully targeted coastal villages in the south of the country whence indentured labourers had departed to Mauritius, imagining that letters to relatives were sure to have found their way back from the one British colony to the other. The two men let their interest be known and were soon inundated with offers from the locals, among them supposedly genuine specimens of both the one penny and two pence 'Post Office Mauritius'. Bratt stored the rarities in the back of his gold watch, a round fob. Unfortunately for the two stamp hunters, their room was expertly thieved while they slept and the watch, with its precious contents, was stolen. Offering a large reward resulted in the apprehension of the thief and the watch, but the thief had been beforehand in opening the back of the watch himself and, on finding what looked to be two dirty little scraps of paper that he feared might assist in identification of the item, he disposed of them by fire.

Major Evans was probably the only visitor to Mauritius, once the existence of the 'Post Office' was known, to return from the island in possession of a specimen, the hunt rewarded. Numerous others tried and failed, it would seem, on the evidence of an article entitled 'Combing an Island for Postal Treasures', published in *Stamp Collecting* in 1933. This was written by Edward Mosely, a South African philatelist who had visited Mauritius several times in the preceding years. He declared that 90 per cent of the island's exports were sugar, rum and aloe fibre, and that forged stamps made up the other 10 per cent! Mosely noted quite sincerely that 'Of the white population probably one in three that I met either (a) had had a Post Office Stamp, (b) had sold a collection to the Prince of Wales, now King George, when he visited the island as a middy, or (c) had had a father, grandfather, uncle, father-in-law, or some relation who came under (a) or (b), and from whom he had inherited the remains of said collection.' While in the island, Mosely was approached on numerous occasions by those offering to sell him specimens of the 'Post Office' and other early Mauritian stamps.

One of the 'Post Office' which Mosely was shown was a brilliant sample of the orange-red one penny, its colour rich and its margins so large 'one could have driven a bicycle if not a motor-car round the stamp'. The philatelist was tempted to buy both specimens shown him by a Monsieur K, for the purchase 'would have made me the proud possessor of the treasures and entitled to take the rank as one of the dozen owners of a "Post Office"', a mantle to be coveted. It transpired, however, that the deceased father of Monsieur K, a local judge, had practised art in his spare time, and, being also a stamp collector, liked to amuse himself by sketching likenesses of the 'Post Office' in pencil. The judge would then carefully paint them and fix them in his stamp album, clearly labelled as copies. His son was not so scrupulous. After numerous approaches during his stay to view marvellous collections, Mosely concluded, 'The value of early Mauritius has had a good Press in the island.'

Philatelic finds and tales of fortunes reported in the press always galvanized a new generation of collectors into action, sending people in search of childhood albums or badgering their elderly relatives to hunt out old trunks and other caches of correspondence. The publicity which accompanied the local finds of Madame Duvivier and Henry Adam back in the 1890s would surely have flushed out any remaining genuine copies of the 'Post Office' stamps in Mauritius. No more were found in the island.

Noted Mauritian philatelist Albert Rae, writing in *Mauritius Illustrated* in 1914, put the rarity of specimens down to a number of local factors, including the appetite of white ants, the humidity and 'the many great fires which have ruined so many valuable properties in the island'. Then there were probably the usual reasons: retirement or removal resulting in a clearing out of years of accumulations of paper documents.

But could there still be copies of 'Post Office' stamps somewhere in Mauritius, France or India, the three most likely places? Robert Walser of Paris thought so in the 1930s, preferring the route of the archives for his stamp hunting. Working on the theory that at least half the known specimens of 'Post Office' stamps were found among the records of the firm of Borchard in Bordeaux, and that the most prized of all 'Post Office' items was also found among business records in the archives of Ducau and Lurguie, he approached Monsieur Blondel, the proprietor of the piano firm of Erard. The nineteenth-century inhabitants of Port Louis were known to be great aficionados of the piano, and the Erard brand was noted in contemporary travel narratives on Mauritius.

Walser's idea was good and he did find twenty-four letters addressed to the Maison Erard from Mauritius in the period 1847–8, but none, unfortunately, were franked with stamps. Similarly, in relation to the Jerrom letter, Norman Williams chased up the British and Foreign Bible Society connection and learned that Reverend Banks (the letter writer, based in Mauritius) wrote several reports to the society back in London. He searched through the society's archives to no avail – none of Banks's reports or correspondence bore any stamps at all.

Finds of valuable stamps occurred occasionally throughout the early decades of the twentieth century when old papers were examined and long-forgotten letters were opened again, revealing unused copies of stamps, sometimes sent for fiscal purposes in lieu of money. They were found in files, overlooked on the uppermost shelves of large bookcases or sometimes in secret drawers of desks when taken to carpenters for repair. A stash of early Canadian stamps was discovered on a number of letters when an old bookcase was being repaired in 1914. The letters were found nailed between two boards on the topmost shelf. In 1920 hundreds of old British stamps, more than forty years old and still intact in sheets or part sheets, were found when an antique mahogany bureau was being taken apart for repairs; the stamps realized hundreds of pounds when auctioned by Harmers in London in April that year.

Reminiscent of the Bonar find, a new 'Post Office' – a heavily obliterated and damaged specimen of the two pence blue – was discovered in France in 1917, reportedly 'in an old box, among a lot of valueless stamps'. Remarkably, the find attracted little or no attention in the press, philatelic or otherwise, despite the fact that it was purchased from the owner by the canny dealer Théophile Lemaire in that same year. Lemaire sold it in 1918 to a collector who remained anonymous and it has never surfaced again, only known from a reference several years later in 1920 in the *Bulletin Mensuel de la Maison Théodore Champion & Co.*, and a passing reference by Brunel in 1928. Less remarkably, it may be that in wartime such a piece of intelligence was trifling. However, although a number of philatelic journals and magazines fell by the wayside or quietly rested during the period of the 1914–18 war, the hobby of stamp collecting continued apace. Unlike many other collecting pursuits, it had in fact, according to *Stamp Collecting* editor Douglas Armstrong, 'not merely weathered the storm of social and economic upheaval, but... actually flourished under the stimulating influence of war issues', confounding its critics.

But after the war was over, the French had other matters, philatelically speaking, on their mind. Thanks to the death of Ferrary in 1917 and his wish that his great collection should go to Germany, the French government now owned the most extraordinary accumulation of stamps ever assembled. It contained all the world's rarities, including Hawaiian 'Missionaries', the only known specimen of the 1¢ British Guiana of 1856 and, it was reported, no fewer than five 'Post Office Mauritius' (he had four). The French had an auction to organize and a new chapter in the fame and fortune of the 'Post Office' stamps was about to be written.

THE BIG-GAME COLLECTORS

---

*The ideal which runs free beyond our reach is the
only beast worth hunting. All the collectors know this.
I can only guess at the strange emotions of the postage
stamp collector, but I have seen him so earnest at his
curious study of watermarks and perforations that I
feel sure he must be as other collectors are. He is not
really content with his complete set of obsolete
Tomboland provisionals; his soul, as he gums these
things into his album, is nourished by the phantom
hope that he will one day collect the lilac octagonal
five cent Oil River Protectorate with the figure
five printed upside-down, a delicious variety of
which the only known example was burned in a
multi-millionare's Chinese gothic villa on
Nob Hill, San Francisco.*

Evening News, London, 1914

So keen were they to have a piece of Philipp la Rénotière von
Ferrary that collectors of every stripe gathered outside the Hôtel
Drouot in Paris one afternoon late in June 1921, in a state of mild
affray. Once the doors to the grand building opened, there was a
mad rush up the stairs, another tussle at the entrance to the auction
room itself and a scramble for the best seats – indeed any seat.
After many months of preparation, Ferrary's stamp collection was

ready to go under the hammer. It was reckoned to be worth more than half a million pounds.

In all, fourteen sales took place between June 1921 and November 1925. There were mixed emotions among the philatelic community about the fate of Ferrary's stamps. Some regretted the breaking up of the world's greatest philatelic collection, more than likely to be the last of its kind assembled. Many saw Ferrary as a philatelic miser, a hoarder unwilling to share his knowledge, his collection dubbed the 'philatelic graveyard'. And yet, had his final wish been honoured, like Tapling's, the preservation of the collection in one of the world's greatest postal museums would have been a greater gift to philately than the occasional exhibition of those treasures during his lifetime. An American commentator opined of the fate of stamps in such circumstances, 'not one philatelist in a hundred would have seen them, and the general public would have hurried by unknowing'. But the continued use and permanent exhibition of the Tapling Collection, now in the British Library, gives the lie to such sentiments. There are degrees of willingness to share, and not all philatelists were, or are, as sainted in this respect as the critics proclaimed. What Ferrary's detractors really wanted was the opportunity to own the best pieces themselves.

Stamp collecting remained a popular hobby, and part of the attraction for the many who attended the Ferrary sales must have lain in the mystique surrounding the man himself and the collection he took fifty years to accumulate. Some of the British dealers and philatelists in attendance were bemused at the high prices realized for some of the stamps, when choicer and more reasonably priced specimens of the same stamps could be had in London. One reason espoused for so much French participation in the buying was their desire for investment in 'things not likely to be taxed or confiscated'. But the attraction of the rarities was understandable and undeniable. Ferrary really had cornered the market in rare stamps – aptly dubbed 'Ferrarities' by philatelic journalist Fred Melville – and some of these would feature in their own special sale later in 1921.

Only one of the men who would vie for dominance in the Mauritius market in the first half of the twentieth century was in attendance himself when the first of Ferrary's 'Post Office' came up for sale in October 1921 – the tobacco magnate Maurice Burrus (1882–1959). Anglo-American businessman Arthur Hind (1856–1933), like George V, preferred to stay at home and send an agent to bid on his behalf. One of the most important Mauritius collectors at that time, Alfred Lichtenstein (1876–1947), was by then more interested in the other early issues of the island.

Lichtenstein had already risen to philatelic prominence in 1917, when he acquired whole portions of the collection of George Worthington, becoming overnight one of the major 'Post Office' owners. Among Worthington's Mauritius treasures were the Jerrom letter to Bombay and the letter fragment to the Port Louis lawyer Caunten.

Alfred Lichtenstein (on the left, looking down at his papers) and Théodore Champion (seated in the centre with a pointed beard) at one of the Ferrary sales in the 1920s.

The tall American was another whose interest in stamp collecting was life-long, having begun as a schoolboy in Brooklyn in the 1880s. Lichtenstein later attended the University of Berlin, and turned the knowledge and abilities acquired from his chemical studies there into a thriving business, Analine Dies and Chemicals, before selling out in 1921 to the Swiss company which became Ciba-Geigy. His growing wealth undoubtedly facilitated his ability to purchase and build up collections of his favourite stamp countries – British North America, Mauritius, Cape of Good Hope, the Swiss cantons, Uruguay and Argentina – much of which he made available to other philatelists for research. Lichtenstein was a generous collector, his treasures always a focal point of major stamps exhibitions, lent 'for other people's pleasure and instruction'. A big man, he dominated photographs taken of himself standing among his philatelic brethren at the many international stamp shows at which he was called to judge.

One of the newer breed of philatelist, Lichtenstein preferred the specialist route. He was more interested in the quality than the quantity of his holdings. He took what he wanted from Worthington's collection and sold the rest. And he hadn't been tempted previously when two more 'Post Office' stamps came on to the market in 1920.

These were used one penny and two pence stamps from Émile Lalanne's collection, owned by the motor-racing family of Mors since 1896. They were purchased at auction by the French dealer Théodore Champion (1873–1954) for his own collection. Like the dealers Peckitt and Lemaire, Champion had been a stamp collecter from an early age; the child's hobby had developed into the man's profession. Champion had already been in business as a stamp dealer for eighteen years, but his purchase of the two Mauritian rarities, according to a *Stamp Collecting* feature on the Maison

Champion in 1922, 'brought him prominently into the limelight'. There was certainly a cachet attached to ownership of the 'Post Office' stamps and their purchase was a wise investment for a dealer, not in the least for the publicity that such acquisitions bought.

Lichtenstein was satisfied with the three 'Post Office' stamps he owned and Champion was seemingly so with the two in his possession. The auction floors of Europe were now cleared for the battle for supremacy in the Mauritan rarity stakes (and rarity stakes generally) between Arthur Hind and Maurice Burrus. Although the general feeling among philatelists was that the likes of Ferrary had had their day – the specialists like Lichtenstein now holding sway – both Hind and Burrus, by their large purchases at the Ferrary sales, proved themselves in disagreement; indeed, Burrus's passion saw him become one of the largest purchasers at the sales. More than 25 per cent of Ferrary's collection ended up in Burrus's home in Lausanne in Switzerland, ironically the place where Ferrary had spent his last days in exile from the greater part of his collection.

Arthur Hind hadn't taken up the hobby seriously until he emigrated to America from Bradford, England, in 1890. He ran a successful plush fabric manufacturing business in Utica, New York, specializing in imitation seal fur and alpaca plush for coats, and upholstery fabrics for car manufacturers. With success came more time for recreation and Hind became interested in philately. The characteristics which drove him to seek fortune far from home asserted themselves in the voracious manner in which he pursued his new sport. He bought entire collections and had to have the best, thus his preference for unused stamps. He was also fond of the 'unusual' over the 'general run' of stamps – in short, it seemed, anything that would make him stand out. His purchases at the

Ferrary sales certainly achieved that and the press were keen for any information on him. Physically he was described as 'a genial, stocky, thick-set gentleman about sixty, with ruddy complexion, blue eyes, light hair bordering on grey, and a close-cropped sandy moustache'. Philatelically he was described as 'the Ferrary of America'.

As with Lichtenstein, Hind was generous in lending his collections to exhibitions. Some would later characterize him as a man more interested in the prestige of owning the greatest collection of the world's stamps, but the dealer Alexander Séfi disputed this. Séfi recalled many happy days spent visiting the collector. It wasn't just the 'pure joy of possession' for Hind:

> I have watched him and sat with him at his stamp work, in his home at Utica, where, wrapped in a voluminous dressing-gown, he would spend the entire day in his simple study, working upon his collection, the whole of which was immediately available a few steps away, in the strongroom built in the wall just behind where he sat. I remember one day that we never left the room from 9.30 in the morning until tea time; lunch, as was his wont, consisting of a few sandwiches as we worked.

Maurice Burrus was a different proposition. Born in St-Croix-aux-Mines in the Alsace region of France, he was an earnest collector and had been since the age of seven. His early interest in stamps and his love of stamps on cover were helped along by his family's ancient business antecedents and the hoards of old correspondence in the family attics. One of the first pieces in his collection came from an uncle who had been going through the family's business correspondence. Burrus had a penchant for things small, including miniature books. He also had a fine sense of history, which led him to support archaeological digs in Provence and underpinned his attitude toward philately. The collector's aim, according to Burrus, was 'to reassemble the whole of the stamps issued in one country, in a certain part of the world, or if possible, of the whole universe, and not to estimate the value of stamps according to their beauty of engraving or design'. He sought stamps in fine condition but was not averse to stamps which had 'done duty' (used stamps) in his efforts to attain this goal.

Resident in Europe, it was easier for the multilingual Burrus to get to the Ferrary sales in Paris. It would have been hard for him to stay away. Ferrary's stamps were available for inspection beforehand, and Burrus wanted to satisfy himself in some cases that they were genuine. When the one penny and two pence 'Post Office' were brought out by the auctioneer on the afternoon of 14 October 1921, the first honours went to Burrus. (Hind would have been less keen on these specimens, as they were both used.) These were the first two 'Post Office' stamps discovered, used together and cut from the same letter by Madame Borchard. They had spent fifteen years in Judge Philbrick's possession (1866–81) before being hoarded away in Ferrary's great collection for forty years (1881–1921). They would remain in Burrus's possession even longer.

Hind's energies at this time were focused on gaining possession of the unique 1¢ British Guiana of 1856. This stamp was the biggest game around, philatelically speaking, and Hind's agent, Hugo Griebert, successfully outbid Burrus for it at a later Ferrary sale in 1922. With Lichtenstein, Hind and Burrus, all very wealthy men in the market for rarities, records kept being broken with each auction. At more than £7,000, the price paid for the 1¢ British Guiana stamp eclipsed all others. Burrus later claimed to have overheard Griebert, Hind's agent, discussing the price he was prepared to pay for the 1¢ British Guiana. Thus armed, Burrus knew when to drop out of the bidding, but not without having pushed his rival to a ridiculous price for a stamp which Burrus himself strongly believed to be a forgery and had had no intention of purchasing. (His aim, Burrus said, was to teach the buyer, then unknown to him, a little lesson in order to curb the foolishness of falsely inflating the prices and spoiling it for everyone – always have a limit.)

In the meantime, since the demise of Ferrary, another two deaths had occurred in the ranks of the 'Post Office' collectors. Henry Duveen died late in 1919 and Brunet de l'Argentière (who purchased the Bordeaux letter from Lemaire in 1903) died late in 1921. Duveen's collection only came back on to the market three years after his death and was sold over a four-year period from 1922. Hind again paid high prices, acquiring much of Duveen's collection, including unused specimens of the one penny and two pence 'Post Office'.

There is some confusion about the sale of de l'Argentière's collection, which contained the superlative Bordeaux letter bearing both the two pence and one penny 'Post Office' stamps. The Williams brothers claimed that Lichtenstein bought de l'Argentière's collection in 1917, citing C. J. Phillips in the *Collectors Club Philatelist* (whom they disagreed with on a number of other points), a claim repeated consistently since 1940. But the firm of Séfi, Pemberton and Co. wrote of purchasing much of the collection early in 1922, after de l'Argentière's death. It seems more likely that Lichtenstein bought the collection after its owner's death in 1921, reserved the pieces he wanted for himself, then offered the rest to Séfi, Pemberton and Co., as he had earlier with Worthington's collection. Messrs Séfi and Pemberton did buy large amounts of the collection but turned down the Bordeaux letter because of 'slight damage' to one of the stamps. This is important to note, because it explains Lichtenstein's otherwise curious private sale of the Bordeaux letter to Arthur Hind in 1922. If Lichtenstein had acquired the Bordeaux letter in 1917, why would he have parted with such a magnificent item after only five years, when the Jerrom letter stayed in his family's possession for more than fifty years? Such an action might suggest that he had doubts about the Bordeaux letter's genuineness. But, if Lichtenstein only acquired the letter some time in 1921 or 1922, then it makes more sense that he should weigh up its value against his criteria and, not being an overly selfish collector, decide that three 'Post Office Mauritius' in good condition were sufficient to his needs.

Whatever the reason, Lichtenstein parted with the Bordeaux letter. Séfi later regretted his missed opportunity and Hind very much enjoyed ribbing the dealer about it. Being in possession of the 'best' collection was important to Arthur Hind. When George V showed him the brilliant 'Blue Mauritius' in 1923, a year after Hind had secured the Bordeaux letter, Hind is reported to have fired back with almost schoolboy-like glee, 'I have a pair!'

If the younger Burrus felt irked at missing out on the Bordeaux letter he didn't show it, for he was known to be every inch the gentleman, and at twenty-six years Hind's junior, there was time enough to wait.

At another Ferrary auction in Paris in April 1923 Burrus successfully bid for an ex-Borchard used two pence 'Post Office'. This had been in Baron de Rothschild's possession for twenty-one years (1872–93), then reposed in the Ferrary collection for a further thirty years (1893–1923). Champion purchased the last of Ferrary's 'Post Office' at the same auction, a fine unused one penny, replacing the heavily obliterated one penny in his personal collection, which he later sold.

By 1923 six of the twenty-five known 'Post Office' stamps were permanently out of circulation, displayed in public collections (the British Museum and Reichspostmuseum in Berlin) and in the British Royal Collection. Hind owned four, and Lichtenstein and Burrus each owned three. Champion probably still had three in his personal collection, while another two graced the collection of Dutchman Henry Manus. Specimens of both values are thought to have been in the collection of the Swedish-American collector Hans Lagerloef some time after 1912. The heavily obliterated ex-Borchard one penny once owned by the Bordeaux collector Schiller, which first came to light in 1897, was languishing anonymously in private hands until acquired some time between 1919 and 1933 by a Mr Cox of Scotland. The damaged two pence found in 1917 and sold by Lemaire had already disappeared into anonymity for good.

By the early 1920s numerous philatelists had a story about a 'Post Office' that had slipped through their fingers. One such tall tale was published in the Christmas number of *Stamp Collecting* in 1919, under the heading 'The Stolen "Mauritius": A True Story'. It was written by Leon de Raay, a South African philatelist, and tells of the author's youthful stamp collecting days back in Amsterdam, around 1884, when he and his friend Frank Miller, 'with more money than brains', decided to take off on a tour of the Continent on a philatelic odyssey.

The first port of call was Brussels, where they stayed with a lawyer friend of de Raay's, to whom they communicated their philatelic passion. This friend, Monsieur Carmenteuil, told the author 'that he must have some old letters among his parchments, also of an old client from Havre, and, on hearing this, we naturally could not allow him a minute's peace before he showed us the letters'. They found a letter from Mauritius addressed to the client from Le Havre, 'with a stamp affixed, of which we had never seen a specimen before, and therefore could not explain, having, instead of the words POST PAID on the left-hand side, the words POST OFFICE – a superb copy in bright vermilion colour'.

De Raay was made a present of the Mauritius stamp, and the following day the two friends set off for Paris and the Jardin de Luxembourg, where the French philatelic fraternity gathered to exchange and sell stamps. Approached by a man, stamp album in hand, the friends made a few transactions and de Raay thought to show the Frenchman the Mauritius stamp. 'He turned pale when he caught a glance of it, but collecting himself, he indifferently said that it was a poor forgery of a stamp that never existed.' The Frenchman offered to buy it for the small sum of five francs, but de Raay refused and the friends thought no more about the business until discussing their purchases with their Parisian host, knowledgeable in matters philatelic, later that evening. It transpired that the two friends had been duped in their transactions with the Frenchman, a rascal who had surely known the value of the rare Mauritius stamp, which the host recognized and was sure would fetch a thousand francs.

All of this seems plausible, the youth of the two friends perhaps excusing their limited philatelic knowledge – by the early 1880s the 'Post Office Mauritius' stamps were well known in philatelic circles and well documented, thanks to Dr Legrand and Major Evans.

But the story then takes an incredible turn. Later that night, asleep and dreaming of stamps and rarities, the author awoke to the sensation of someone breathing over him, the muzzle of a revolver pressed to his forehead and a handkerchief pressed to his nose, shortly after which he lost consciousness. He woke to find Frank Miller no longer there and all the drawers in the room they shared turned out – his precious stamps gone. Days passed and the police were unable to solve the mystery of Frank's disappearance. On the day before de Raay was to leave Paris he spied the Frenchman who had tried to dupe them when they first arrived. The author called out to him and the man panicked and ran into the path of a horse and carriage, was crushed under the wheel and taken away to hospital. Later that evening a message was brought around to de Raay's abode, requesting his immediate attendance at the bedside of the injured man. A deathbed confession ensued:

It appeared that Renaud (that was his name) on first seeing my 'Mauritius' was filled by the desire of possessing it. Seeing how futile it was trying to get it from me by fair means, he decided to obtain it by other means, and, shadowing me to the door, discovered where I lived. He thereupon went to the Prefecture of Police and denounced my friend, Frank Miller (who he thought was the owner, although I had shown him the specimen), as a Prussian spy, coming to Paris to get at the plans of the defences of that city.

At the time I write of, France was in very strained relations with Prussia, and the city swarmed with secret spies and detectives. Renaud, knowing this, was sure, by denouncing Frank, to receive a reward, and offered his help to arrest Frank. This was gladly accepted, but the Prefect, not wishing to make any commotion in these troublous times, ordered that the arrest should be done with the utmost secrecy. Renaud, with a sergeant and some secret policemen, came in the dead of the night into the house, and, before Frank could utter any cry, was duly chloroformed and bound, and all his belongings were taken away. Renaud explained to the men accompanying him that the secret plans were undoubtedly concealed in some place, but, as the friend of the Prussian spy also slept in the same room, one of the men should hold a pistol to his head to keep him quiet. In the meantime, Renaud opened the drawers and took the coveted treasures, which he secreted about his person, and handed instead to the sergeant some plans he had in his own possession, which he would have sold later to the Prussian Government.

Renaud wrote out his confession and promptly died. The stamps were on his person when he was brought into the hospital and before expiring he returned them to de Raay, who, with the written confession, was thus able to liberate his poor friend from the clutches of the Prefecture. The author gave his friend the one penny 'Post Office Mauritius' as a souvenir, and at the time he was writing claimed that it still hung, framed, in Frank Miller's possession.

Could the story possibly be true? Leon de Raay was a respected philatelist and seemingly had no reason to stretch the truth. However, the avowed purpose of this Christmas number of *Stamp Collecting* was to increase the circulation of the magazine and create interest in the hobby, to be achieved through a rich 'pudding' of philatelic fare through 'various articles, stories, and phantasies' of light character. With this in mind, 'The Stolen Mauritius' should be read with indulgence. De Raay in fact cribbed the early sections of the story from a certain Jabez Jones's recollections of similar wanderings, published in the *Stamp-Collector's Magazine* back in 1864.

Crime in relation to the Mauritian stamps was not unheard of.

Walter Nathan, another respected philatelist, wrote of a tale of fraud, also from before 1890, in a series of reminiscences for the *Stamp Collectors' Fortnightly*. He had seen an advertisement from a gentleman who claimed to have had much correspondence with Mauritius and the Australian colonies during the period 1847–57, and who was prepared to part with six of the 'Post Paid' and a pair of the 'Post Office'. The philatelist decided to look into it and duly presented himself at the private address in north London, and with difficulty found himself a seat in a crowded room, surrounded by 'South Pacific canoes and weapons, Maori nulrullas, Japanese enamels, Chinese gongs, ivories, jade and brass work... thrown together in chaotic heaps'. He was, it seemed, in the abode of a well-travelled and eclectic collector. The owner of the stamps, an elderly gentleman, launched into 'a long story of his birth, education and travels' when the thought suddenly occurred to Nathan that 'perhaps I was being mesmerised (hypnotism was a word which had not then dribbled from medical circles into general use), and I sat up alert'. Informing the gentleman that he should like to see some stamps, Nathan was then told that the owner had *six* 'Post Office Mauritius'. While the owner was search-ing for the stamps among the clutter, a knock came at the door. It was a telegram purporting to be from Philipp von Ferrary, offering £100 for each specimen of the 'Post Office' stamps. The elderly gentleman was unable to find the stamps and Nathan paid £5 for the stamp album he had been examining in the meantime. He offered £110 for a single specimen of the 'Post Office' and the owner promised to call on Nathan on the morrow to show him the 'Post Office' stamps (presuming he could find them among the clutter). Perhaps he never did find them, for Nathan never saw the gentleman again. When he opened his £5 purchase at home, he found that all the good stamps contained in the album had been removed from under his very nose. 'I think,' Nathan mused, 'that old gentleman missed his walk in life when he forsook the certain fortune he would have secured as a conjurer, for I never saw a neater trick done with more celerity on any public stage.'

A curious echo of supposed hypnotism to perpetrate a philatelic fraud occurred (perhaps) many years later in Vienna, in January 1921. Workman Franz Raaber believed himself 'the lucky possessor of 7 Mauritius stamps of 1847, amongst which a specimen of the famous blue 2d was supposed to figure':

> Raaber's tale ran that a man had called on him, who styled himself president of the Vienna collectors' society and who swindled him by changing the genuine blue stamp, and giving instead a less valuable copy in exchange. The aforesaid Raaber also did not hesitate to place the matter before the police. The latter, however, in the course of investigations made clear that Raaber had been a victim of a well known hypnotical authority called Andrussen, who was able to exercise such influences over him that Raaber dreamt the whole affair. So swindle and exchange had been only dreams; probably the possession of Mauritius stamps, too.

Probably, yes; but that the stamps – and particularly the two pence blue – should figure so prominently in this delirium of fortune indicates that they had a very strong and widespread hold over the public imagination by the early 1920s. It was the secret dream of much of the population (the European population at least) to discover a specimen or two themselves.

Raaber's strange tale was reported in the *Philatelic Magazine* in April 1921, under the heading 'Hypnotism and the Blue Mauritius'. While the claim to possess no fewer than seven specimens of rare

Mauritius stamps was intriguing, it was the possible inclusion of the two pence blue which appealed to the contemporary audience – the 'Blue Mauritius' again confirming its popular status.

As a subject for the philatelist, Mauritian stamps have always been tightly held and hoarded by collectors. Few, if any, of the 'Post Office' stamps would come back on to the market until another death occurred among the ranks of their prominent owners.

Another two specimens of the stamps were taken off the market permanently in 1927 when they were donated to the Swedish Postal Museum in Stockholm. Hans Lagerloef (1880–1952) was a generous philatelist and donated many of his collections during his lifetime to institutions, including the Smithsonian. The one penny was the stamp originally found by Monsieur Noirel of Port Louis on some old newspapers, subsequently owned by Arthur de Rothschild for twenty-three years (1870–93) and Ferrary for around nineteen years (1893–1912). It was obliterated with part of a rectangular PAID hand stamp. The two pence specimen owned by Lagerloef was finer, with only the faintest of red postmarks, and was one of the stamps found by Madame Borchard and sold by Madame Desbois. It had been owned by Perinelle for eleven years (1870–81) before spending more than thirty years in Ferrary's collection (1881–1912). Ferrary had let it go to an American dealer in exchange for another coveted stamp (the 'Boscawen'), and it was some time after this that Lagerloef purchased both the values of the 'Post Office'. He did so, it seems, with the intent of gifting the stamps to their ultimate home, for he didn't want his own country's postal museum to be outshone by the Reichspostmuseum in Berlin. Established in 1906, the Swedish Postal Museum still considers the two Mauritius stamps their greatest treasures.

There was little movement of any kind in the 'Post Office' market for some years after the Ferrary sales were completed. Some time between 1920 and 1940, Théodore Champion sold the lesser of his two one penny 'Post Office' to a collector who remained anonymous, that specimen not coming back on to the market for almost seventy years. The early 1930s saw the deaths of two key Mauritius collectors, Henry Manus in 1931 and Arthur Hind in early 1933. Manus was the Dutch collector who owned the only ball envelope still in private hands, the one addressed to young Henry Adam. Manus had owned the envelope since 1909, and this, along with one of the best unused specimens of the two pence blue, was sold on 10 March 1933. They were both bought by the British dealer Tom Allen, who paid large sums for them, particularly given the financial climate of those Depression years. A few years later, Allen sold both items to King Carol of Romania, the second king to own a 'Post Office Mauritius'.

Arthur Hind's interest in stamps began to wane once he felt that his collection was complete. He had tried to sell his holdings intact in 1929, but found no buyers forthcoming after the stock market crash. Hind died of pneumonia in March 1933, at the age of seventy-seven, at his home in Miami, Florida. Curiously, in his will he left his wife dwelling, jewellery, furniture and paintings but *not*, he stipulated, his stamp collection. He also left the instruction that if his wife contested the will she should get nothing. Mrs Hind did, however, eventually manage to secure a third of the sale value of the stamp collection, which was on the market by November of that year. The first auction was held at the Waldorf Astoria Hotel in New York. The sale didn't reach the heights expected, even allowing for the straitened times – it emerged that Hind was a careless philatelist who had used thick glues and tapes to fix his stamps and covers in albums, affecting their condition.

As with the Ferrary collection, a series of Hind auctions took place over several years. The Mauritius portion was scheduled to be auctioned by the dealer Charles J. Phillips (by then based in New York) in March 1934, but the London firm of Harmers, representing a syndicate of Hind's relatives back in England, negotiated directly with the executors and purchased Hind's entire remaining British and foreign collection out from under Phillips's nose. Harmers' prize was immediately whisked away in an armoured car to the SS *Majestic*, waiting at the New York docks, to return to England. Eleven auctions took place in London at Harmers in their New Bond Street galleries between April 1934 and June 1935, but the one which attracted the headlines, of course, was the fourth sale of British Africa, containing the Mauritius portion.

The sale room, as on that famous occasion at Puttick and Simpson thirty years before, was crowded. According to *The Times's* report, 'philatelists, both amateur and professional, including buyers from France, Germany, India, Italy, and the United States', turned out in force and the bidding was spirited. The Mauritius stamps were the *pièces de résistance*. The Bordeaux letter was knocked down to Edgar Mohrmann 'on behalf of a private collector'. Paying less for the cover than Hind had in 1922, the private collector was none other than the ever patient Maurice Burrus. Of the sale Mohrmann later recalled, 'One of the most outstanding moments in my life was the occasion when Monsieur Burrus instructed me to purchase for him the World famous cover bearing copies of the Post Office Mauritius 1d and 2d... I paid the sum of £5,000 and in 1934 that was a sensational figure and in consequence my purchase received tremendous publicity in the press and I was interviewed like a "film star".' (Advertising his business in the American journal *Collectors Club Philatelist* later that year, Mohrmann declared himself, somewhat ambiguously, 'Buyer of the world's rarest philatelic piece since Ferrari'!)

With his purchase of the Bordeaux letter Burrus now owned five 'Post Office Mauritius'. Robson Lowe, who later auctioned the 'Burrus Mauritius', fondly recalled his visits to the collector: 'He would almost certainly bring out the cover on each occasion. It was one item he treasured most of all.'

Although the prices realized at the Hind auction for the 'Post Office' stamps were lower than in the boom years of the early 1920s, they were still considered high given the Depression in America and the number of stamps for sale at the one time. Hind's four 'Post Office' were the most sought after of their kind. In addition to the Bordeaux letter bearing both values of the 'Post Office', Hind had also owned fine unused specimens of the one penny and two pence. These stamps had not suffered in his care and were still beautifully fresh in appearance, the colours as rich as the day Barnard had printed them in 1847. They were significant because so few 'Post Office' were known in this pristine condition. Only one other unused one penny was known and three unused two pence. (Two of the unused two pence were already permanently off the market, in the Royal Collection and the British Museum.) Thus far Hind's 'Post Office' had shared the same pedigree. Both stamps were found by Madame Borchard in Bordeaux, the two pence one of the first ever found, in 1865. The one penny was among the stamps Madame had put aside for a rainy day, which had come too soon, in 1869. Bordeaux collector Lalanne aside, all subsequent owners of these two stamps – Avery, Duveen and Hind – had died still in possession of their prize. Once obtained, it seemed only death would part a collector from an unused 'Post Office'.

But at the Hind auction in 1934 the unused pair went their separate ways. Ernest de Silva, a collector based in Colombo, bought the one penny, and a European dealer bought the two pence. This time the two pence fetched a significant £1,000 less than its one penny sibling, which a report in *The Times* put down to its being slightly cut into. In tight financial times, condition became even more important; in the case of this two pence, however, it was a mere quibble. The lower price paid probably resulted from a dearth of competing collectors with sufficient funds.

The unused two pence 'Post Office' bought at the Hind Mauritius sale changed hands once more in 1938, bought by English dealer Tom Allen on behalf of a European collector. Apart from this, no 'Post Office' stamps came on to the market for almost ten years.

Fittingly, on the eve of the centenary of the 'Post Office' stamps, an unrecorded specimen of the one penny was discovered in a collection in Folkestone in England, but made its bow to little applause. This was perhaps on account of its poor condition – the stamp was heavily cancelled, although the Queen's profile and the word 'Office' were clearly visible. Nor was it on cover, like the majority of 'Post Office' stamps found between 1897 and 1903. As with the Bonar discovery, this 'Post Office' was thought to have come into the owner's possession some time in the 1870s, much earlier than its 'discovery'. It is said to have been found in India and returned with its owner to England at a later date.

In celebration of the 'Post Office' centenary, the Mauritius

The one rupee Mauritius stamp issued to celebrate the centenary of the island's first British colonial postage stamps.

government issued four commemorative stamps – in 1948. A rather hideous confusion of orange, mauve, green, blue and brown, the designs incorporated the original two 'Post Office' stamps and the head of George VI, bearing the values 5, 12 and 20 cents and 1 rupee. The designs were ready in time, by September 1947, but the stamps themselves were not. Louis Dardenne had engraved the last locally produced stamps in 1859, and all subsequent Mauritius stamps were, and are, produced outside of the island itself. In fact, the Mauritius government had originally ordered stamps from England back in 1847, but grew tired of waiting for them and so the 'Post Office' were commissioned locally. Nothing much had changed in 100 years.

Late in the centenary year another one penny 'Post Office' was found, this time by Mr R. Haydock, a stamp dealer in Perth, Australia. Sadly for Mr Haydock, on being shown a photograph of the stamp, the Williams brothers, who had been studying the history and provenance of the 'Post Office' stamps for some years, declared it a forgery. Perhaps it was the same stamp documented in the *Australian Stamp Journal* back in 1913, found by an elderly lady in Perth and never acknowledged as a true specimen.

When the one penny 'Post Office' owned by Mr Cox of Scotland came back on to the market in 1933, experts expressed their concerns. This was the stamp found in 1897 in the collection of a man named Schiller, who is said to have acquired it through an exchange with Madame Borchard as early as 1864–5. Due to its condition it never attained the high prices of some of the other 'Post Office' stamps, and the Williams brothers aptly described it as 'the unpopular black sheep in the popular "Post Office" Mauritius flock'. It had no margins, was cut into on one side and the word OFFICE was barely visible through the barred cancellation, which obscured most of the Queen's head and her profile. (The profile was an important feature in identifying the more obvious forgeries.) After its sale in 1933 this stamp was sent to the Royal Philatelic Society in London for closer examination. One of the society's objects was 'the detection and prevention of forgeries and frauds'. To that end they had set up an expert committee in 1893, a year when forgeries were increasing noticeably on the London market. Mr Cox's 'Post Office' was refused a certificate of genuineness because somebody had tried to repair a defect in it and because the cancellation was so heavy. The society felt itself unable to pronounce a definite opinion and the new owner returned the stamp to the auctioneers. The experts of the committee did not believe the stamp to be a forgery but from that time on it could only be sold 'as is', with no guarantee of genuineness. It is still accepted as one of the canonical twenty-six 'Post Office Mauritius'.

This poor one penny specimen continued to change hands in Germany regularly over the next few years. H. R. Harmer, who had auctioned the stamp in 1933, believed that the stamp was being used as a means of smuggling currency. ('To-day many serious business men in more disorganised countries consider stamps as the safest portable security of international value,' Alexander Séfi had noted some years previously.) The black sheep of the 'Post Office' family was eventually purchased by a Bavarian philatelist in 1952 and hasn't been seen since.

Very Much in Love with Mauritius Stamps

Later, as he progresses, he will find the path diverges,
when he is left to make his own choice, whether for the
stiff and arduous climb to Mauritius, which, as a
child said of Mount Everest, 'people cannot climb very
high without resting'; or, if he has enough ballast,
steer his barque for the Capes, or occupy his business
in a country which presents easier possibilities.

Rev. C. S. Morton, 'On Garnering',
Stamp Collecting, 1922

The walls of the Reichspostmuseum were bare. The little metal display case that had contained the two 'Post Office Mauritius', along with six other rare stamps of British Guiana and Hawaii, was gone. During the Second World War valuable items from the Reichspostmuseum had been first removed to the safety of a vault in the Reichsbank in Berlin, and early in 1945 were taken to a mineshaft in Eisleben. Some items were recovered after the war ended, but Germany's most beloved philatelic treasures disappeared.

An unnamed person reportedly offered two 'Post Office' stamps for sale in the Zoo district of Berlin in 1955, thought to be the specimens missing from the Reichspostmuseum, but the mystery of the missing 'Post Office' stamps would remain unsolved for some years yet.

Rumours surfaced occasionally of new finds of the 'Post Office' stamps – in Vienna in 1955 and in Australia in 1956 – but none turned out to be genuine. The problem of forgery was not new. It had been part of the business of stamps from the very first, and philatelists, keen and canny, were well aware of this. Publications on philatelic forgeries, such as *Forged Stamps: How to Detect Them*, appeared almost simultaneously with the first philatelic journals. Not only were the fledgling philatelists thought a little odd for collecting dirty scraps of paper, they were also viewed suspiciously by postal authorities. Fraud could be perpetrated against postal issuing authorities on a grand scale by forging current stamps for postal use. In consequence some looked askance at the efforts of philatelists to document forgeries. Doing so was certain to provide a model for forgers. But the stamp collector who delighted in detail was the best possible insurance against this. As Major Evans commented in 1907, minute study was a means to an end. The value of philatelic research lay in 'the discovery of fresh facts in the history of the stamps studied and of their manufacture and production, and fresh points that may enable us the better to cope with the forgeries and frauds that beset collectors of all kinds'.

Forgers aimed not only to defraud the post office, but to loosen the purse strings of collectors. However, the intent to deceive and defraud, inherent in forgery, is an accusation not so easily levelled at the earliest practitioners of the art in the philatelic field. It all gets rather murky at the beginning of the hobby, before great sums of money came into play. With the advent of albums such as the Lallier, which reserved spaces for all the world's stamps, there was an expectation that all those spaces could be filled and an understanding that there were probably not enough genuine stamps to do so. To fill this gap, the *Stamp Collector's Magazine* had speculated in 1863 that stamp clubs would form 'to reprint curious and

The original case containing the two 'Post Office Mauritius' and other rare stamps which belonged to the Reichspostmuseum in Berlin. The case and its contents disappeared at the end of the Second World War.

obsolete stamps'. The writer of those words made no distinction between a genuine stamp, created by legitimate stamp-issuing authorities for postal use, and imitations or facsimiles of those stamps; he clearly did not share the concerns of the authors of *Forged Stamps: How to Detect Them.* To some, facsimiles were fine if marketed as such. The Spiro brothers, who ran a lithographic business in Hamburg, Germany, began producing very good imitations of stamps in 1864 and advertised them as facsimiles. Although the brothers did not intend to deceive with these productions, once out of their creators' hands the stamps took on a life of their own. As they passed from hand to hand their origins became obscured, so much so that the British philatelic press began describing these 'philatelic weeds' in great detail, warning against them in 1871. The Spiro brothers had stopped making facsimiles by 1880. But another German firm, the Senf brothers in Leipzig, took up the mantle and produced facsimiles, marked and marketed as such, throughout the 1880s.

Jean-Baptiste Moens would write to postmasters asking for stocks of obsolete stamps – stocks which had legitimately been printed for postal use but not used up before other issues took their place. As early as 1862 Moens is known to have also requested that stamps be reprinted from their original printing bases, if those articles of production were still in existence. (Stamps thus produced would be considered official reprints.) Both Moens and Edward Stanley Gibbons even purchased original lithographic stones and electrotype plates of stamps first issued in the 1860s in order to commission private reprints well into the 1890s. By this time such practices were condemned. As one chronicler of the history of philatelic forgers has noted, obituaries – usually the main source of biographical detail on the early dealers and collectors – never tell the whole story. Philately was, after all, a gentlemanly pursuit and no obituary of Moens was ever going to describe the great Belgian dealer as a forger. But by later standards, like a number of other respected dealers from the earliest days of collecting, he came close.

While many collectors, such as Henry Duveen and Arthur Hind, preferred their stamps in an unused condition, free of cancellations, other collectors came to value used stamps for the stories they could tell and the evidence they provided. On being offered an unused one penny 'Post Office' in 1909, the Prince of Wales wrote to his philatelic adviser that he had come to the conclusion 'that £2,000 was a ridiculous price to ask for the 1d Post Office Mauritius, especially as one could not swear that it was an unused one & I have a genuine one on the envelope'. The Prince liked his stamps unused. He was mostly concerned in this instance about the price (the money could be better spent on other stamps he needed), and was not suggesting that this one penny 'Post Office' was a forgery. Possibly the Prince was suspicious of the beautifully clean state of this specimen and thought it might have been cleaned to remove traces of a cancellation. (Some stamps are more valuable with cancellations and some without.) Whether used or unused, the King-in-waiting, like all collectors by this time, wanted a genuine stamp. His conclusion in this case – 'They are quite welcome to it in America.'

There are many fine lines in the practices of stamp collecting. Soaking a used stamp in water to dislodge it from its support is a legitimate process and can also make a stamp seem brighter, newer, as surely happened with James Bonar's specimen. Sometimes stamps might be altered to improve their appearance, with no intent to make them more valuable (apparently). This is considered a repair, as in the case of the one penny 'Post Office' that came before the Philatelic Society's expert committee in the 1930s. A repair can be as crude as removing stray specks of ink, or colouring in a spot missed in the printing process. Stamps can also be immersed in certain chemical solutions to brighten their appearance and cleanse them of cancellations. It becomes problematic when any of these things are done to genuine stamps to make them seem more valuable than they really are. (Ferrary was sometimes duped by these 'chemical varieties'.) So it is also with the removal – and addition – of cancellations. As the value of cancellations for determining periods of use and genuineness came to be understood, so more cancellations were forged, applied to both genuine and forged stamps. There are examples where genuine lettersheets or envelopes have been fraudulently brought together with genuine stamps, tied to the covers by forged cancellations. These covers are described, rather mildly, as 'improved' or 'enhanced'.

In the nineteenth century, illustrations in the early philatelic journals were not reproduced from photographs, but from engravings copied from originals. These illustrations were often then copied from journal to journal. Sometimes the illustrations were seasoned with imagination. George Herpin had not even seen a 'Post Office Mauritius', or confirmed its existence, when he reproduced a two pence 'Post Office' in 1865. His description arose from hearsay and in his bogus illustration the word 'Office' was superimposed on to an example of a later 'Post Paid' stamp, the so-called 'Sherwin'.

Most of the illustrations and descriptions of stamps which appeared in these journals were derived from specimens in the publishers' own stock. Philatelic facts, remember, had to be gleaned from the stamps themselves, from those that had happened to survive. Sometimes a forgery might inadvertently make its way into the collection of a dealer-publisher and subsequently be illustrated as a legitimate issue. But usually in these cases it didn't take long for sharp-eyed readers with similar specimens to enter the discourse and issues of genuineness were usually resolved – a happy outcome.

A less beneficial by-product of this illustration process was the existence of the original dies of these facsimile versions of stamps. (Dies are the original piece of metal, or other material, on which a stamp design is engraved, usually before being multiplied on to a printing base, from which sheets of stamps are then produced.) They could of course be used not only for illustration purposes in the journals, but to print stamps. As publisher of *Le Timbre-Poste*, Moens had many of these dies and they were sold along with his remaining stock when he retired in 1900. Reprints from them are known, but who made them is not.

Dies for the one penny and two pence 'Post Office Mauritius' must have been among these. Moens appears to have first illustrated the 'Post Office' stamps in *Le Timbre-Poste* in January 1870. Although they do look like 'Post Office' stamps when compared with the originals Moens was working from – the first two found – it is very easy to tell the difference, in the lettering (the s particularly) and in the Queen's profile. It may be that Moens's illustration dies are the source of the first forgeries of the 'Post Office' stamps.

After James Bonar's rediscovery of the brilliant 'Blue Mauritius' in his childhood collection in 1903 there were only a few more 'Post Office' stamps discovered and pronounced genuine – the two pence, apparently found in France in 1917, and the one penny found in England in 1946. Two one penny forgeries on a fragment of an envelope were doing the rounds in the 1930s, eventually coming before the expert committee of the Royal Philatelic Society in London, who confirmed their dubious status. (In the interim between this item being denounced in the *Philatelic Magazine* in 1935 and its being presented for examination to the expert committee, somebody had removed the flaps, which indicated the piece was clearly from an envelope. Envelope usage was far less common in 1847, so making this forged piece appear more like a lettersheet than an envelope was a further attempt to 'enhance' it.)

Familiarity with engraving processes helped in detection of the better forged stamps. The 'Post Office' stamps were worked from copper plates, where the quality of the printing differs from those worked from lithography stones. In the opinion of the Royal Philatelic Society's expert committee, the printing process was the usual giveaway in detecting forged 'Post Office' stamps, as was the Queen's profile (nobody ever seemed to get it quite right). Photo-lithographic forgeries were another matter. This process used photographic methods to transfer a copy of the image to the engraving plate. These would look identical to the originals (if an original or good photograph of one was available to the forger), so only a knowledge of inks and printing processes, and a feel for paper, were useful in the expertizing process of these kinds of forgeries.

Another 'Post Office' surfaced in 1952 and did eventually make it into the pantheon of the genuine stamps, albeit relegated to no man's land and assigned the cataloguing appellation of 'Limbo I'. It was a used one penny, with four clear margins, cancelled with a thick black pen in the form of a cross. The provenance of the stamp was hazy and, unlike most of the other genuine 'Post Office' stamps, news of the stamp does not appear to have made it widely into the philatelic press. It was said to have been acquired by a Belgian banker some time in the 1890s, then purchased by René Berlingin, a wealthy Belgian collector, in 1940. A most unattractive specimen, it was chemically treated to try brightening its appearance and to remove the heavy pen cancellation, repairs which only made the stamp look worse. The condition also made it more difficult for expertizers to consider the stamp genuine, because it had been tampered with. Berlingin might ultimately have had doubts about this stamp, or perhaps like other 'Post Office' collectors he sought to improve his Mauritius holdings by buying or trading up, for he parted with the defective one penny some time after he acquired two finer specimens from King Carol of Romania in April 1950.

Only a few other 'Post Office' stamps changed hands during the 1950s, including, at separate times, the highly desirable unused pair once owned by Arthur Hind. Harry Nissen, an English dealer, purchased the unused two pence in 1951. In 1957, in partnership with one W. E. Lea, Nissen also obtained the near-perfect unused one penny specimen, paying a then record price for a single stamp at a British auction – £4,500. The little orange-red stamp had generously been gifted by Ernest de Silva to the Young Men's Buddhist Association, whose interest in the stamp, to be expected, was purely financial, not philatelic.

Alfred Lichtenstein had died unexpectedly at the age of seventy in February 1947, the year of the 'Post Office' centenary, but collectors had to wait another twenty years before his Mauritius stamps came back on to the market. On his death Lichtenstein's collection had passed to his only child, Louise Boyd Dale. Philately was bred in her veins and by the time she was fourteen she had delivered a lecture on the Bordeaux stamp issues of France to the prestigious Collectors Club of New York. She went on to become an internationally renowned philatelist in her own right and, like her father before her, was invited to sign the Roll of Distinguished Philatelists. Lichtenstein's collection did not remain intact. Portions of it were sold off in the mid-1950s and in the years before Louise Boyd Dale's own death in 1967. She added no 'Post Office' stamps to the collection, which had no need of them, but did retain the Mauritius portion and improved it – particularly the 'Dardenne' holdings, on which her father had been working when he died.

Maurice Burrus remained the prince among 'Post Office' collectors, holding five specimens at the one time. He was so well known that an envelope addressed to 'M. Burrus, Philatelist, London' from an elderly lady who lived in outback Australia reached him at his picturesque home in Lausanne, Switzerland, and was much treasured by the recipient, containing a few 'kangaroo' stamps for his collection.

Burrus decided to sell his collection towards the end of the 1950s. In his later years he became crippled by arthritis and was no longer able to enjoy the pleasure of handling his stamps. The New Orleans dealer Raymond H. Weill made an offer of $4 million, but Burrus refused. Weill remembered how Burrus had chided him that

Americans thought nothing of spending $7 million on a couple of aeroplanes and that he valued his collection more highly than that. But the asking price went unmet and Maurice Burrus died on 8 December 1959 before effecting the sale of his collection. The magnificent assemblage was eventually sold through seventy-five auctions and private treaties that took place over a five-year period from 1962.

The 'Burrus Mauritius' was auctioned on 1 October 1963, almost four years after Burrus's death, in the Prince Edward Suite of London's Piccadilly Hotel. The Piccadilly was chosen for its superior accommodation, as interested buyers were expected to flock to London from around the world to attend the sale. The Prince Edward Suite was commodious enough to allow 100 buyers to be seated at tables to inspect the stamps. The most prestigious lot of all was auctioned first, the Bordeaux letter, which had been in the Burrus collection for almost thirty years. Raymond Weill bought it on behalf of a client for £28,000. The second lot, the first specimens of the 'Post Office' ever found by Madame Borchard, the one penny and two pence originally from the same letter, was knocked down for £8,250. The last of the 'Post Office' stamps to be auctioned was a fine used specimen of the two pence, which Burrus had purchased from the Ferrary sale back in 1923.

Hiroyuki Kanai, who would become the last of the great 'Post Office' collectors, was not among the buyers of that issue at the Burrus sale, although he did make purchases of the other classic Mauritius stamps. Born in 1925 to wealthy parents in Amagasaki, Japan, Kanai began collecting at the age of five. He still remembers the Greek stamps, from around 1930, which his father gave him, taken from business correspondence. By the time he was thirteen he considered himself a serious collector, and during his twenties moved away from general collecting, specializing in British

Colonials and Japanese classic issues. Kanai was ambitious to be considered one of the world's greatest philatelists and Mauritius, with its degree of difficulty, held great appeal. (Kanai clearly loved a challenge. When one present-day philatelist expressed the desire to an old Mauritius hand of taking up that challenge, he was met with raised eyebrows and a look that said, 'Do you *really* mean you're going to do Mauritius?') He set himself a task with the 'Post Office', to see how many of the twenty-six reported specimens he could acquire, intent on bettering Burrus's tally of five at the one time.

On 21 March 1963, the beautiful unused one penny 'Post Office' that had passed through the hands of Avery, Duveen, Hind and de Silva, was once again on the market. The Royal Philatelic Society of London had considered this specimen to be 'unquestionably the finer of the two recorded unused examples'. It had been sold several times since leaving the possession of Nissen and Lea, who had acquired it in 1957, and was only up for auction again in 1963 because the present owner, a man named Gilbert, found himself in considerable debt as a result of losing millions on the New York Stock Exchange. Gilbert was a curious collector. Prior to his share losses he had been a very wealthy man. He preferred to rent rather than buy Old Master and Impressionist paintings to adorn his walls, but liked to pay for his stamps outright. For four years he was the proud possessor of this unused one penny 'Post Office', which he reportedly framed and hung between his hired paintings. The stamp was eventually taken by Gilbert's creditors and put up for auction at Harmer, Rooke & Co. in London. Hiroyuki Kanai successfully bid for his first 'Post Office' and the stamp was again in the news, the managing director of Harmer appearing on the BBC *Today* programme. At £8,500, it was the highest price yet paid for a single British Commonwealth stamp.

Kanai was now on the trail of an unused specimen of the two pence 'Post Office' to match. The firm of Stanley Gibbons had acquired one some time in the early 1960s. This was the stamp that had been purchased by Henry Nissen back in 1951, destined to end up paired with the beautiful unused one penny specimen Kanai already possessed. Gibbons had previously bought these two stamps from Piet Lataudrie back in 1893 for £680. They had been discovered by Madame Borchard and had always been sold together – to Desbois, Lalanne, Lataudrie, Gibbons, Avery, Peckitt, Duveen and Hind – until they were bought separately in the breakup of the Hind collection in 1934. Kanai purchased the two pence 'Post Office' from Gibbons in 1965 and now owned incomparable specimens of both values in an unused condition. After thirty years apart, and a procession of owners, the two stamps were together again, in the care of one who understood their significance.

The formidable collection held by Louise Boyd Dale, known as the Dale-Lichtenstein collection, was sold during the period 1968–71, following Louise Boyd Dale's death. For the first time in fifty years philatelists had the opportunity to become the owner of the Jerrom letter to Bombay, bearing the pair of one penny 'Post Office' stamps, and the fine example of the two pence 'Post Office' on part cover (the Caunten fragment). Lot 1 of the first Dale-Lichtenstein auction, 21 October 1968, was the prize of the collection, the Jerrom letter. After a five-way bidding war, the Raymond H. Weill Company of New Orleans became its new owners, paying the headline-grabbing amount of $380,000. This was the highest price paid for a philatelic item to date. The Weill brothers bid on their own behalf, seated up the back of the New York auction room to keep an eye on the competition, afterwards declaring that they were 'representing no one but ourselves'.

Interviewed after the sale, the brothers stated, 'We have a great elation when we buy a rare cover like this, and a great dejection when we sell it.' They were in no hurry to sell and kept the letter for twenty years. 'My brother and I love stamps,' is how Raymond summed it up.

Kanai was one of the underbidders and never did purchase the Jerrom letter, which he considered the most beautiful of all the 'Post Office' covers.

The Weill brothers also purchased the Caunten fragment. In the same year they bought the Bordeaux letter for the second time. (They had previously purchased the letter from the Burrus sale in 1963 on behalf of a client.) The brothers did indeed love stamps, but they were also businessmen. Three years later Kanai owned both pieces, paying another record-breaking price for the Bordeaux letter – 120 million Japanese yen – once more the highest yet paid for a philatelic item.

The Japanese collector had only a used one penny to acquire and his 'set' would be complete – single unused and used specimens of both values, and the two combined on the unique Bordeaux letter. In December 1971 Kanai finally realized his dream of becoming the 'greatest' of all the Mauritius collectors, pipping Maurice Burrus, when he purchased the Adam ball envelope from a Stanley Gibbons sale in New York. Referring to himself obliquely, Kanai later stated, 'The greatest number of "Post Office" stamps that has ever been held by a single collector or collection is six... but, of course, this applies to the modern philately only.' Ferrary had owned six 'Post Office' stamps between 1893 and around 1912, so the modern-era rider was a neat exclusion. Nevertheless, Kanai now owned six of the eighteen specimens not in permanent collections – a third of the available market.

Using his extensive collection as the basis, Kanai began

researching the postal history of the little island in the Indian Ocean. In 1971 he was asked to expertize the pen-cancelled one penny 'Post Office' that had entered the 'Post Office' pantheon in 1952. Kanai found the condition very poor and declared the stamp genuine but repaired. He published the results of his research in a small book in Japanese in 1976, which he later extensively revised and published in English as *Classic Mauritius.* 'I am,' he wrote in the preface, 'very much in love with Mauritius stamps.'

Possessed of a strong stamp-collecting culture, the Germans too had always been a little bit in love with the 'Post Office Mauritius', particularly the two pence blue, known as 'die Blaue Mauritius'. One German 'Post Office' owner puts this down to his nation being 'number one in the world when it comes to paying attention to quality and being fascinated by history'. A novel entitled *Die Blaue Mauritius* was published in Berlin in 1939, following on the enormous success of the 1937 film *Der Man, Der Sherlock Holmes War.* Set in 1910, the comedy featured Heinz Rühmann and Hans Albers, two of Germany's most popular actors, as private detectives pretending to be Holmes and Watson on the trail of four stolen Mauritius stamps. In time 'die Blaue Mauritius' came to mean something rare and valuable and the phrase is still current in Germany. Fish, flowers, a shade of marine paint, a BMW model, even a blue potato – all have been named in honour of the two pence stamp.

The nation's loss of its two 'Post Office' stamps during the war only strengthened the love affair. The stamp-collecting community cherished the hope that the stolen stamps might one day turn up, which they did some thirty years later in unlikely circumstances.

International philatelic exhibitions bring together the know-ledgeable and the interested from all over the world. Institutions and private collectors are usually generous in lending their treasures to these exhibitions and the great rarities are often on display at them. Dealers and collectors congregate, and much business is done, including the sale of rare stamps. Would it be the place to attempt to sell stolen stamps, rare and well known? In the summer of 1976 somebody attempted to do exactly that at the seventh International Philatelic Exhibition in Philadelphia.

A man approached Robson Lowe, a London stamp dealer, with a curious metal case containing eight of the world's rarest stamps from British Guiana, Hawaii and Mauritius. The man, who wished to remain anonymous, wanted half a million dollars for the lot. Lowe was not yet sure of his facts and, on returning to London, consulted his dog-eared copy of the Williams brothers' *Stamps of Fame* (or 'Stamps of Ill Fame', as the dealer liked to refer to it). Only then did he realize the significance of what he'd been offered. One of the Mauritian stamps was a two pence 'Post Office' on a letter to a certain Ducau and Lurguie of Bordeaux. They were the Reichspostmuseum's missing rare stamps, lost for some thirty years. Lowe alerted the Philatelic Fraud Squad at Scotland Yard and was instrumental in retrieving Germany's favourite philatelic treasures. In America the following year, Lowe was once more contacted by the man and the English dealer duly passed these details on to the American authorities.

The 'owner' chose to hand the stamps over and accept a reward from the West German government for their recovery. He had been a soldier in the US Army stationed in Germany during the Second World War and claimed that in the days following the end of the war he had helped a German couple leave Soviet-occupied territory for a safer place. The stamps were a gift in return for this help. However, after the soldier's death in 1980 it was revealed that he had been stationed at Eisleben, where the Reichspostmuseum's treasures had been stored for safety during the war, entrusted with the task of organizing the Allies' withdrawal. His title to the stamps was problematic at best.

As a result of both East and West Germany claiming the stamps, the US government retained them and they remained in America until the reunification of Germany in 1990. In poor condition, the eight stamps were returned to the custody of the Museumsstiftung Post und Telekommunikation in Bonn and were seldom displayed until they were able to be returned to the postal museum in Berlin. Between the end of the war and reunification, both Germanys had established postal museums in East and West Berlin. These were eventually brought together and, after much renovation, the new Museum für Post und Kommunikation opened in Berlin in 2000. The corporate identity of the museum is blue, in honour of its most famous tenant, the 'Blue Mauritius', and at night the magnificent glass cupola which crowns the museum is illuminated by blue lights.

Real and imagined, crime was inseparable from the little Mauritian stamps. Fiction writers from the 1890s onwards had spun tales around the 'Post Office' stamps in novels, short stories and poetry. *Die Blaue Mauritius*, published in Germany in 1939, was probably the first full-length novel to take the stamp as its subject. The dearth of new discoveries in the twentieth century gave rise to the occasional rumour of such and saw the publication of another two novels, both involving crime and the 'Blue Mauritius'.

The first, published in 1952, was *Billy Bunter and the Blue Mauritius*, part of the famous Billy Bunter series by Frank Richards, about a large and irritating British schoolboy. Young Billy Bunter and his friends from Greyfriars School overhear Sir Hilton Popper muttering away to himself about the voracious demands of the

British tax office, which causes him to resolve to sell 'the stamp'. 'My stamp!' Sir Hilton cries mournfully. 'My Blue Mauritius! The gem of my collection! There is no other resource! The Blue Mauritius will have to go.' Sir Hilton had bought the stamp in his younger days for £500, 'a great bargain at the time'. Since then the stamp had increased in value to £2,000, its 'scarcity value' the author calls it. Alas for Sir Hilton, at the very moment he is contemplating his lovely stamp one last time, standing in his garden waving it about for all the world to see, the stamp is snatched by a thief (Slim, 'a snapper-up of other people's property') who, hotly pursued by Bunter and friends, takes refuge within the walls of Greyfriars School, where he happens upon the rooms of Bunter himself. Spying Bunter's big gold watch on the table, the thief, rather than filch the watch, hides the stamp inside the watch casing, meaning to return and retrieve it once the bustle has died down. After much bumbling, dimwittedness and the exclamation, 'We know all about the Blue Marumptious, sir –!' the schoolboys finally realize what has all along been under their nose, in Bunter's watch:

'Great pip!' gasped Peter.

'Oh, gad!' said the Bounder.

'My only hat!'

'The stamp –!'

'The jolly old Blue Mauritius –!'

'Eureka!'

'The Eurekafulness is terrific!'

They had more than half expected it. But it was a thrill to see it. And there was no mistake about it. It was a postage-stamp: once upon a time worth the humble sum of twopence: worth, at the present moment, at least two thousand pounds, and probably more.

So the stamp is returned to Sir Hilton, and Bunter and his friends go on to star in further adventures.

The second novel appeared a few years later in 1954, *The Blue Mauritius* by Vernon Warren. The Thriller Book Club version had a wonderfully lurid dust jacket. The stamp (*a* stamp – it is all wrong for a two pence 'Post Office', except that it is blue) featured on the book's spine, with a bloodied dagger through it.

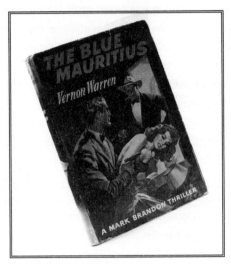

The Blue Mauritius by Vernon Warren.

Brandon is a private detective based in Chicago. Business is quiet in the Windy City and murders are thin on the ground. Late one night, in the process of winding down his business, Brandon receives a visitor with a strange proposal. 'Mr Brandon, have you ever wanted something so badly that you would have done anything to get it?' His visitor, the detective speculates, has money problems; that, or 'it must be a dame'. 'No,' continues the stranger, 'it isn't a woman or anything like that. Tell me, have you ever heard of the Blue Mauritius?' 'Well,' responds Brandon at length, 'let me see, Mauritius is an island somewhere, isn't it? Mebbe it has something to do with that, huh?'

The twist in this piece of fiction, however, is that the 'Blue Mauritius' of the title is not one of the twelve known specimens of the two pence blue. The visitor continues:

A few weeks after that primitive Post Office opened on that remote island, the man on duty found a sheet of blue stamps in amongst the reds. He didn't pay any attention at first, merely thinking that a sheet of twopennies had been shuffled in with the pennies. Later on in the day, though, he got around to wondering how they could have gotten mixed up and when he took a closer look he discovered that they weren't twopenny blues at all. They were penny reds – printed in the wrong colour.

The postal employee was ordered to destroy the errors, which he did, save one that he kept as a souvenir, and this is the object of the mysterious visitor's desire.

It turns out that he once owned the stamp but, finding himself in financial difficulties, sold it for $150,000. He now has the funds to buy it back, but the new owner won't sell, so he wants Brandon to steal it. The detective refuses to undertake the commission, end of story... perhaps.

Brandon crosses paths with a stamp collector at a party and decides to pursue a few inquiries in relation to the 'Blue Mauritius'. He learns the further history of the stamp, which was acquired by a sea captain and lost around the turn of the century, but rumoured to have been sighted in India, China, Australia, Mexico and Tibet. Eventually turning up again, it was sold to one Douglas Craig.

Brandon decides to warn Craig about the mysterious visitor, but is too late. Arriving at Craig's apartment, the detective finds him dead. Nothing appears to have been stolen and the stamp is still in Craig's safe, but Brandon correctly suspects that it is a fake, switched by the killer for the real thing (a suspicion which he keeps to himself).

Brandon smokes out the killer by running an advertisement in the personal columns of the newspaper, leading the killer to believe that the stolen stamp was also a fake and that Brandon has the real McCoy, with a certificate of authenticity to prove it. The story progresses, loose ends are tied up and Brandon, ultimately taking advantage of the moment, switches the fake 'Blue Mauritius' for the real one and keeps it himself:

> I ain't in this racket for the good of my health, bub, and even though there was a warm blank check waiting for me over on Lake Shore Drive, there's nothing like a stand-by for a rainy day.
>
> As if you wouldn't have done the same.
>
> And then some.

Both authors must have had a nodding acquaintance with the 'Post Office' story and an understanding of the ways of stamps. The Bunter tale has shades of the story of the two stamp hunters in India, who lost a 'Post Office' when the watch in which they had been keeping the stamp for safety was stolen. A genuine 'Blue Mauritius' was too predictable a subject for the author of the American detective novel, so he came up with the twist of a one penny blue. Colour errors such as this did occasionally occur in stamp production and they were often worth a great deal of money.

But why the constant fascination with the blue? As the Williams brothers pondered in *Famous Stamps*, who ever heard of the 'Red

Mauritius'? Fourteen examples of the orange-red one penny 'Post Office' (fifteen if 'Limbo I' is counted) are known and twelve of the two pence blue, hardly a reason for the one to be favoured over the other in the popular imagination. Perhaps it was just that the rich blue of the two pence was a more brilliant colour, and the fame that the blue 'Post Office' had acquired back at the time of the Bonar sale, due to its high cost and purchase by a future king, was still resonant. 'The Red Mauritius' as a phrase doesn't have the same currency.

There had been one short story published in 1922 in the *Scout* magazine titled 'The Red Mauritius', again revolving around a theft of a 'Post Office'. A year later another short story entitled 'The Red Mauritius' appeared on the other side of the Atlantic in the pulp fiction magazine *Detective Tales*, in the company of such stories as 'The Green-eyed Monster', 'The Murder on the Bus' and 'Pressed While You Wait'. In the irony of the ephemeral (*Detective Tales* was true pulp fiction – printed on cheap paper, featuring unknown writers, with a short life span and published by a small firm), copies of this magazine appear to be rarer than the 'Post Office' them-selves and seem only to have survived in the realm of the committed private collector.

A mere four pages, the story is set in 'Metropolis', a fictional London. One Lord Alscot of Berkshire owns a rare stamp issued in 1847, known as 'the Red Mauritius' and valued at more than £2,500. Nothing of the stamp's origins is related, nor does its blue sibling rate a mention. Lord Alscot's safe is burgled and the stamp is found to be missing (while precious family jewels remain untouched). A burglar is apprehended on the premises by a friend of the Lord who happens to be visiting the house; the burglar swears to the police that he did not steal the stamp, but is convicted anyway. Enter Scotland Yard detective Roger Wade, once innocently imprisoned himself and on a mission to right injustice. He is approached for help by a friend of the imprisoned burglar. It transpires that the real thief was the Lord's visitor friend. He had long been infatuated with the Lord's wife, even before her marriage, and stole the stamp because Lord Alscot values it more than his wife. By taking away the one thing the Lord values, the would-be swain hoped to inflict on Alscot the same mental agony under which he himself labours. The stamp is recovered by the end of the story and Wade effects the innocent burglar's release.

A number of one penny 'Post Office' stamps had come on to the market in the early 1920s, and were the first specimens, blue or red, to do so in more than a decade, perhaps explaining their fleeting appearance in fiction at this time. One penny and two pence used specimens sold together at the Ferrary sale in October 1921, and another pair in unused condition had been bought by Hind in 1923. Théodore Champion bought a single one penny from the Ferrary sale in April 1923 for £2,100, and although this was too late a date to have inspired Malcolm Field, the author of 'The Red Mauritius' (the story was published in *Detective Tales* in February 1923), the price realized shows that he was close to the mark about the current market value.

It would be over fifty years before the less well-known 'Red Mauritius' featured in another story, again a crime novel focusing on the theft of a 'Post Office' stamp. This was *The Case of the One-Penny Orange* by Howard Fast (writing under the pseudonym E. V. Cunningham), first published in 1977.

Masao Masuto, a Zen Buddhist detective, works for the Beverly Hills police force in Los Angeles. Investigating the death of a stamp dealer, the only clue Masuto turns up is the letters P and M scrawled in the dealer's daybook. Suspecting that the theft of a stamp might be involved ('Not the stamps one buys at the post office to mail a letter, but stamps that people collect with greed and passion'), the detective visits his elderly father-in-law, Ishido, a stamp collector, to ask 'is any stamp worth an act of murder'. From Ishido he learns about a famous one penny stamp from Mauritius, issued in 1848. PM, Penny Mauritius.

But 1848? Was the author mistaken? Had he not done his home-work? No. Howard Fast turns out to be the most knowledgeable of the authors to write the stamps into the pages of fiction, explaining the engraver Barnard's role, the theory that the OFFICE inscription might have been an error and the discovery of the original plate. The 'mistake' proves merely a device to propel Masuto to another dealer who declares that 'The One-Penny Orange of 1847 is the most valuable postage stamp in the world' and there is 'a whole history of murders to gain possession of stamps'. Masuto ponders, 'But what gives a tiny bit of paper such value?' The dealer replies:

… it's the collector who gives it such value. If he did not desire it with demonic ferocity, well then, what would its value be? Nothing. And why does he value it? Mainly because of its rarity. When he has it, he has something that no one else or almost no one else in the world has. Why does one pay seventy thousand dollars for a Rolls-Royce? To have what few others have… a stamp accumulates a mythology, thieves who try to steal it, kings and oil barons who vie for it, murderers who kill for it.

It transpires that the murdered dealer is really a Nazi war criminal (a former SS captain at Buchenwald) and there ends up being a connection between his death and a robbery which Masuto had been called to the previous day. The burgled woman's father, who died in Buchenwald, had been in publishing before the war and published the German edition of the famous Gibbons stamp catalogue. Masuto speculates that, unbeknown to the woman, her parents had left her something of great value, no less than a used one penny Post Office Mauritius on cover, more valuable than the stamp on its own, worth perhaps $300,000. The murder of the dealer is never formally solved, although Masuto suspects the burgled woman (whom he has fallen a little in love with) in a convoluted scenario that doesn't bear repeating. The fate of the stamp is not determined. Presumably it has vanished into the ether of unrecorded and criminal ownership. Of philately one is left to reflect, along with Masuto, 'A peculiar profession for a pathological madman to finish with.'

MILLION-DOLLAR QUESTIONS

Of that there is no possible doubt,
No possible, probable shadow of doubt,
No possible doubt whatever.

Gilbert & Sullivan, *The Gondoliers*, quoted in
Stanley Gibbons Monthly Journal, 1890

With his publication of the carefully documented biographies of the 'Post Office Mauritius' in 1899, Jean-Baptiste Moens ended his long association with the famous stamps, retiring not long after. There were further attempts to bring the biographies up to date. The London-based Williams brothers, journalist Maurice (1905–76) and barrister Norman (1914–99), keen philatelists, took over this role during the 1930s, continuing the tradition of numbering the stamps individually, so rare and important was each new discovery. Norman completed the final update of the 'Post Office' biographies in 1997, some sixty years after the brothers had first published their 'Post Office' research. In this final work – the *Encyclopaedia of Rare and Famous Stamps* – there is no suggestion that Williams had any doubts about the genuineness of the canonical twenty-six 'Post Office' stamps. He only relegated the very poor specimen of the one penny known from 1952 to a 'special category' because 'certification by a recognised expertising authority has never been obtained'. This was 'Limbo I'. Williams donated the correspondence for the brothers' earlier book *Famous*

Stamps to the British Library's Philatelic Collections in 1988 and the remainder followed after his death in 1999. But whispers of forgery linger in these papers.

Williams was less circumspect about 'Limbo I' in his correspondence than he later was in print, describing it as 'Berlingin's nonsense' (René Berlingin had owned the stamp between 1940 and some time in the 1950s). The writer thought it was probably a 'much doctored' specimen which had been reprinted from the 'Post Office' plate before it disappeared in the 1930s. At the same time Williams was speculating on this, in the late 1980s, a number of rumours about the status of some of the 'Post Office' stamps were doing the rounds in philatelic circles.

One of Williams's correspondents, a dealer, unable to express an opinion himself without actually examining the stamps, said that he had been told by a 'reliable source' that four of the accepted 'Post Office' were very good lithographic forgeries. Another correspondent (also a dealer) passed on the rumour – with the rider 'all good fun' – that most of the stamps with a certain cancellation were thought to be forgeries made by or for, and/or sold through, Moens.

'All good fun' does not seem quite the right expression. Williams, by now in his seventies, may have inclined to a similar feeling and it does not appear from the records he left, or the text of the *Encyclopaedia*, that he pursued the truth (or otherwise) of these rumours. One expert in early Mauritius stamps has expressed doubts about the genuineness of some of the 'Post Office' discovered after 1900, while an astute millionaire collector of early Mauritius postal history, easily able to afford a 'Post Office', has, in the last ten years, declined to buy one of the canonical twenty-six because he was convinced it was forged. Could it really be that more than a third of the known 'Post Office' stamps, long accepted as genuine, are forgeries?

In addition to 'Limbo I', the stamps which stand accused are these: the used one penny in Berlin's postal museum; two used one pennies now in private collections; the Adam ball envelope; the brilliant unused two pence in the British Royal Collection, no less; both Bordeaux letters; the one penny discovered in 1917; and the two pence discovered in 1946. Back in the 1970s a German expert suggested that even Tapling's unused two pence, now in the British Library, was worth a closer look.

The difficulty in all this is that the accusers seem dismissive (sometimes even unaware) of the stamps' documented history and disinclined to consider issues of provenance. Nor have they in most cases examined the stamps themselves, relying instead on photographs. In the case of the one penny discovered in 1917, which has not been seen or heard of since Lemaire sold it the following year, no photograph of the stamp appears to have been taken. (It is the only 'Post Office' not illustrated in the *Encyclopaedia* – the Williams brothers tried hard to get good reproductions of all the stamps.) Without examining the stamps closely in the flesh and getting a feel for the paper and how the ink lies on the surface, one of the key indicators of the genuineness of the 'Post Office' stamps is lost.

What if anything is suspicious about the accepted twentieth-century discoveries?

The existence of the plate, if indeed the plate itself is not a clever forgery, certainly complicates matters. Colonel Colnaghi's good title to the plate was never established. A suspicious mind might point to the obvious family connection between the Colonel and the long-established British firm of Colnaghi's, dealers in fine prints. But all such a connection might explain is the interest of the Colonel (and the great-aunt he said gave him the plate) in an arte-fact of the engraving process as an object of curiosity. According to the auctioneer H. R. Harmer, after the plate's discovery, an employee of David Field, who had purchased the plate from Nevile Stocken in 1912, is believed to have taken the plate to Paris. Reprints from this time are known and were made in black, in orange-red (both values) and in deep blue (both values). Harmer was one of the last people to see the plate when he took charge of its travel arrangements to the International Stamp Exhibition held in Berlin in 1930. Reprints from the plate are also thought to have been taken at this time. A very curious plate-related piece was once part of Kanai's collection and the Dale-Lichtenstein collection before that. It has been suggested that it is a proof from the plate made close to the original production date of the stamps in 1847, unique in that the two pence has been printed in blue and the one penny in orange-red on the same piece of paper. (When the Paris reprints were made around 1912, the plate was inked in only one colour at a time, resulting in the anomalies of orange-red two pences and blue pennies.) The catalogue description of this curiosity (offered for sale along with the rest of Kanai's Mauritius collection in 1993) simply states, 'This is obviously an important piece in telling the final and definitive story of the "Post Office" issue.'

Then there are very good reproductions, notably those made by French dealer Victor Perron before the First World War. It is thought that Perron, having obtained one of the Paris reprints from Colnaghi's plate, created a duplicate plate from this reprint, using a photo-etching process. There was no intent to defraud in this case, and Perron numbered his reproductions and marked them on the back as such. But the whereabouts of this plate is also now unknown.

The existence of these early-twentieth-century reprints and reproductions might give credence to an assertion that the three discoveries after 1912 are forgeries, possibly some of these reprints. Williams thought as much in relation to 'Limbo I'. But the reprints were made too late to have been used in forging Bonar's famous 'Blue Mauritius' and the schoolboy's Bordeaux letters.

Could it be that the plate brought to light by Colnaghi had been used for reprinting purposes much earlier than its purported rediscovery in 1912? Colnaghi told the government commission of inquiry into the plate's disappearance, presumably under oath, that the plate had been in his possession since some time in the 1880s. There is no reason to doubt him, except for the widely varying statements from the numerous post office employees and the odd journalist back in Mauritius who were also interviewed by the commission. Might Colonel Colnaghi's plate be merely a copy created from the model of the genuine stamps? Or, if Moens was truly a dastardly forger, might not the Colonel's plate have once belonged to Moens, and the Colonel have only acquired it since the dispersal of Moens's stock upon the dealer's retirement from business in 1900? The plate's rediscovery in 1912 also followed coincidentally on the death of Madame Desbois earlier that year. Perhaps she had had a plate made based on the genuine 'Post Office' stamps which had passed through her hands, and on the dispersals and disposals that inevitably follow death, the plate had been released? Speculation aside, a satisfactory conclusion might be reached only if the plate resurfaces and is subjected to critical scrutiny and appropriate scientific analysis.

Patrick Pearson, a member of the Royal Philatelic Society's expert committee and chairman of the Fédération Internationale de Philatélie Forgeries Commission, has warned collectors that 'they should take care to examine their material, even if items have a lengthy and distinguished provenance'. Physical examination remains paramount.

Jean-Baptiste Moens.

What role, then, does provenance play in these sorry scenarios of possible forgery? There are no stamps which have lengthier or more distinguished – and, importantly, documented – provenances than the 'Post Office Mauritius'. That much of the crucial early information on the history of the discovery of the 'Post Office' stamps in the nineteenth century came from Jean-Baptiste Moens should be no deterrent to accepting the basic truth of what he says. He does not appear to have been a gullible or basically dishonest man. In terms of his own philatelic research, Moens couldn't abide the unacknowledged copying from his journal *Le Timbre-Poste* that occurred frequently in the early days. He even invented a fake stamp to catch out the plagiarists, reporting it in the pages of *Le Timbre-Poste* then watching news of it go forth and multiply in the pages of some of his publishing rivals. Some of the accusations made against him of dubious early practices remain 'alleged' only and can't be proven, while others should be understood in the context of the times. He deserves the benefit of the doubt.

The provenance of the stamps known and recorded up to 1899 by Moens seems straightforward and key points can be verified by independent research. The story of the Borchards – the major source of the 'Post Office' stamps – tallies with the recorded facts: Adolphe Borchard did live in Bordeaux, was married and did die in 1869; and his involvement with commercial shipping to Mauritius in 1847–8 gives him an unassailable reason to be in receipt of genuine Mauritius correspondence, whether bearing 'Post Office' stamps or not. The used one pennies under suspicion (one in Berlin's postal museum and two in private collections) and the two pence in the Tapling Collection at the British Library all originally came from Madame Borchard and only two of these passed through Moens's hands. Was Moens, or indeed anybody in the philatelic world of the 1860s, capable of the deception required to take the genuine circumstances of the Borchards and turn this to good account by setting up Madame as a front for laundering forged 'Post Office' stamps? The answer is probably not.

However, the circumstances surrounding the discovery of the Bordeaux letters have always been a little more problematic because part of the provenance – the identity of the person who found them, important in determining genuineness – remains a provocative mystery. Lemaire, the dealer who bought both letters in 1903, may have transacted his business through an intermediary (a common enough occurrence now), not with the 'schoolboy' himself. He may never have known the identity of the original finder; in the pages of his own journal he described the owner only as an 'amateur'. And yet, could the French dealer have been complicit in the creation of what may be early examples of 'enhanced' or 'improved' covers? At this distance Lemaire too must be given the benefit of the doubt. He was much committed to the philatelic life, serving as a juror at many philatelic exhibitions, and he probably couldn't afford to knowingly associate himself with dubious merchandise.

An expert on philatelic forgeries, *not* however an expert on Mauritius, has suggested that the Bordeaux letter bearing the single two pence stamp now in Berlin's postal museum is rather dubious and may be 'enhanced'. The reason given is that there is no Mauritius cancellation anywhere on the front of the letter, and the Boulogne cancellation (added at the letter's point of entry into France) shows a break where it connects with the stamp. Food for thought perhaps? But this opinion was not derived from a physical examination of the item itself – merely from an illustration of the front of the letter in an exhibition catalogue. Hennecke, curator of the Reichspostmuseum at the time of its acquisition of the Bordeaux letter, had already raised the issue of the apparent lack of a Mauritius cancellation 100 years earlier in correspondence with Lemaire. He too had only seen a photograph of the letter at that point and later satisfied himself as to the piece's authenticity upon physical examination. Awareness and understanding of the ways and means of forgery are not skills exclusive to the twenty-first century expertizer.

Peter Ibbotson, an expert on Mauritius and author of *Mauritius Postal History and Stamps*, raised no such alarm in his 1994 article on the two Bordeaux letters. He acknowledged his reliance on illustrations of the front of Berlin's prize and concentrated on researching the movements of the ship which had carried it, the *Mischief.* These accorded with the Boulogne entry postmark on the letter. Ibbotson probably assumed that a Mauritius cancellation, such as the circular date stamp used on the ball envelopes, would be found on the back, as one is on the Bordeaux letter bearing both the two pence and one penny 'Post Office'. (There is indeed a

MAURITIUS POST OFFICE cancellation on the back of Berlin's Bordeaux letter.)

There seems no reason to doubt the authenticity of the letters themselves. The movements of the two ships which carried the letters tally with the postmarks, Messieurs Ducau and Lurguie were wine merchants in Bordeaux, and Edward Francis & Co. (the senders) were merchants in Port Louis. Regardless of whether the Bordeaux letter now in Berlin has been enhanced by the addition of a 'Post Office' (genuine or forged) the cancellations it acquired along the way tell the right story. And what reason would there be in 1903 to take a genuine letter and enhance it with a 'Post Office'? At this time being on cover made no difference to the price.

If there is a query over Berlin's Bordeaux letter, then the same should be asked of the other Bordeaux letter, *the* Bordeaux letter bearing both two pence and one penny 'Post Office' stamps. On the surface it seems more problematic, despite the stamps bearing a Mauritius cancellation (the boxed PENNY POST). Peter Ibbotson has pointed out that there was no such rate as three pence for overseas letters from Mauritius; however, his speculation that the sender may have thought an extra penny was needed to cover the delivery of the letter from the post office to the ship in the harbour might explain the anomaly. Stamps were still a novelty and this use of three pence worth of stamps was not unique. The first two 'Post Office' stamps found by Madame Borchard some forty years earlier were also used on the same envelope, tied together by a boxed PAID cancellation. When the Bordeaux letter was sold from Kanai's collection in 1993, the authenticity of all lots was guaranteed by the auctioneers, who had consulted widely with the major Mauritius experts. In the opinion of these gentlemen, the Bordeaux letter was 'truly the megastar in the philatelic firmament', 'probably the most desirable item in existence' for those interested in covers, routes and rates. It is 'beyond compare', and philately's 'greatest item'. One imagines that the mystery buyer who paid millions of dollars for it trusted their judgement.

Cancellations come into play in considering the genuineness of the Adam ball envelope too. The Adam envelope differs in two respects from the Marquay and Duvivier envelopes, in the cancellation used and the date sent. All three bear the boxed PENNY POST hand stamp in various positions on the upper left of the envelopes. In addition, the stamps on the Marquay and Duvivier envelopes are both cancelled with the large circular MAURITIUS POST OFFICE hand stamp, dated 21 September 1847. The stamp on the Adam envelope is cancelled only with a boxed PAID hand stamp; the large circular MAURITIUS POST OFFICE hand stamp has been used on the back of the envelope, dated 27 September 1847. And yet, is it really so surprising – and hence a reason for suspicion – that items sent six days apart might be cancelled differently? The envelopes may not even have been cancelled by the same postal clerk, and each clerk undoubtedly had his quirks and preferences in the discharge of this duty. On the Mauritius covers still existing from this period there are many variations in the application of cancellations.

In speculating on issues of letter rates and cancellations, it is worth considering a Spanish example related by postal historian Denis Vandervelde. Reflecting on the challenges and joys of postal history – 'interpreting the evidence on mail... of what actually happened' – Vandervelde cited the example of a 10 centimos franking appearing in addition to the documented normal rate on mail sent from Bilbao in 1873. The port of Bilbao was then under seige because of the Carlist Wars and ships found their task of delivering mail difficult. Vandervelde was at a loss to explain the meaning of this additional sum until a Spanish philatelist subsequently informed him that he 'knew nothing of Spain': the additional 10 centimos was obviously a bribe to the ship's captain 'to run the gauntlet of artillery fire'. There is always a variety of possible, if not so exciting, explanations.

One of the used pennies which became the subject of rumours belongs to the postal museum in Berlin and once belonged to Dr Legrand. An early authority on Mauritius, the doctor had made a careful study of as many of the earliest issues from the island as he could get his hands on back in 1869, examining six 'Post Office' stamps at the one time (his own two, Judge Philbrick's used pair and Émile Lalanne's unused pair). When the 'Post Office' stamps were first reported, Moens, remember, like most others, was sceptical about their existence. Philatelic pioneers such as himself and Legrand were always watching out for any discrepancies in the look of the stamps or their general appearance regarding inks and papers. All six of the 'Post Office' stamps examined by Legrand can be traced back to Madame Borchard, but only Legrand's used one penny stands accused because, it seems, of the heavy cancellation, which obscures much of the stamp. All of the used pennies similarly the subject of rumour bear the same cancellation (a circular cancellation of twelve solid bars), known to be in use in Mauritius from at least 1848, and probably late 1847, given their use on some of the 'Post Office' stamps. All of the cancellations are heavily applied and more or less obscure the Queen's profile. But obliterating a stamp to avoid its being fraudulently reused is the point of cancellation. Once again, the degree to which this was done, whether heavily or with a light hand, was very much the prerogative of the postal clerk. The clerks were probably directed to apply the cancellations with vigour to compensate for the poor quality of the stamping ink: the Colonial Postmaster of Mauritius complained in 1861 that 'the Postage Stamps are not so perfectly cancelled as to render it impossible for the obliterating mark being removed by a cleansing process – thus opening a door to fraud'. Or perhaps too those clerks whose origins were French rather delighted in heavy-handed obliteration of the little portraits of the English monarch.

Then there is the specimen, so often described as 'brilliant', whose magical discovery and sale to a future king secured the fame and fortune of all its siblings, 'the Blue Mauritius' now reposing in the British Royal Collection. Are the condition and the circumstances of the stamp's discovery too good to be true? Possibly, although cleaning stamps to improve their appearance was considered the same as polishing the best silver. Such finds were not limited to the world of philately. Might not the date Bonar said he acquired it as a schoolboy – 1864 – have been chosen to accord with the first documented discoveries in Bordeaux, in order to add a veneer of legitimacy? If the stamp were a forgery perpetrated by Bonar, then this would have been a good idea, but the date could equally be a coincidence, and is unsurprising given the rise of interest in the hobby of stamp collecting at precisely that time in Scotland.

When one starts to look for evidence of forgery in the 'Post Office' story, much (in some cases) can be made from the muddled evidence in favour of such a conclusion. But it is easy to allow the imagination free rein. With a lifetime's experience of philately and its protagonists, David Beech, head of the British Library's Philatelic Collections, believes (good-naturedly, no criticism implicit here) that 'philatelists are rather prone to coming up with complicated answers and hypotheses to simple questions'. Therein lies much of the challenge and the enjoyment of philately. Does this mean this or does it mean that? Physical examination of the stamps reveals so much, but the circumstances of the production of the stamps and their subsequent discovery by philatelists must also come under close scrutiny.

Has scientific testing anything to offer in the expertizing of the 'Post Office' stamps, or will it only muddy the waters further? A technique known as Raman microscopy may be of use. Tapling's two 'Post Office' stamps, now in the British Library, were tested using this technique in 2003. The one penny 'Post Office' on the Marquay ball envelope and a two pence described as unused, originally discovered by Madame Borchard, were both analysed alongside a twentieth-century Perron two pence 'Post Office' reproduction and a pair of two pence 'Post Paid' forgeries. (The forgeries were produced by photogravure and appear different upon examination to the originals produced using an engraved copper plate.) Previous scientific efforts to unlock the secrets of stamps have skimmed the surface, literally looking for signs of cleaning and the removal of postmarks. The Raman microscopy technique directs laser light on to the surface of the stamps and gathers information about the pigments used, and how they sit on the paper, how the ink mingles with the paper fibres. Concentrating on the blue stamps, testing revealed noticeable differences in the way the forged 'Post Paid' stamps responded to the light, attributable to the different printing processes used. This is thought to be a more reliable indicator than the composition of the pigments themselves, for the genuine, reproduction and forged stamps all used Prussian blue. The paper used in Madame Borchard's two pence also revealed blue crystals between the fibres, missing in the reproduction and forged stamps. Sometimes these crystals were added to paper at the manufacturing stage to brighten the appearance of the paper and stop it from yellowing over time. Both the British Library's 'Post Office' stamps, considered genuine, contained these crystals, confirming at least that they were printed on the same or similar paper.

How useful these findings will be in determining the genuineness of the known specimens of the 'Post Office' stamps won't be clear until more of the stamps are submitted for testing; however, with a billion-dollar annual global market in philatelic rarities, it is unlikely that 'Post Office' owners will be rushing to find out.

Despite being very much in love with Mauritius stamps and pleased to be the owner of the most 'Post Office' at one time (in 'modern' times at least), Hiroyuki Kanai sold the Caunten fragment privately in the early 1980s. His Mauritius collection as complete as he felt it needed to be, he directed his interests elsewhere and in 1986 turned his entire Mauritius holdings over to the Swiss auction house of David Feldman. He parted with it, he said, 'only to satisfy the collectors who are dreaming to own one of these beautiful stamps'. But given that Kanai stipulated the collection be sold as a whole, this intention was not realized. A private consortium bought the lot, undoubtedly as an investment, in 1988.

Five years later, the private consortium called their investment in and the entire Kanai collection, as sold in 1988, was once again consigned to David Feldman. On 3 November 1993, at the Hotel International, Zurich, the Mauritian rarities were dispersed to a new generation of collectors. The sale was widely anticipated and reported in the press, particularly in Europe, where interest in the 'Post Office' stamps remains strong. The sum realized by the Bordeaux letter again stunned the world, selling for close to $4 million. It was the highest price paid to that date for a philatelic item and nothing has come close since. The letter was bought by a mystery woman, described as plump and dark-haired. She was unknown to any of the experts present and was thought to have been acting for someone else. When asked her identity by journalists immediately after the sale, she replied in 'slightly accented' English, 'No comment'.

The Adam ball envelope fetched approximately $1.1 million, and the unused specimens of the one penny and two pence, $1.1 and $1.2 million respectively. The interest in these two stamps was heightened by the mystery of the whereabouts of the other unused specimens. Kanai's unused one penny was now the only one known, as its unused sibling had not been seen since the Second World War. Of the four unused specimens of the two pence, one was in the British Royal Collection, one was in the British Library and the other had not been seen for some twenty years. Consequently, Kanai's unused 'Post Office' were highly desirable prospects for collectors.

Following the spectacular success of the Kanai Mauritius sale, several unaccounted-for, unused 'Post Office' stamps were tempted out of hiding and back on to the market. Seven months after the Kanai sale, in July 1994, a postal and telecommunications museum in The Hague purchased the remaining unused two pence. The Dutch were thrilled with their acquisition, only a few years short of the 400th anniversary of their claiming the little Indian Ocean island for their own and naming it after Maurits van Nassau. In an exhibition to celebrate the first public display of their own 'Blue Mauritius' the museum displayed old maps of Mauritius supplied by the Rijksarchief and detailed the particular Dutch connections of this two pence. It had first been shown in The Hague many years ago at an international stamp exhibition, lent by its then owner, Dutchman Henry Manus.

In 1995 the unused one penny and used two pence once owned by Théodore Champion (which had changed hands privately several times since the 1920s) were sold by private treaty through the French auction house of Bernard Behr to a collector identified only as Western European. In 1996 the Jerrom letter was bought by an Italian dealer, and the following year the Adam ball envelope came back on to the market. All remain in private hands.

The 150th anniversary of the 'Post Office' stamps in 1997 was celebrated in Mauritius by the issue of commemorative stamps, once again produced offshore by security printers and removed in every respect from the circumstances of production of the island's famous first foray into postage stamps.

Also in honour of this occasion, the German Federal Republic Printing Office rekindled its acquaintance with the non-genuine variety, engaging two master engravers to create new facsimile engravings of the 'Post Office' stamps on copper plates, based on proofs taken from the lost plate. They were advertised in philatelic journals as souvenirs for £18.

By this time, nine of the 'Post Office' stamps were in permanent collections in postal museums, the British Library and British Royal Collection. The remaining stamps were in private hands. The whereabouts of more than half of these are unknown; one stamp has not been seen since 1952 and another since 1918.

'Post Office' owners now are more likely to protect their anonymity because of concerns over the theft of what are looked upon as investments. Accordingly, it is difficult to know whether any other than financial motives drive these collectors. They are as elusive as the 'Post Office' stamps themselves.

Dealers have always been among this company, tempted into 'Post Office' ownership by the cachet it confers and because in many cases collecting and dealing are in their genes. A number of past and present dealer-owners are the third and fourth generations to run the family stamp business. What has changed is that their ownership of the 'Post Office' stamps is more selectively known.

One Western European 'Post Office' owner began purchasing stamps in the 1960s as a way to diversify his considerable investments. His collecting was purely speculative, although part of what had driven both Hind and Kanai also underlay his interest, to see whether he could better others, in his own country at least. And yet, stamp collecting brought this chequebook collector a sense of order that had been missing in his life and he says that he would not have missed the experience for the world. He had fallen a little under the spell of philately, thanks to the final purchase for his collection, some twenty years after having begun it: the crown jewel, the signifier of belonging to an exclusive club – the Blue Mauritius.

While the likes of Tapling and even the specialist Lichtenstein seem to have, of necessity, had their day in terms of the breadth and depth of collecting, serious (and cashed-up) collectors have not left the field to the investors. Complementing the Mauritius portion of the Tapling Collection on display at the British Library is a significant collection of Mauritius postal history on cover, on long-term loan to the library from present-day collector Vikram Chand.

Some of Chand's favourite Mauritius pieces are harder to see, as they remain with him, framed and hung in his neat, well-appointed office in the Plaza on Singapore's steamy Beach Road. Born in 1962 and brought up in Japan, Vikram Chand began collecting at eleven, encouraged by his grandmother, a lover of art and antiques. Stamp collecting then proved a cheaper alternative. Chand still has the first stamp he purchased, a Penny Black. Reading a biography of Hiroyuki Kanai one day, the young collector realized that the subject was Mr Kanai, the man who lived next door. Kanai's love of classic Mauritius stamps rubbed off on the boy Vikram, as did the attitude: if you want to collect, go for the best you can. Chand determined on collecting postal history – usually covers or other pieces bearing philatelic markings – fascinated by the emphasis on researching rates and routeings. In the field of Mauritius philately, the detail of routeings – how mail travelled from Mauritius to Egypt, for example – was one of the few challenges remaining to the true philatelist serious about research and furthering knowledge. In this respect, Chand is closest in spirit to Tapling and Lichtenstein. A wealthy man (tall, dark and handsome to boot – a philatelic standout, it must be said), Chand established a fund through the British Library to encourage research on nineteenth-century philately. In a gesture reflective of the meaning and value he finds in his hobby, Chand named the fund after his children.

But there is a gaping hole in Chand's collection – he lacks a 'Post Office'. It was he who had the opportunity to buy one and declined, as he was not convinced the proffered specimen was genuine. But in common with most who know the 'Post Office' story, he shares the hope that one day a new specimen might be unearthed and that he might be the person to do it.

To that end (as yet to no avail) he has run advertisements in newspapers in India, encouraging locals in the ports known to have supplied immigrant labour to Mauritius in the 1840s to hunt among their family papers for the treasured red and blue stamps. India was a logical choice, given the amount of trade in human and other cargo that had passed between the two British colonies. Port Louis was regularly visited by ships from Calcutta in the period between late September and November 1847, bearing mainly rice for the port. In return any one of the *Intrepid, Portly, Emily, Braemer, Centaur, Nussur* or *Champion* might have carried a few letters home to merchants and the families of immigrants. For the most part those letters would have shared the common fate of everyday mail – kept for as long as they were of interest or use, then discarded, a process taking anywhere from a day to a generation or two. It would be a similar story in South Africa, Sweden and Sydney, all destinations with nineteenth-century maritime and commercial relationships to the little island in the Indian Ocean.

The survival rate of pre-1860s stamps is low, around 2 per cent. The twenty-six or twenty-seven 'Post Office' stamps now known from the small printing of up to 1,000 is consistent with this figure. But lost works by great artists have been known to turn up in attics, so why not rare stamps? Maybe, just maybe, some sixty years since the last documented find, another 'Post Office' could still be awaiting discovery, far from its birthplace, reposing anonymously in a collection of old correspondence or a forgotten accumulation of old stamps.

It is unlikely that any more 'Post Office' stamps will be found in the island itself. The great publicity generated by the ball envelope finds at the end of the nineteenth century would surely have drawn out any remaining specimens. For similar reasons Bordeaux too, another hotbed of philatelic interest, seems unlikely to yield any more paper treasure from Mauritius.

A fourth ball envelope, in true 'Post Office' fashion, is rumoured to be secreted away in a château in France, in the collection of an old French family formerly resident in Mauritius. But without taking its place alongside its siblings in the 'Post Office' story, what interest or value, financial or otherwise, could such an item really have?

POSTSCRIPT

The carriages that once bowled along the tree-lined Place d'Armes in Port Louis are long gone. In their place old Bedford buses ply the roads, brightly painted in the best traditions of public transport advertising. The march of green cane in the fields is a perfect foil for the multicoloured Smarties bus and the brilliant orange, red, white and yellow splashes of colour on the Chantecleur chicken bus as they roar into the Mauritian capital. These days you arrive in Port Louis by road and miss the seaboard view. But the bus has its advantages, affording glimpses of the *maisons créole* normally hidden from view at street level behind high stone fences or fancy iron railings, sandwiched and abandoned in between shops and filling stations. Built of wood, with high pitched roofs, shuttered French windows and verandas ornamented with wooden lacework, they are the *ancien régime*.

The streets of the town have undergone several changes of name, from French governors and events from Napoleon's campaigns, to English sirs and queens. Take the main street, which runs from the Port Louis harbour, beginning at the Place d'Armes (according to some guidebooks, or Place Bissoondoyale according to others). Now bearing the name Queen Elizabeth Avenue up to Government House, the street becomes Intendance Street before a slight crook, turning into Jules Koenig Street (a twentieth-century Franco-Mauritian politician) and then Pope Hennessy Street (a nineteenth-century British governor). The street continues, nameless, right through to the Champs de Mars racetrack, over the track itself into the centre of the course. The shifting balance of racial relations in the twentieth century has seen yet more French (and British) names fall by the wayside to Seeneevassens, Seetul-singhs and the Sir Seewoosagur Ramgoolam street – all more telling of the island's history than the M2 autoroute, which now cuts a dangerous path between the town itself and the harbour.

Although it was said that when the British left Mauritius a precariously balanced boulder on top of Pieter Both, the island's tallest mountain, would topple off, it failed to do so when the country finally gained its independence in 1968. The mountain still soars to the same distinctive peak overlooking the town, along with its sibling, Le Pouce. Lady Gomm loved her view of these mountains from the rooms at the back of Government House and she painted their silhouettes, framed by the window of her room, in her sketchbook. This is what she wanted to remember of her time in Mauritius. Despite many hopeful searches by her family since, not a single specimen of the little red and blue stamps, or any souvenir of her marvellous ball, has been found among her effects.

In an old nineteenth-century stone building close to the harbour a few rooms are given over to the Mauritius Postal Museum. Thematically arranged stamps line the walls and speak of sugar factories, mountains, men and machinery, and the ubiquitous dodo. Somebody has gathered as many of the old obliterators and hand stamps as possible, and there they are, including EATEN BY RAT.

Bois Cheri, Blue Mauritius vanilla tea, available from the Bois Cheri tea factory and duty free at Mauritius's international airport.

A short account of the 'Post Office' stamps welcomes the visitor, but the museum, unsurprisingly, has no originals, only reproductions.

Over the busy road and facing the harbour there is a small shop selling the usual souvenirs, including packets of stamps. The name of the shop is Blue Penny, as it has been for as long as the owner can remember, dating back, he thinks, to its days as a café in the early decades of the twentieth century, serving the sailors in the harbour. It is a phrase peculiar to the island, long in use, familiar to the locals and sniffed at by philatelic sticklers who point out that the single penny 'Post Office' is red not blue. But Mauritians will go on calling their stamps exactly what they please, as they should. It matters not.

Exporting to an international market, the Bois Cheri tea factory prefers the more widely known appellation 'Blue Mauritius' for its fragrant blend of vanilla tea. Perversely, the company celebrates this most famous philatelic event by reproducing the *wrong* stamp on the silvery tea-bag packets – one of the subsequently issued two pence 'Post Paid' stamps – because it bears the 'correct' inscription.

Much of the patrimony of Mauritius is scattered throughout the world, in private and public collections from Stockholm to Canberra. After the Adam ball envelope left the island in 1899 only the memory of the 'Post Office' stamps remained. But, although a mystery woman walked away with the Bordeaux letter from the Kanai sale, Mauritius walked away with the brilliant unused penny and two pence 'Post Office' stamps. A private consortium consisting of the Mauritius Commercial Bank and fifteen other Mauritian companies were determined to repatriate national treasures to the island. They pooled their resources to buy a number of rare Mauritian stamps, including the matchless unused 'Post Office' pair. These were the stamps which had begun their travels many lifetimes ago, journeying first to Bordeaux and the Borchards, and then through the hands of English, American, Sri Lankan and Japanese collectors, before returning to the island courtesy of the winning bid made by a Mauritian accountant. Not long after the sale, Kanai himself finally made the journey to Mauritius. Members of the local philatelic society and the curator of the Mauritius Commercial Bank's collection took the one-time 'Post Office' collector all around the island to see the old post offices and to visit the engraver Barnard's grave.

The two unused 'Post Office' stamps, which remained locked away except for a brief outing in the 150th anniversary year, were destined to be the centrepiece and namesake of a purpose-built museum in Port Louis – the Blue Penny Museum – a project of the Mauritius Commercial Bank. Built in the style of an old Creole mansion, the museum is tucked away behind the main waterfront complex of Port Louis, not so very far from the harbour or the site of the old post office on the Place d'Armes. Inaugurating the new museum in November 2001, the Prime Minister of Mauritius, Sir Anerood Jugnauth, declared, 'What is rightfully a Mauritian heritage is also a priceless universal treasure. Because of its rare value, the Blue Penny could have ended up in the private collection of a foreign billionaire. How happy and proud are we to see it back home in our capital city!'

But there was a certain irony in their display. 'If you hurry upstairs now, you will see the Blue Penny stamps. They are only illuminated temporarily; at 11 o'clock they rest.' In a dark little room, a line of classic red and blue stamps of Mauritius sparkle behind glass in low light on the black walls. Occupying the corner of the room, and the focal point of this display, are the two 'Post Office' stamps. When they slip back into darkness to preserve them from the effects of light, the spotlight switches to two identical copies beside them. Not so long ago, neither the copies nor the genuine stamps were labelled. The genuine stamps, you might have been told, were the pair on the left.

GLOSSARY

Both L. N. and M. Williams's *The Postage Stamp: Its History and Recognition*, Penguin, Harmondsworth, 1956, and L. N. Williams's *Fundamentals of Philately*, American Philatelic Society, State College, Pennsylvania, revised edition, 1990, were used in the compilation of this glossary. The latter stretches to more than 800 pages.

BLOCK A group of three or more stamps that have not been separated from one another, forming a block: that is, joined over more than one column or row (as opposed to a strip – multiple stamps in a single horizontal or vertical row). A numerical qualification is usually given, such as 'block of five'.

CANCELLATION Markings applied by hand or machine by postal authorities to stamps in order to prevent reuse. Cancellations can also indicate the post office processing the mail and the date processed. The term is often used synonymously with POSTMARK. The study of cancellations is of great philatelic interest, for cancellations tell much of the story of the use of stamps and travels of mail.

CLEANED A cleaned stamp has had cancellations or other marks removed by a cleaning process (by the use of certain chemicals or by boiling in water). This can be done with or without fraudulent intent.

COVER The envelopes or outer wrappings of mail.

DIE The original piece of metal, or other material, on which a stamp design is engraved, usually before being multiplied on to a printing base, from which sheets of stamps are then produced.

ENTIRE A complete envelope, letter sheet or other postal item, still intact, bearing postmarks and stamps.

ERROR An accidental mistake made or occurring during the manufacturing process of stamp production, as opposed to an artist's error made during the design process. If the 'Post Office' inscription were considered an error, it would be an artist's error. I have used the term more generically in this book.

ESSAY Artwork submitted for a proposed stamp design which may or may not subsequently be accepted for use.

ISSUE A particular stamp or related group of stamps put into official postal use at the same time.

LETTER SHEET A single sheet of paper with the contents written on one side, folded up into a rectangle resembling an envelope, with the address inscribed on the front and sealed at the back. Common before the use of envelopes became widespread later in the nineteenth century.

MULTIPLE Any group of stamps not separated from one another.

OBLITERATION *See* CANCELLATION. As the word suggests, obliteration usually implies that the cancellation is heavy and defaces much of the design.

PERFORATION Small holes, usually circular, punched out around stamps to aid their separation from one another. The number of perforations per unit length on a stamp can differ from issue to issue and printing to printing.

PLATING   The reconstruction of the make-up of the original plates used to print stamps, usually using pairs, strips or blocks of stamps as a point of reference.

POSTAL HISTORY   The history of the posts, with an emphasis on re-searching rates and routeings, or as one postal historian describes it, 'interpreting the evidence on mail... of what actually happened'.

POSTMARK   *See* CANCELLATION.

PROOF   Impressions taken from the original engraving (die) in order to check the design before mass production. Proofs are not sold to the public.

REPRINT   Impressions taken from the original plates (also known as the printing base) after they have been withdrawn from use (when the stamp issue is no longer current).

TIED   The physical connection between stamps and covers, and to each other, evidenced by the application of cancellations or other postal markings to both elements.

UNUSED   The condition of stamps which have not been cancelled. A stamp may have been postally USED but escaped cancellation, and may then be described as unused.

USED   A stamp which has been used for its intended purpose on mail and bearing evidence of that.

VARIETY   May generally refer to a stamp, or commonly to stamps, differing from other stamps of the same issue, sometimes as the result of printing methods.

Biographies of the Stamps

These condensed biographies are based on those originally compiled by Jean-Baptiste Moens, continued by others, including L. N. and M. Williams, as published in L. N. Williams's *Encyclopaedia of Rare and Famous Stamps*, David Feldman, Geneva, Vol. 2, 1997. They have been edited and added to by me (a few errors have been corrected), with permission of David Feldman. Consult Williams's footnotes for detailed sources and note that in some cases these are misleading.

Moens, in his 1899 biographies, gave the nineteen stamps then known identifying numbers in the form of Roman numerals, assigned in order of their discovery. The Williams brothers followed this system in their revised and updated biographies published in the 1930s and 1940s, but this was changed to Arabic numerals with publication of the *Encyclopaedia*. The numbering sequence was reorganized in order to make a distinction between denomination (one penny, two pence, one penny and two pence used together) and state (unused, on cover, used). I found the traditional numbering and sequencing used by Moens easier to follow for the purposes of this book, so have restored it here to aid the general, rather than specialist, reader. Where a date is not known or is uncertain this is indicated by (?).

I and II

1d and 2d. Used. Cancelled with one impression of PAID in a rectangle. The upper left-hand corner of the 1d is defective. The two stamps were used on one letter; they were separated, but joined again after 1881.

1847   Used on a letter to Borchard at Bordeaux.

1864   Found by Madame Borchard. Albert Coutures obtained the two stamps in exchange for two Montevideo 'suns'.

1865   Dealer Jean-Baptiste Moens bought Coutures's collection, valuing the two 'Post Office' stamps at Fr.100 (£4) each.

1866   Judge Philbrick bought the two stamps for Fr.500 (£20).

1881   Philipp von Ferrary bought Philbrick's collection, including the two 'Post Office' stamps, for Fr.100,000 (£8,000).

1921   Maurice Burrus bought the two stamps at the second Ferrary sale in Paris for £2,172.

1963   Dealer Wilhelm Bartels bought the two stamps at the Burrus sale for £8,250.

1964   Bought by a European collector.

1985   Sold by dealer Wolfgang Jakubek for 1,955,000 DM (£521,333). Private hands.

III

2d. Unused. The stamp is cut into slightly at two places. It is thinned in the centre of the back, but only over a small area. There is a slight crease, running from the o of TWO to the s of POST, but it is visible only on the back.

1847   Used on a letter to Borchard at Bordeaux.

1865   Found by Madame Borchard. The stamp was acquired by the dealer Madame Desbois.

1866   Madame Desbois sold the stamp to one of Bordeaux's major stamp collectors, Émile Lalanne.

1893   Piet Lataudrie bought Lalanne's collection through the agency of Marcel Pouget for Fr.60,000 (£2,400) in July. A month later the British firm of Stanley Gibbons Ltd bought III, along with X, for £680, advertising their purchase as the highest price ever paid for two stamps. They were then bought together by collector William Avery.

1909   Dealer W. H. Peckitt bought Avery's collection (Avery died in 1908) for £24,500. Henry Duveen bought both III and X, paying partly in cash and partly by the exchange of XX (the Adam ball envelope) and VI.

1923   Arthur Hind bought III and X through the agency of C. J. Phillips for about $30,000. (Duveen's collection came back on to the market in 1922, three years after his death in 1919.)

1934   Auctioned by H. R. Harmer in London at the Hind sale (Hind died in 1933) and purchased by a European dealer for £1,500.

1938   Auctioned by H. R. Harmer again and purchased by dealer Tom Allen on behalf of a European collector.

1951   Bought by dealer H. Nissen, who later sold it.

1964(?) Acquired by Stanley Gibbons Ltd.

1965   Bought by Hiroyuki Kanai.

1986   Consigned with the Kanai Mauritius collection to David Feldman.

1988   Sold to an anonymous buyer.

1993   Auctioned by David Feldman in Zurich and purchased by a private consortium of Mauritian companies for SFr.1,725,000 ($1,150,000).

2001   Blue Penny Museum opened in Port Louis, Mauritius, purpose-built for the permanent public display of 'Post Office' stamps III and X.

IV

1d. Used. Cancelled with part of PAID in a rectangle. The upper left-hand corner has been added. There is a tear at the E of POSTAGE and another tear into the second F of OFFICE. The lower right-hand corner is damaged and there are several thin spots.

1868   Found by a Monsieur Noirel of Port Louis, Mauritius, among an auction lot of old newspapers purchased at a public sale, then purchased by T. Lionnet.

1870   Bought by dealer Jean-Baptiste Moens for Fr.100 (£4)

in July and sold to Arthur de Rothschild in October for
Fr.500 (£20).

1893　Philipp von Ferrary bought Rothschild's collection for
Fr.140,000 (£5,600).

1912　Acquired by Warren H. Colson of the New England
Stamp Co.

19(?)　Hans Lagerloef bought both IV and IX.

1927　Lagerloef gifted the two stamps to the Swedish Postal
Museum in Stockholm.

V

2d. Used, on piece of the original envelope, addressed to
'H. Caunten, avocat, au Port Louis'. The stamp is cancelled with
PAID in a rectangle and has been repaired at the foot.

1847　Used on a letter to H. Caunten at Port Louis.

1887　Henri Adam Junior obtained the piece from Caunten.
Albert Rae then purchased it for 300 Mauritian rupees
(£23).

1889　Rae consigned his collection to a Parisian dealer for
Fr.12,500 (£500), from whom the 'Post Office' piece
was bought by a certain Perrissin for Fr.4,000 (£160).
(The Parisian dealer, according to Rae himself in
Mauritius Illustrated in 1914, was a Monsieur Le Roy
d'Etionnel, not Monsieur Ch. Roussin, as stated by
Moens in 1899.)

1890   Offered for sale by Whitfield King & Co. at the
        London Philatelic Exhibition in May for £200, but not
        sold. Dorsan Astruc purchased the piece from Perrissin
        in June for Fr.3,500 (£140) – one of the few times a
        'Post Office' was sold at a loss. P. Mirabaud purchased
        the piece from Astruc in July for Fr.3,750 (£150).

(?)   Bought by the American George Worthington.

1917   Alfred Lichtenstein bought part of Worthington's
        collection, including the Mauritius portion.

1947   Louise Boyd Dale inherited the Lichtenstein collection
        on the death of her father.

1968   The Dale-Lichtenstein collection was auctioned by
        H. R. Harmer (Boyd Dale died in 1967) and the piece
        was bought by Raymond H. Weill Co.

1970   Acquired privately by Hiroyuki Kanai from H. R.
        Harmer.

1982   Acquired by a German collector.

VI

2d. Unused. There is a blue spot over the letters AU of MAURITIUS.
The design is cut into at the bottom right.

1847   Used on a letter to Borchard at Bordeaux.

1869   Found by Madame Borchard (in 1869 or earlier). The
        stamp was acquired by the dealer Madame Desbois,
        who sold the stamp to Legrand for Fr.250 (£10).

1897   Dealer Théophile Lemaire bought Legrand's collection in July, valuing VI and VII at Fr.30,000 (£1,200). Both VI and VII sold later that year to Jules Bernichon for Fr.46,500 (£1,860).

1898   Henry Duveen bought VI for £1,200.

1909   Dealer W. H. Peckitt obtained both VI and XX (the Adam ball envelope) from Duveen in part exchange for III and X. Peckitt then sold VI and XX to Dutch collector Henry Manus.

1933   The Manus collection was auctioned by Plumridge (Manus died in 1931) and both VI (£1,750) and XX (£2,400) were bought by dealer Tom Allen.

193(?)   Acquired by King Carol of Romania.

1950   Both VI and XX were sold privately through the agency of Harmer, Rooke & Co. Ltd to Belgian collector René Berlingin.

1971   Both VI and XX were offered for sale at Stanley Gibbons's 'Anphilex' New York auction, but VI remained unsold.

1972   Auctioned by Edgar Mohrmann in Hamburg and purchased by a European collector, the then owner of I and II.

1994   Purchased by the PTT Museum, The Hague, which later became the Museum voor Communicatie (Dutch Museum for Communication).

VII

1d. Used. Completely obliterated with a cancellation of parallel bars.

1847	Used on a letter to Borchard at Bordeaux.
1869	Found by Madame Borchard (in 1869 or earlier). The stamp was acquired by the dealer Madame Desbois.
1870	Madame Desbois sold the stamp to the dealer Jean-Baptiste Moens, along with VIII and IX and some other Mauritian stamps, for Fr.500 (£20). Legrand subsequently purchased VII for Fr.250 (£10).
1897	Dealer Théophile Lemaire bought Legrand's collection in July, valuing VI and VII at Fr.30,000 (£1,200). Both VI and VII sold later that year to Jules Bernichon for Fr.46,500 (£1,860).
1901	The Reichspostmuseum, Berlin, obtained VII through the agency of German dealer Philipp Kosack as an exchange. The stamp, along with seven others (including XXIII, the Bordeaux letter bearing the single two pence 'Post Office'), was placed in a wall-mounted, glass-fronted, lead display frame.
1943	The frame was moved to the safety of the Reichsbank's vaults in Berlin.
1944	The frame was moved to a mineshaft in Eisleben (situated in what later became East Germany), but was not recovered at the end of the Second World War.

1976   A former US army soldier offered the frame and its contents to British dealer Robson Lowe at an international stamp exhibition, an offer reported by Lowe to Interpol.

1977   The former soldier surrendered the frame to the US Customs Service. The frame and its contents were claimed by both East and West Germany.

1990   Upon the reunification of Germany, the US government handed back the frame and it was placed in the Museumsstiftung Post und Telekommunikation in Bonn.

2000   A new Museum für Post und Kommunikation opened in Berlin and the stolen stamps, including VII and XXIII, returned to public display.

VIII

1d. Unused. Cut close at upper left-hand corner. There is a light patch at the right-hand foot of the A in MAURITIUS.

1847   Used on a letter to Borchard at Bordeaux.

1869   Found by Madame Borchard (in 1869 or earlier). The stamp was acquired by the dealer Madame Desbois.

1870   Madame Desbois sold the stamp to the dealer Jean-Baptiste Moens, along with VII and IX and some other Mauritian stamps, for Fr.500 (£20). A Monsieur Perinelle subsequently purchased VIII and IX for Fr.950 (£38).

1881   Moens repurchased VIII and IX for Fr.3,000 (£120) and sold them to Philipp von Ferrary for Fr.5,500 (£220).

1923   Dealer and collector Théodore Champion bought VIII and IX at the sixth Ferrary sale in Paris for Fr.143,350 (£2,100) to replace XI, which he then sold.

196(?) Changed hands privately, together with other items from the Champion Collection.

198(?) Bought by the French dealer Bernard Behr for his personal collection, from an anonymous owner based in the US.

1995   Sold through Bernard Behr to a Western European collector (probably German).

IX

2d. Used. There is a faint red postmark infringing the lower left corner and the tops of the letters PO of POST.

1847   Used on a letter to Borchard at Bordeaux.

1869   Found by Madame Borchard (in 1869 or earlier). The stamp was acquired by the dealer Madame Desbois.

1870   Madame Desbois sold the stamp to the dealer Jean-Baptiste Moens, along with VII and VIII and some other Mauritian stamps, for Fr.500 (£20). A Monsieur Perinelle subsequently purchased VIII and IX for Fr.950 (£38).

1881   Moens repurchased IX and VIII for Fr.3,000 (£120)
        and sold them to Philipp von Ferrary for Fr.5,500
        (£220).

1912   Warren H. Colson, of New England Stamp Co.,
        acquired IX in exchange with Ferrary for the
        'Boscawen', a unique American stamp.

19(?)   Hans Lagerloef bought both IX and IV.

1927   Lagerloef gifted the two stamps to the Swedish Postal
        Museum in Stockholm.

X

1d. Unused. The stamp is not cut into at any place. There are two
thinnings on the back: one is under the mount; the other is a hardly
visible spot.

1847   Used on a letter to Borchard at Bordeaux.

1869   Found by Madame Borchard (in 1869 or earlier). The
        stamp was acquired by the dealer Madame Desbois.

1870   Émile Lalanne, one of Bordeaux's major stamp
        collectors, obtained the stamp from Madame Desbois
        for services rendered in helping her to dispose of a lot
        of stamps.

1893   Piet Lataudrie bought Lalanne's collection through the
        agency of Marcel Pouget for Fr.60,000 (£2,400) in July.
        A month later the British firm of Stanley Gibbons Ltd
        bought X, along with III, for £680, advertising their

purchase as the highest price ever paid for two stamps. They were then bought together by collector William Avery.

1909   Dealer W. H. Peckitt bought Avery's collection (Avery died in 1908) for £24,500. Henry Duveen bought both X and III, paying partly in cash and partly by the exchange of XX (the Adam ball envelope) and VI.

1923   Arthur Hind bought bought X and III through the agency of C. J. Phillips for about $30,000. (Duveen's collection came back on to the market in 1922, three years after his death in 1919.)

1934   Bought by A. E. de Silva of Colombo.

1957   Sold on behalf of the Young Men's Buddhist Association, to which it had been presented by de Silva. Bought jointly by H. Nissen and W. E. Lea.

19(?)   Peter Holcombe, while a director of J. A. L. Franks Ltd, bought the stamp for £7,000 and sold it to a collector in New York for £8,250.

1962   The collector in New York fell on hard times after losing millions on the Stock Exchange on the day known as 'Black Friday' and the stamp was taken in part payment of a debt.

1963   Auctioned by Harmer, Rooke & Co. Ltd and bought by Hiroyuki Kanai for £8,500.

1986   Consigned with the Kanai Mauritius collection to David Feldman.

1988   Sold to an anonymous buyer for $850,000.

1993   Auctioned by David Feldman in Zurich and purchased by a private consortium of Mauritian companies for SFr.1,610,000 ($1,073,340).

2001   Blue Penny Museum opened in Port Louis, Mauritius, purpose-built for the permanent public display of 'Post Office' stamps III and X.

XI

2d. Used. Cancelled with obliteration of parallel bars.

1847   Used on a letter to Borchard at Bordeaux.

1865   Found by Madame Borchard, along with XII. Both stamps were acquired by the dealer Madame Desbois.

1866   Madame Desbois sold the stamps to one of Bordeaux's major stamp collectors, Émile Lalanne.

1893   Piet Lataudrie bought Lalanne's collection through the agency of Marcel Pouget for Fr.60,000 (£2,400) in July.

1896   E. Mors, of motor-racing fame, bought both stamps (XI and XII) for Fr.42,000 (£1,600).

1920   Both stamps (XI and XII) were bought by the French dealer and collector Théodore Champion.

19(?)   Some time before 1940, Champion sold XI only to an anonymous collector.

1988 Auctioned by Hervé-Chayette Laurence Calmels, Paris, for Fr.1,019,405 (£97,086).

1992 Auctioned by Harmers of London and sold to a German collector for £198,000.

XII

2d. Used. Cancelled with what appears to be PDAI in a rectangle and also part of a circular postmark reading PAUILLAC 2 JANVIER 1848.

1847 Used on a letter to Borchard at Bordeaux.

1865 Found by Madame Borchard, along with XI. Both stamps were acquired by the dealer Madame Desbois.

1866 Madame Desbois sold the stamps to one of Bordeaux's major stamp collectors, Émile Lalanne.

1893 Piet Lataudrie bought Lalanne's collection through the agency of Marcel Pouget for Fr.60,000 (£2,400) in July.

1896 E. Mors, of motor-racing fame, bought both stamps (XI and XII) for Fr.42,000 (£1,600).

1920 Both stamps (XI and XII) were bought by the dealer and collector Théodore Champion.

196(?) Changed hands privately, together with other items from the Champion Collection.

198(?) Bought by the French dealer Bernard Behr for his personal collection from an anonymous owner based in the US.

1995 Sold through Bernard Behr to a Western European collector (probably German).

XIII

2d. Used. Cancelled in the lower left-hand corner with part of a large circular postmark. The stamp is damaged at the bottom and the lower right-hand corner is cut.

1847 Used on a letter to Borchard at Bordeaux.

1869 Found (in 1869 or earlier) by Madame Borchard, who exchanged the stamp with Martineau, a Bordeaux collector (in 1869 or earlier).

1872 The stamp was acquired by the dealer Madame Desbois, then bought by Jean-Baptiste Moens for Fr.100 (£4) in September. Moens sold it to Arthur de Rothschild four days later for Fr.600 (£24).

1893 Philipp von Ferrary bought Rothschild's collection for Fr.140,000 (£5,600).

1923 Maurice Burrus bought the stamp at the sixth Ferrary sale in Paris for Fr.49,350 (£720).

1963 Bought by the firm of Stanley Gibbons Ltd at the Burrus sale for £3,300.

1972   Displayed by Stanley Gibbons Ltd in Brussels at Belgica '72, from which it was sold to a collector in Bermuda for £22,000.

XIV

2d. Unused. The stamp has been repaired and part of the inscription at the foot crudely redrawn.

1847   Used on a letter to Borchard at Bordeaux.

1865   Found by Madame Borchard, who later (date unknown) exchanged the stamp with, or sold it to, a Bordeaux collector.

1875   The owner sold the collection to the dealer Madame Desbois for Fr.500 (£20). The 'Post Office' stamp was extracted and bought by Jean-Baptiste Moens for Fr.300 (£12) in August. Moens sold it soon after to Philipp von Ferrary for Fr.600 (£24).

1886   Ferrary exchanged the stamp with Thomas Keay Tapling for, it is thought, a pair of Poonch stamps.

1891   The British Museum received Tapling's collection as a bequest.

1973   Tapling Collection transferred to the British Library.

XV

1d. Used. The stamp is cancelled with a large double-lined circular postmark reading MAURITIUS POST OFFICE, dated 21 September 1847. In addition, the cover bears a PENNY POST mark in a rectangle.

1847	Used on an envelope, which probably contained an entry card to Lady Gomm's ball, addressed to Monsieur Alcide Marquay.
1876	Bought by Edouard Buger for Fr.75 (£3).
1878	Major Evans bought Buger's collection, while in Mauritius, for Fr.250 (£10).
1884	Thomas Keay Tapling bought Evans's collection, the value of the envelope reckoned at £75.
1891	The British Museum received Tapling's collection as a bequest.
1973	Tapling Collection transferred to the British Library.

XVI

1d. Used. Heavily cancelled with an obliteration of parallel bars. The stamp is cut into on the right and has been repaired along the left-hand side.

1847	Used on a letter to Borchard at Bordeaux.
1864	Found by Madame Borchard.

1865   Madame Borchard exchanged the stamp with, or sold it to, a Bordeaux collector named Schiller.

1897   Dealer Marcel Pouget bought Schiller's collection in January, then sold it to G. Kirchner for Fr.10,000 (£400) in April.

1899   Bought by Eugen Lentz for 9,000 German marks (£450).

19(?)   Acquired by Russian collector Frederick Breitfuss (1851–1911), who formed the third greatest general collection, after Tapling and Ferrary, in the nineteenth century.

1907   Stanley Gibbons Ltd bought the Breitfuss collection.

1908   German dealer Philipp Kosack bought the stamp at auction and subsequently advertised it for sale.

19(?)   By 1914, Le Comte de Ramaix, of Antwerp, had paid Fr.18,000 for the stamp.

1919   Bought at auction by F. B. Smith in May and auctioned again in June by Harmer, Rooke & Co., when it was bought for cash, £480.

19(?)   Acquired by A. W. Cox some time between 1919 and 1933.

1933   Auctioned by H. R. Harmer in June, described as 'repaired' and sold for £320. The sale was cancelled after the purchaser submitted the stamp to the expert committee of the Royal Philatelic Society London, who refused to give it a certificate. The stamp was again auctioned by H. R. Harmer in September and sold without guarantee to the dealer Dr Paul Wolf. German dealer Philipp Kosack then bought the stamp for about £500.

193 (?)   Auctioned by Edgar Mohrmann.

1938   Auctioned by Heinrich Köhler, in Berlin, after having changed hands several times in the interim.

1952   Auctioned by Heinrich Köhler and bought by a Bavarian philatelist for 29,700 German marks.

XVII

1d. Used. The stamp is cancelled with a large double-lined circular postmark reading MAURITIUS POST OFFICE, dated 21 September 1847. In addition, the cover bears a PENNY POST mark in a rectangle.

1847   Used on an envelope, which probably contained an entry card to Lady Gomm's ball, addressed to Ed. Duvivier Esq.

1898   Madame Duvivier found the envelope when destroying old papers preparatory to moving house. It was bought by the British dealer W. H. Peckitt for £600 in March, then advertised later in the year for sale by Ostara & Darlow, but was withdrawn before the sale. The envelope was then bought from Peckitt by the Earl of Kintore for £850.

1904   Passed into the Royal Collection.

XVIII and XIX

1d (two stamps). Used on a folded letter, the stamps have large margins and are lightly cancelled with two impressions of an obliteration of parallel bars; also, the right-hand stamp bears part of an impression of '2' in a single-lined circle. The front of the letter bears a crowned MAURITIUS GPO broken double-lined circular postmark dated 4 January 1850.

1850	Used on a folded letter addressed to 'Thos. Jerrom Esqr., Secretary to the Bombay Auxiliary Bible Society, The Esplanade, Bombay'.
1897	Charles Howard bought the letter, together with some others, in an Indian bazaar for a sum reported from between five rupees to £50.
1898	British dealer W. H. Peckitt bought the letter in November for £1,600 then sold it to Vernon Roberts for £1,800.
1905	W. H. Peckitt bought back the letter for £2,000.
1906	American collector George Worthington bought the letter for £2,200.
1917	Alfred Lichtenstein bought part of Worthington's collection, including the Mauritius portion.
1947	Lichtenstein bequeathed his collection to his daughter, Louise Boyd Dale.
1968	The Dale-Lichtenstein collection was auctioned by H. R. Harmer (Boyd Dale died in 1967) and the

Jerrom letter was bought for a record price, $380,000, by Raymond H. Weill Co.

1989   Auctioned by Christie's Robson Lowe in Zurich, but withdrawn from sale at SFr.2,600,000.

1990   Purchased privately by Dr Chan Chin Cheung.

1996   Bought by Guido Craveri, an Italian dealer.

XX

1d. Used. The stamp is cancelled with one impression of PAID in a rectangle. In addition, the cover bears a PENNY POST mark in a rectangle.

1847   Used on an envelope, which probably contained an entry card to Lady Gomm's ball, addressed to 'H. Adam Esq Junr'.

1899   Dealer Théophile Lemaire bought the envelope from Adam for £680. It was then bought for £800 by the British dealer W. H. Peckitt, who sold it to Henry Duveen for £1,080.

1909   W. H. Peckitt obtained both XX and VI from Duveen in part exchange for III and X. Peckitt then sold XX and VI to Dutch collector Henry Manus.

1933   The Manus collection was auctioned by Plumridge (Manus died in 1931) and both XX (£2,400) and VI (£1,750) were bought by dealer Tom Allen.

193(?)   Acquired by King Carol of Romania.

1950   Both XX and VI were sold privately through the agency of Harmer, Rooke & Co. Ltd to Belgian collector René Berlingin.

1971   Both XX and VI were offered for sale at Stanley Gibbons's 'Anphilex' New York auction; the Adam ball envelope (XX) was bought by Hiroyuki Kanai for $174,000 (£73,000).

1986   Consigned with the Kanai Mauritius Collection to David Feldman.

1988   Sold to an anonymous buyer.

1993   Auctioned by David Feldman in Zurich and sold for SFr.1,610,000 ($1,073,340).

1997   Auctioned by David Feldman in Zurich and sold for SFr.2,070,000 ($1,564,630).

XXI AND XXII

1d and 2d. Used together on a folded letter. The stamps are cancelled with one impression of PENNY POST, upside down in a rectangle. In addition, the letter bears the following markings: (on the back) MAURITIUS / POST OFFICE / OC 04 1847, SHIP LETTER / PLYMOUTH, PARIS / 26 DEC 47 (?), BORDEAUX 28 DEC 47; (on the front) BOULOGNE / 26 DEC 47 in red, COLONIES & C. ART.13 in a rectangle. The delivery charge, 90 centimes, is indicated in manuscript on the front.

1847   Used on a letter to Ducau & Lurguie at Bordeaux, sent 'via England'.

1902   Found by a French schoolboy when searching through the firm's correspondence.

1903   Dealer Théophile Lemaire bought the letter for £1,600 and sold it to Brunet de l'Argentière for £1,800.

192(1?)   Alfred Lichtenstein bought de l'Argentière's collection. (See my reasons for this date in Chapter 10.)

1922   Arthur Hind bought the letter from Lichtenstein.

1934   Auctioned by H. R. Harmer in London at the Hind sale (Hind died in 1933) and purchased by dealer Edgar Mohrmann for Maurice Burrus for £5,000.

1963   The Raymond H. Weill Co. bought the letter at the Burrus sale on behalf of a client for £28,000.

1968   The Raymond H. Weill Co. bought back the letter after it had again changed hands.

1971   Bought by Hiroyuki Kanai for 120 million Japanese yen.

1986   Consigned with the Kanai Mauritius collection to David Feldman.

1988   Sold to an anonymous buyer for $3.8 million.

1993   Auctioned by David Feldman in Zurich and purchased by a lady representing an anonymous client for SFr.5,750,000 (£2.64 million, $4 million), which remains, at the time of publication, the highest amount ever paid for a philatelic item.

XXIII

2d. Used on a folded letter. A piece is torn out of the O of OFFICE. The stamp is just touched at the lower left-hand corner by a double-lined ANGL / BOULOGNE / 27 DEC 47 postmark. In addition, the letter bears the following markings on the front: COLONIES & C. ART.13 in a rectangle, and the delivery charges in manuscript. On the back: a large double-lined circular postmark reading MAURITIUS POST… the rest of inscription and date are obscured by a BORDEAUX 29 DEC 47 circular postmark; a red circular English postmark, AL / 25DE25 / 1847, and another rectangular postmark which reads DE24 1847 / LIVERPOOL / SHIP.

1847   Used on a letter to Ducau & Lurguie at Bordeaux, sent 'by Mischief via England'.

1902   Found by a French schoolboy when searching through the firm's correspondence.

1903   Dealer Théophile Lemaire bought the letter for £1,200 and sold it to the dealer Philipp Kosack for £1,400. Kosack then sold it to the Reichspostmuseum, Berlin. For the letter's subsequent history, see biography of VII.

XXIV

2d. Unused. The stamp has large margins and is considered the finest known example.

186(4?)   James Bonar obtained the stamp in Scotland.

1904   Auctioned by Puttick and Simpson in London, where it was knocked down to Mr J. Crawford for £1,450, purchasing on behalf of the Prince of Wales, later George V. The stamp passed into the Royal Collection.

XXV

2d. Used. The stamp is heavily postmarked and damaged. It appears never to have been photographed.

1917   Found in an old box, among a lot of valuable stamps, and purchased by the dealer Théophile Lemaire.

1918   Sold to a collector who remained anonymous.

XXVI

1d. Used. The stamp is heavily cancelled at right-hand side with part of an obliteration of parallel bars. The stamp is cut close and there is a small closed tear on the right.

187(?)   Acquired by a collector, possibly in India, and later brought to England.

1946   Discovered in a collection in Folkestone.

1947   Bought by Frank Godden Ltd.

194(7?)   Acquired by Sir Andrew Clark.

1961   Passed into the collection formed by Sir Denys Lowson.

1976   Auctioned by Stanley Gibbons and bought for £50,000 by René Berlingin, who presented it to his daughter Myriam as a wedding gift.

1977   Auctioned by Edgar Mohrmann and bought for 330,000 DM (£76,726) on behalf of a German collector.

Limbo I

1d. Used. The stamp has four full margins. It was pen-cancelled and attempts to remove the cancellation chemically resulted in the stamp appearing badly printed. In 1971 Hiroyuki Kanai examined Limbo I and pronounced it genuine but repaired.

189(?) Acquired by a Belgian banker named Van Bierbat.

1940   Bought by René Berlingin.

195(?) Sold through the dealer Wilhelm Bartels to the dealer Edgar Mohrmann.

1971   A German dealer offered the stamp for sale to Hiroyuki Kanai, who refused the offer. The identity of the current owner is unknown.

Notes and Sources

There can be no doubt that other forms of amusement,
especially bicycling, have deprived philately of a few
followers, specially during the season. But I can see no
direct danger to philately from this cause. There is
nothing antagonistic in the two. In Paris, for instance,
there is a Philatelic Bicycle Club, to which many
dealers of universal reputation and prominent
collectors belong.

'Is Philately on the Decline?',
Philatelic Journal of India, 1898

Introduction

The quotation 'contribution to the history of human folly' was cited by the Reverend C. S. Morton in 'From Angel Court to Park Lane', *Stamp Collecting,* Vol. 13, No. 10, 13 December 1919, p. 286, the original source given only as a leading London daily newspaper in 1889. For one response to the refrain that the hobby of stamp collecting is dying, see Gary Watson, 'Don't Blame the Children!', *Stamp News Australasia,* Vol. 50, No. 3, April 2003, pp. 58-60. Consult notes following for sources on Mauritius and George V.

Chapter 1: Port Louis, Mauritius, September 1847

Nineteenth-century Port Louis is still very much in evidence in the town's streets and buildings. My descriptions were also informed by reading contemporary travel narratives, particularly Nicolas Pike, *Sub-Tropical Rambles in the Land of Aphanapteryx: Personal Experiences, Adventures, & Wanderings in and around the Island of Mauritius*, Sampson Low, Marston, Low & Searle, London, 1873 (wonderful, wonderful, wonderful); Charles John Boyle, *Far Away, or, Sketches of Scenery and Society in Mauritius*, Chapman and Hall, London, 1867 (the source of the chapter's epigraph); Charles Pridham, *An Historical, Political and Statistical Account of Mauritius and its Dependencies*, T. and W. Boone, London, 1849 (the source of 'bare-headed, the hair twisted…'); *The Journal of Mrs. Fenton; A Narrative of Her Life in India, The Isle of France (Mauritius), and Tasmania During the Years 1826–1830*, Edward Arnold, London, 1901 (the source of 'here the time…'); Rev. Patrick Beaton, *Creoles and Coolies; or, Five Years in Mauritius*, James Nisbet & Co., London, 1859.

The few published sources on the 30 September 1847 ball include a notice about the vehicular arrangements on page one of *Le Cernéen*, 30 September 1847, and Vol. 1 of *The Story of a Soldier's Life; or Peace, War, and Mutiny*, Lieutenant-General John Alexander Ewart, CB, Aide-de-Camp to the Queen from 1859 to 1872, Sampson Low, Marston, Searle, & Rivington, London, 1881. The announcement about Nash's engraving can be found in *Le Mauricien*, 29 October 1847, p. 4. I have paraphrased and translated the observation about the lights in the ballroom from Matou's *Guêpes Mauriciennes*, Henri Plon, Paris, 1861. Although it was made in relation to another Mauritian ball some years later (1858–61), I was sure that Lady Gomm's ballroom could be similarly imagined. Copies of Nash's engraving are said to be in the Mahébourg Historical Museum in Mauritius and owned by the stamp-dealing firm of Harmers in London.

The major Mauritian newspapers published in Port Louis in the period of William Gomm's governorship (1842–9) – *Le Cernéen, Le Mauricien* and the *Mauritius Times* – provided background detail on the social and political life of the time. The Mauritius Blue Book for 1847 was also extremely useful in this respect. My favourite imports, apart from the rhinoceros, were artificial flowers, leeches, playing cards and tongues.

Lady Gomm's own bound copy of the *Mauritius Times* passed out of the family's collection and is now, providentially, in Australia's National Library in Canberra – a discovery which gave me no small thrill. The Gomms' arrival in Mauritius was recorded in *Le Cernéen*, 22 November 1842, p. 3. The major published source on Sir William Gomm is *Letters and Journals of Field-Marshal Sir William Maynard Gomm, G.C.B. Commander-in-Chief of India, Constable of the Tower of London &c. &c. From 1799 to Waterloo, 1815*, edited by Francis Culling Carr-Gomm, John Murray, London, 1881. Richard Carr-Gomm, Tony Carr-Gomm and his wife in London generously shared family details with me. High hopes for Lady Gomm were expressed in *Le Cernéen*, 29 November 1842, p. 4. The badly attended levee was noted in *Le Mauricien*, 26 May 1847, p. 4. Objections to Gomm's military background and other general grumblings appeared in *Le Mauricien*, 29 January 1847, p. 4.

Darwin's brief stop in Mauritius is recounted in *The Voyage of the Beagle*, Chapter 21. For an overview of slavery and Indian immigration in Mauritius, see Marina Carter, *Servants, Sirdars and Settlers: Indians in Mauritius, 1834–1874*, Oxford University Press, Delhi, 1995.

The Antelme story has been oft repeated. In the context of the 'Post Office Mauritius' story, it has been related in Alfred S. de Pitray's *The 'Post Office Mauritius' and its Legend*, Editions de l'Océan Indien, Mauritius, completed 1975, published 1990. See also Raymond d'Unienville, 'La nuit du 15 juillet 1847', *Gazette des Iles,*

December 1997. The quotation 'finished an eloquent plea...' is my translation from the French, *Le Cernéen*, 17 July 1847, p. 2. For information about the winter assemblies, see *Le Mauricien*, 18 June 1847, p. 3. The pun 'Loge de la Triple/triste Espérance' is not mine. It was described thus in *Le Cernéen* by Plickford in his 'Feuilleton' column, 17 July 1847, p. 2. The report on the bad-mannered young men appeared in *Le Mauricien*, 23 July 1847, p. 4.

CHAPTER 2: MESSAGE IN A BOTTLE

General information about the philatelic history of Mauritius can be found in Peter Ibbotson, *Mauritius Postal History and Stamps*, Royal Philatelic Society London, London, 1991; Hiroyuki Kanai, *Classic Mauritius: The Locally Printed Postage Stamps 1847–59*, Gibbons, London, 1981; Edward B. Proud, *The Postal History of Mauritius*, Proud-Bailey Co. Ltd, East Sussex, 2001. I consulted *Bolton's Mauritius Almanac and Official Directory* (1854, 1858), Mauritius Civil Service Almanacs (1867–78) and the Mauritius Blue Books (1840, 1847, 1848, 1853) for specific details of the Mauritius postal service and staff.

The details about Verhoeff, generally noted in Ibbotson, can be found in the *Bibliography of Mauritius (1502–1954), Covering the Printed Record, Manuscripts, Archivalia and Cartographic Material*, compiled by A. Toussaint and H. Adolphe, Port Louis, Mauritius, 1956, E974, p. 629. See also E965–E976. The details of Altham and the dodo, cited in Ibbotson, can be found in the *Proceedings of the Scientific Meetings of the Zoological Society of London*, 19 May 1874, p. 307, and 16 June 1874 ('On a Living Dodo Shipped for England in the Year 1628', Alfred Newton, pp. 447–9).

Postmaster Brownrigg's explanation about missing the mail can be found in Mauritius Archives series RA909, 3 October 1847. My main sources of information on Brownrigg came from reading his official correspondence in the Mauritius Archives and from the paper printed on the circumstances of his dismissal from the public service in Mauritius: 'Mr. Brownrigg. Return to an Address of the Honourable The House of Commons, dated 24 May 1855; – for, A "Copy of all Despatches and Correspondence connected with the Removal of Mr. J. Stuart Brownrigg from the Office of Postmaster General of the Island of Mauritius, on the 9th day of June 1853." Ordered by The House of Commons, to be Printed 11 July 1855'. This is the source of 'an indefatigability and zeal…', p. 39. Brownrigg, I think, was very hard done by. It was he who believed that courier work was suitable for less physically able convicts, an opinion given in a letter to C. J. Bayley, Mauritius Archives series RA1006, 19 October 1849, cited in Clare Anderson's useful *Convicts in the Indian Ocean: Transportation from South Asia to Mauritius, 1815–53*, Macmillan, London, 2000, p. 45. The source of 'Noxious effluvia coming…' was a letter from Brownrigg to the Colonial Secretary, Mauritius Archives series RA967, cited in Jean-Marie Huron, 'Location of Port Louis Post Office 1847', *Mauritius Philatelic Society News Bulletin*, No. 18, April 2001, p. 46. His urgent request for a carpenter can be found in Mauritius Archives series RA909, No. 8?89, 1 October 1847. His plea for numbering the houses can be found in Mauritius Archives series RA909, No. 8650, 24 September 1847.

Pridham (1849, p. 267) was the source of the 'gay display of jewellers…' quotation, and it was Pike (1873, pp. 429–30) who so looked forward to the monthly mail packet. Beaton (1859, pp. 8–9) described the reverberations of the evening gun; his aural observations were brilliant (both he and Boyle, in Mauritius some years apart in the 1850s and 1860s, commented on the pianos). I've been entering houses backwards at night ever since learning of and understanding this belief from my Mauritian husband.

Information on the daily duties of the postal staff and the quotation 'repair immediately to the Post Office...' can be found in the Post Office Rules and Regulations in *Bolton's Mauritius Almanac and Official Directory*, 1858, p. 203. Armed with contemporary and current maps of Port Louis, Governor Cole's 1828 Ordinance No. 30, 27 February 1828, 'For establishing a new Nomenclature of the Streets of the Town of Port Louis and its Suburbs', from the Public Record Office, Kew, London, CO 171/3, was a surprisingly enjoyable read.

The Reverend Cyril Shadforth Morton (1884–1947) never seems to have visited Mauritius but certainly travelled there in his mind. A prize-winning philatelist, he wrote a number of detailed articles on the early stamps of Mauritius, the strength of his work lying in his willingness to delve into Public Record Office and Colonial Office files and to trawl the contemporary Mauritius newspapers. He had an eye for a good anecdote – in fact picked the eyes out of them – and all subsequent writers on this period owe the following, in his translation, to a series of articles he published in *Stamp Collectors' Fortnightly*, 'The Post Office at the Mauritius': 'general rush to an opening...', *Le Mauricien*, 5 November 1849, p. 4, and Bayonet's response to this criticism, *Le Mauricien*, 16 November 1849, p. 4, cited in *Stamp Collectors' Fortnightly*, No. 780, 31 January 1925, p. 46; 'In a small shop...' and 'We have traced...', *Le Cernéen*, 24 September 1852, p. 2, cited in *Stamp Collectors' Fortnightly*, No. 781, 14 February 1925, p. 66.

Time and opportunity (or lack thereof) meant I relied on a secondary source for Gomm's visionary comment on the flying machines: 'The Story of Air Mauritius', *Mauritius Philatelic Society News Bulletin*, No. 18, April 2001, p. 28.

Brownrigg came under fire from the editors of *Le Mauricien*,

13 August 1847, p. 4 ('Mr Brownrigg is responsible...'), and the 'anonymous letters containing calumnies...' were noted in *Le Mauricien*, 26 July 1847, p. 4. For 'The Public complain of the Post...' and 'letters written which have no object...' the source is again the Reverend Cyril, from *Le Cernéen*, 27 July 1847, cited in 'A Study of the Early Postal Issues of Mauritius', *London Philatelist*, Vol. 33, 1924, pp. 220–21.

Details on Barnard's life are taken from Harold Adolphe and Raymond d'Unienville's 'The Life and Death of Joseph Osmond Barnard, Stowaway, Engraver, Stevedore and Planter', *London Philatelist*, Vol. 33, No. 985, December 1974, pp. 263–6. The description of the stamps comes from Captain E. B. Evans, 'The Stamps of Mauritius', *Philatelic Record*, Vol. 2, No. 14, March 1880, p. 20, also the source (Vol. 2, No. 15, April 1880, p. 31) of 'Mr. Barnard did not...'.

Stanley Gibbons' stamp catalogues are a good place to begin a study of the world's postage stamps. I worked with *Stanley Gibbons' Simplified Stamp Catalogue*, 1952 and *Stanley Gibbons Limited Priced Catalogue of Stamps of Foreign Countries*, Part II, 1927, on my desk.

CHAPTER 3: TO PHILATELIC FACTS, WHICH ARE USUALLY DRY

The Times 1841 and *Punch* 1842 anecdotes are often repeated in histories of stamp collecting. I read numerous of these, listed in the bibliography, as well as many of the early British stamp journals. My source was Fred Melville's *New A.B.C. of Stamp Collecting*, Melville Book Company, London, 1922, pp. 16–17. Melville (1883–1940) was one of, if not *the*, most prolific, enthusiastic and entertaining of the twentieth-century propagandists of philately, with more than 100 books to his credit when he died in his early fifties. Another enjoyable introduction to the hobby of stamp collecting, as practised in the twentieth century, is L. N. and M. Williams's *The Postage Stamp: Its History and Recognition*, Penguin, Harmondsworth, 1956. The *Philatelist*, 1 December 1866, Vol. 1, p. 2., is the source of the quotation 'the double charm of being very euphonious...'

A copy of Booty's rare 1862 catalogue, *The Stamp Collectors Guide: Being a List of English and Foreign Postage Stamps with 200 Fac-simile Drawings*, H. & C. Treacher, Brighton, sold at Cavendish Auctions, sale 626, 6 September 2002, Item 2088, for £2,600. The auction note is the source of the half a million hoard of stamps figure: http://www.cavendish-auctions.com/sale626_6sep02/A2080_2159.html (accessed 21 January 2004). In the tradition of the lucky find, the catalogue was found in the back of an old stamp album at a church charity sale and had a 50p price tag on it: http://www.thefrasers.com/nessie/news/nesspaper102602.html (accessed 21 January 2004).

For more on the early stamps of Mauritius, see Hiroyuki Kanai's *Classic Mauritius* and the catalogue *Mauritius Classic Postage Stamps and Postal History, Including the Entire Collection Formed by Hiroyuki Kanai, R.D.P., F.R.P.S.L*, 3 November 1993, David Feldman SA, Geneva, 1993. Herpin's article, 'Des Timbres de l'Île Maurice', appeared in *Le Collectionneur de Timbres-Poste*, No. 9, 15 March 1865, pp. 50-55, and the unsigned riposte, 'Des Timbres de Maurice', followed in *Le Timbre-Poste*, No. 29, May 1865, pp. 34-9. The correspondence concerning requests from various postmasters for specimens of current Mauritius stamps in 1865 can be found in Maurtius Archives series RA 1800.

The descriptions of Moens come from his obituaries in the *London Philatelist*, Vol. 17, No. 197, May 1908, pp. 113-21. Moens's brother-in-law Louis Hanciau recalled the 'found among the papers' anecdote in 'Old-Time Memories', *Stanley Gibbons Monthly Journal*, Vol. 17, No. 200, 28 February 1907, p. 167; the descriptions of Legrand come from his obituary in the *London Philatelist*, Vol. 21, No. 247, July 1912, pp. 177–8; Moens and Hanciau (for it must have been them) renounced their doubts about the existence of the 'Post Office' stamps in *Le Timbre-Poste*, No. 35, November 1865, pp. 87–8. I used Williams's translation (*Encyclopaedia*, Vol. 1, 1993, p. 178) of Moens's statement 'This famous "post-office"…', from 'Les Timbres "Post Office" de Maurice', *Le Timbre-Poste*, November 1865, p. 88.

Legrand's 'Post Paid' and 'Post Office' articles, written under the name Dr Magnus, were 'Timbres de Maurice', *Le Timbre-poste*, January 1869, pp. 5–8; 'Les Timbres Post Office de Maurice', *Le Timbre-Poste*, January 1870, pp. 5–8. The *Stamp-Collector's Magazine*, Vol. 3, 1 April 1865, p. 56, is the source of the quotation 'to bring to light the old Mauritius'.

CHAPTER 4: NO ROOM IN MADAME'S LALLIER

Staff at the Archives Municipales de Bordeaux and the Bibliothèque Municipale de Bordeaux were very helpful. Details about the impact of the weather on Bordeaux shipping can be found in the supplement to the *Mémorial Bordelais*, 1 October 1847. My impressions of Bordeaux, experienced during a few warm September days in 2003, were supplemented by Charles Higounet, ed., *Histoire de Bordeaux*, Univers de la France et des Pays Francophones, Toulouse, 1980; Henry Gradis, *Histoire de Bordeaux*, Calmann Lévy, Paris, 1888; Albert Rèche, *Dix Siècles de Vie Quotidienne à Bordeaux*, Seghers, Paris, 1983; Albert Charles, *La Révolution de 1848 et la Seconde République: A Bordeaux et dans le Département de la Gironde*, Éditions Delmas, Bordeaux, 1945; Paul

Perrein, *Images d'Autrefois de Bordeaux et de la Gironde*, Pierre Fanlac, Périgueux, 1984; John Murray's *Hand-Book for Travellers in France*, London, 1844 and 1864 editions. The *Mémorial Bordelais* newspaper was also invaluable (July, September–December 1847), as were the Bordeaux *Almanach* and *Annuaire* for 1847 (confirming the identity and location of key persons, for the delightful list of professions and the information about the postal procedures).

The source of the 300 to 400 collectors figure is Georges Brunel, *Ce Qu'était la Philatélie en 1867*, Yvert & Cie, Amiens, 1930, p. 8. The first serious account of the 'Post Office' stamps, by Jean-Baptiste Moens, 'Encore les Post-Office de Maurice', can be found in *Le Timbre-Poste*, No. 438, June 1899, pp. 87–93. Justin Lallier's *Postage-Stamp Album Illustrated with Maps* was first published in Paris by A. Lenègre, 35 R. Bonaparte, 1862. It was Fred Melville who described the Lallier as 'second only in veneration and respect to the Family Bible'.

Details of addresses for Coutures and Borchard came from the *Annuaire* for Bordeaux, 1864 and 1869; other personal details about the Borchards come from the Bordeaux census for 1866. Specific shipping details relating to Borchard, Serizier and Laffitte come from the *Mémorial Bordelais*, 14 July 1847 and 28 December 1847. The Mauritius Blue Book for 1847, and shipping details and advertisements from *Le Cernéen* for July and September–December 1847, provided the other side of the story. For Lalanne, see 'Lalanne, Émile (1831–1909)', obituary extract from *Revue Numismatique*, 1909, pp. 520–21, http://www.archivesmonetaires.org /dossiers/biographies/notices/lalanne.html (accessed 25 October 2004).

James Strachan's *The Recovery and Re-manufacture of Waste-paper*, Albany Press, Aberdeen, 1918, was a gem, but archivists and historians be warned, it will make you weep. Madame Desbois's story about the waste-paper merchant and the Mauritius stamps was given in *Gazette des Timbres*, Vol. 12, July 1874, p. 104, appeared in translation in the *Stamp-Collector's Magazine*, Vol. 12, July 1874, p. 104, and was cited in part in Williams's *Encyclopaedia* (Vol. 1, 1993, p. 181). I used Williams's translation (*Encyclopaedia*, Vol.1, 1993, p. 189) of Madame Desbois's 'the winding-up of his business...' from Moens's classic 1899 article. Further details about Madame Desbois came from the Bordeaux census for 1866 and the Bordeaux Annuaire. Small obituaries on her were published in *L'Echo de la Timbrologie*, No. 459, 15 February 1912, p. 101, and *Le Timbre-Poste*, Vol. 3, Nos. 16–17, 20 May 1912, p. 199. The source of Madame Desbois's 'I have entirely given up...' was the *Gazette des Timbres*, referred to in the *Stamp-Collector's Magazine*, Vol. 12, p. 104, July 1874, cited in Williams (*Encyclopaedia*, Vol. 1, 1993, p. 181).

Albert Rae's information on Noirel was published in 'Encore les Post Office de Maurice', *Le Philatéliste Francais*, May 1900.

Louis Laffitte had providentially been researched by members of Généalogie et Histoire de la Caraïbe in France: see 'G.H.C. Numéro 66: Décembre 1994 Page 1215', http://www.ghcaraibe.org/bul/ghc066/p1215.html (accessed 14 October 2004).

Chapter 5: Major Evans's Tour of Duty, Mauritius 1876–9

Biographical sources on Major Evans include: the *Philatelic Record*, Vol. 5, No. 72, January 1885, pp. 225–6; 'Major E. B. Evans', *London Philatelist*, Vol. 31, No. 364, April 1922, pp. 79–81; Ron Negus, 'Eminent Early Collectors: Edward B. Evans', *British Philatelic Bulletin*, Vol. 39, March 2002. His classic series of articles 'The Stamps of Mauritius', written as Captain E. B. Evans, RA, can be found in the *Philatelic Record*, Vol. 2, No. 13, February 1880, pp. 6–8;

Vol. 2, No. 14, March 1880, pp. 17–20; Vol. 2, No. 16, May 1880, pp. 48–52.

A report (in English) of the annual meeting of the Royal Society of Arts and Sciences in Port Louis was given in the *Mercantile Record and Commercial Gazette*, 29 August 1878, p. 2. Evans's talk was reproduced in full in that same journal on 30 August 1878, p. 2 (as was his account, as 'Cheth', 'Our Special Representative at the Theatre Royal Line Barracks'). Nineteen persons gathered for the forty-ninth anniversary meeting. Also on the agenda that day were a discussion on the life of Georges Cuvier and notes on the Aldabra giant tortoises sent by Dr Günther of the British Museum.

Brownrigg's letter of 2 May 1848 is in Mauritius Archives series RA967. His letters from 1847 can be found in Mauritius Archives series RA909. For sources on Brownrigg and Barnard, see notes given for Chapter 2. Lumgair's 'Mauritius Memories' appeared in the *Stamp Lover*, Vol. 1, No. 10, March 1909, pp. 253–5. Moutoussamy's history was compiled from a number of sources, including Bolton's Mauritius Almanac, the Mauritius Blue Books (1840–78) and Mauritius Archives series RA534 and RA2368.

CHAPTER 6: ALL, ALAS! DISCONTINUED BY DEATH

Philbrick: see 'Death of His Honour Judge Philbrick', *London Philatelist*, Vol.19, No.228, December 1910, p. 284; 'Frederick Adolphus Philbrick', *London Philatelist*, Vol. 20, No. 229, January 1911, pp. 1–3.

Rothschild: see 'Death of Baron Arthur de Rothschild', *London Philatelist*, Vol. 13, No. 146, February 1904, p. 40; Henri de Rothschild, *Les Timbres-Poste et Leurs Amis*, Théodore Champion, Paris, 1938, pp. 49–53 (source of the quote 'I no longer...', my translation); information from the Rothschild Research Forum,

'Brief Biography: Arthur (1851–1903)', http://www.rothschildar chive.org/research/?doc=/research/articles/XArthur (accessed 24 March 2005).

Ferrary: see the man himself, 'A Protest', the *Philatelic Record*, Vol. 5, No. 59, December 1883, pp. 199–200 (the source of 'abandoned all present and future claims' and 'Although, unfortunately, it was not granted…', p. 199); 'A Protest', the *Philatelic Record*, Vol. 6, No. 69, October 1884, p. 177; 'A Protest', the *Philatelic Record*, Vol. 6, No. 70, November 1884, pp. 200–201. See also Pierre Mahé, 'My Souvenirs: Reminiscences of a Veteran', *Stanley Gibbons Monthly Journal*, Vol. 16, No. 182, 31 August 1905 (the source of 'unpardonable!', p. 29); Fred J. Melville, 'The Fortunes of Ferrary', *Stamp Lover*, Vol. 14, Nos. 2–3, July–August 1921, pp. 29–40 (the source of 'I only saw him once…', p. 31); Georges Brunel, *Ce Qu'était la Philatélie en 1867*, Yvert & Cie, Amiens, 1930, pp. 12–15; Charles J. Phillips, 'Philipp La Rénotière Von Ferrary: One of the Greatest Collectors', *Stamps*, Vol. 1, No. 2, 24 September 1932, pp. 45–7, 61 (the source of 'I would sooner buy one hundred forgeries…', p. 46); Carlrichard Brühl, *Geschichte der Philatelie*, Georg Olms Verlag, Hildesheim, 1985, pp. 169–98; Carlo Bitossi, 'Riches and Charity: The Duke and Duchess of Galliera', *Journal of European Economic History*, Vol. 23, No. 2, Fall 1994, pp. 397–409; 'The Hôtel Matignon: Historical Background', http://www.archives.premier-ministre.gouv.fr/juppe_version1/ ENG/VIRT/HISTVIRT.HTM (accessed 28 October 2004).

Tapling: see editorials in the *Philatelic Record*, Vol. 13, No. 148, April 1891, pp. 69–71 (the source of 'It will be remembered of him…', p. 71) and Vol. 13, No. 149, May 1891, pp. 93–97 (the source of 'The changes of life are many…', p. 95, and 'fully contemplated…', p. 96); 'The Tapling Collection', *London Philatelist*, Vol. 12, No. 142, October 1903, pp. 229–30. On the philatelic dinner attended by Ferrary and Caillebotte, see the *Philatelic Record*, Vol. 6, December 1884, p. 223. The comment on the Tapling display, 'So great is the reputation…', appeared in the *London Philatelist*, Vol. 12, No. 142, October 1903, p. 230.

Image: see 'The Late Mr. W. E. Image', *London Philatelist*, Vol. 12, No. 142, October 1903, pp. 241–42.

For the state of play in philately in the 1880s and 1890s, see the editorial on the sale of Legrand's collection, 'The Old Order Changeth', *London Philatelist*, Vol. 6, No. 70, October 1897, pp. 277–8, 290 (on the change in the practice of the hobby, and the source of 'for a larger sum than he has expended…', p. 278); 'Death of Dr. Legrand', *London Philatelist*, Vol. 21, No. 247, July 1912, pp. 177–78; plus various editorials and articles in the *Philatelic Record*: Vol. 2, No. 20, September 1880, pp. 99–100; Vol. 3, No. 25, February 1881, pp. 1–2; Vol. 4, No. 47, December 1882, pp.189–91 (the source of 'Were the rarer stamps less hoarded…' and 'unattainables', p. 190); 'Newspaper Twaddle', Vol. 9, No. 98, March 1887, pp. 38–9 (the source of the 'vast chasm' comparison, p. 38). See also Hubert Haes's letter to the editor, 'The Fiftieth Anniversary of Penny Postage', *The Times*, 11 January 1890, p. 12.

For more background on French philately see Pierre Mahé, *Les Marchands de Timbres-Poste d'Autrefois et Leurs Catalogues*, Yvert et Tellier, Amiens, 1908, pp. 173–9. See also 'Death of M. Pierre Mahé', *London Philatelist*, Vol. 22, No. 254, February 1913, p. 39.

Biographical notes on Albert Rae and William Charles Rae can be found in Allister Macmillan, *Mauritius Illustrated*, W. H. & L. Collingridge, London, 1914, p. 443, which also contains an article by Albert, 'The Famous Stamps of Mauritius', pp. 316–23.

Williams's *Encyclopaedia* was again useful, as was Moens's 1899 account (the source of 'judging two Post Office sufficient to his happiness…', p. 90, my translation), while Stanley M. Bierman's

The World's Greatest Stamp Collectors, Frederick Fell Publishers, New York, *c.* 1980, was useful for bibliographic references.

CHAPTER 7: PRETTY PHILATELIC FAIRY TALES

Much of my feeling for stamp collecting as practised in Britain in the 1880s and 1890s comes from page-by-page scanning of the contemporary British philatelic literature, which the Royal Philatelic Society of Victoria kindly allowed me to remove from their library and read at my leisure, sat up late at night as I imagine many of the original readers would have. Applying the same depth of research to the French and Belgian literature, as I would have liked to do, was impossible given access to holdings. One day...

The epigraph to this chapter, about the would-be philatelic bridegroom, is perhaps another one of those philatelic fairy tales. Williams included it in the *Encyclopaedia* (Vol. 1, 1993, p. 202), citing a South African correspondent in *Stamp Collecting*, Vol. 132, No. 3, 7 December 1978, p. 345, who in turn was quoting the *George & Knysua Herald* of 1 July 1891. Williams also reported the story as appearing in *Vanity Fair* in 1891. The citation in *Stamp Collecting* claims that the advertisement appeared in a Mauritian newspaper called the *Monitor*. According to Toussaint's *Bibliography of Mauritius (1502–1954)*, no newspaper of that name was published in the island. Which *Monitor* might it have been? Nearby Réunion, still a French colony, had a newspaper, *Le Moniteur*, at this time. Perhaps the original correspondent, as they sometimes are, was in error. I have not trawled through *Le Moniteur* to find out. Interestingly, Williams misquotes this advertisement (unless he was quoting the *Vanity Fair* version, in which case it would have been helpful of him to say so). He says, 'the possessor of the blue two-penny stamp of Mauritius'. As given in *Stamp Collecting*, this reads, 'the possessor of the Blue Penny (*sic*) stamp of Mauritius'. The *sic* is the *Stamp Collecting* correspondent's, no doubt a cautious man. It is a usage, as explained in the postscript, that hardline philatelists frown on, but one that has been current in Mauritius for a long, long time.

Rumours about the plate, 'Alleged Reprinting of the Early Mauritius Stamps', appeared in the *London Philatelist*, Vol. 2, September 1893. The quotation 'A friend of the editor of the Paris *Figaro...*' comes from 'A Pretty Philatelic Fairy Tale', *Stamp Collectors' Fortnightly*, Vol. 2, No. 42, 18 April 1896, p. 171, and a similar version of this story appeared in the *Philatelic Journal of Great Britain*, Vol. 6, No. 62, 10 February 1896, p. 25. The *London Philatelist* (Vol. 6, No. 71, November 1897, p. 325) discussed the prestige of the stamps in 'The Post Office Mauritius'.

Contemporary and later sources on Howard's find of the Jerrom letter include: 'Encore deux!', *Le Timbre-Poste*, No. 429, September 1898, pp. 138–9; 'Two More "Post Office" Mauritius', *London Philatelist*, Vol. 7, No. 82, October 1898, pp. 269–70; 'More "Post Office" Mauritius', *Philatelic Record*, Vol. 20, December 1898, p. 272; 'Encore les Post-Office de Maurice', *Le Timbre-Poste*, No. 438, June 1899, pp. 91–2; 'Encore les Post-Office de Maurice', *Le Timbre-Poste*, No. 441, September 1899, pp. 141–2; Charles J. Phillips, 'The Pedigree of Rare Stamps', *Collectors Club Philatelist*, Vol. 18, No. 4, October 1939, pp. 263–73; C. H. Harmer, 'The "Thos. Jerrom" Mauritius Letter', *London Philatelist*, Vol. 78, No. 913, January 1969, pp. 10–12; 'Post Office Mauritius 1d.', *Philatelist*, Vol. 43, No. 3, December 1976, pp. 74–5; L. N. Williams, 'Mauritius 1847 1d. – The Letter Writer and the Recipient', *Philatelist*, Vol. 43, No. 6, March 1977, pp. 172–3. I used Williams's translation (*Encyclopaedia*, Vol. 1, 1993, p. 199) of Moens's statement 'To buy a stamp for 25,000 francs...', from 'Encore les Post-Office de Maurice', *Le Timbre-Poste*, No. 438, June 1899, p. 92.

Contemporary and later sources on the find of the Duvivier envelope include: 'Another "Post Office" Mauritius', *London Philatelist*, Vol. 7, No. 78, June 1898, pp. 168–9; *Philatelic Journal of Great Britain*, Vol. 9, No. 90, 15 June 1898, p. 116, cited in 'Over £1,000 for One Stamp: Mr. Peckitt pays Big Money for the Penny "Post Office" Mauritius', *Stamp Collectors' Fortnightly*, 9 July 1898, p. 191; 'Mr. Peckitt's Thousand-pounder', *Stamp Collectors' Fortnightly*, 23 July 1898, p. 195; 'Encore les Post-Office de Maurice', *Le Timbre-Poste*, No. 438, June 1899, p. 91; 'Encore les Post-Office de Maurice', *Le Timbre-Poste*, No. 441, September 1899, p. 142; Allister Macmillan, *Mauritius Illustrated*, W. H. & L. Collingridge, London, 1914, p. 317; L. Halais, 'Duvivier, L. A. Aimé (1858–1922), *Dictionary of Mauritian Biography*, No. 7, December 1942, pp. 205–6. Mr Pope's story of the figure paid for the Duvivier envelope, 'A Chat on Mauritius and Its Stamps', was reported in the *British Guiana Philatelic Journal*, Vol. 1, December 1906, p. 5.

Cerne's letter to the editor, 'To Philatelists', appeared in the *Westminster Gazette*, 26 July 1897, p. 3, following on from an article a few days previously, 'A Monster Stamp Collection to be Opened by the Duke of York' (22 July 1897, p. 5), which described the one penny and two pence 'Post Office' stamps as the rarest in the world, due to a printer's blunder in the wording.

Sources on Henry Adam and the Adam find include A. Toussaint, 'Adam, Charles Félix Henry (1829–1907)', *Dictionary of Mauritian Biography*, No. 10, July 1943; 'Post Office Mauritius by the Score', *London Philatelist*, Vol. 8, No. 92, 1899, pp. 208–9; 'Encore les Post-Office de Maurice', *Le Timbre-Poste*, No. 441, September 1899, p. 142; Williams, *Encyclopaedia*, Vol. 1, 1993, pp. 196, 199–200, Vol. 2, p. 140.

For Peckitt: see 'Leading London Dealers: VII – Mr. W. H.

Peckitt', *Philatelic Journal of Great Britain*, Vol. 2, 1 February 1892, pp. 31–2 (source of the quotations 'old Continentals...' and 'There are gems brighter...'); Theodore Buhl, 'Editorial Interviews: Mr. W. H. Peckitt', *Philatelic Record*, Vol. 21, No. 1, January 1899, pp. 4–5; L. N. and M. Williams, *The Postage Stamp: Its History and Recognition*, Penguin, Harmondsworth, 1956, p. 79.

The Ventom, Bull and Cooper sale was reported in *The Times*, 'Sale of Postage Stamps', 28 October 1895, p. 13. The hobby of stamp collecting was described as 'the spoilt darling of the drawing rooms' in 'Philately in the New Century', *Stamp Collectors' Fortnightly*, Vol. 6, No. 153, 19 January 1901, p. 178. On auctions and the value of stamps, see Walter Nathan, 'Reminiscences of a Philatelist', *Stamp Collectors' Fortnightly*, Vol. 6, No. 150, 8 December 1900, p. 154. Some have wondered whether tales of murder for possession of rare stamps are merely tales: the murder of Gaston Leroux was widely reported in the philatelic press – for example, 'Discovery of Another Philatelic Crime', *Stamp Collectors' Fortnightly*, Vol. 2, No. 48, 25 July 1896, p. 250.

The story from London's *Evening Standard* in 1891, 'We can understand a new or unique orchid...', was cited in the *Philatelic Record*, Vol. 13, No. 150, June 1891, p. 143; in response, the sentiments 'A unique orchid would...' and 'These values do not...' followed on p. 144. The gripe 'simply because they bore the misprint "Office"...' originally appeared in the *Hastings Times*, cited in *Stamp Collectors' Fortnightly*, Vol. 4, No. 90, 5 March 1898, p. 112. The philatelic press reported that there were stamps rarer than the 'Post Office' in: '£1026 for a Pair', *Stamp Collectors' Fortnightly*, Vol. 2, No. 29, 2 November 1895, p.36; 'The New "Rarest Stamp" in the World', *Stamp Collectors' Fortnightly*, Vol. 2, No. 40, 4 April 1896, p. 161; 'Rarer than the Post Office Mauritius', *Stamp Collectors' Fortnightly*, Vol. 6, No. 152, 5 January 1901, p. 165. Charles J. Phillips later elaborated in '19th Century Stamps that are Rarer than the Post Office Mauritius', *Stamps*, Vol. 2, No. 1, 17 December 1932, pp. 17–18.

The observation about nourishing covetousness, materialism and filthy stinginess was made in *Mekeel's Weekly Stamp News*, cited in 'Pecuniary Interests in Collecting', *Stamp Collectors' Fortnightly*, Vol. 2, No. 28, 19 October 1895, p. 24. The tongue-in-cheek plea for an SSSSSS was made in a letter to the editor, *Stamp Collectors' Fortnightly*, Vol. 4, No. 96, 28 May 1898, p. 165. The Hammarskjöld anecdote has recently been retold by Christer Brunström, 'The US Hammarskjöld Invert', *Stamps News Australasia*, Vol. 50, No. 3, April 2003, pp. 44–5. Lastly, the notion that 'In rare stamps, as in other things in life, "kissing goes by favour"' belongs to W. E. Hughes, 'Rarity and Some of its Attributes', *Stamp Collecting*, 20 September 1924, p. 526, and is shared by me.

CHAPTER 8: THE SCHOOLBOY AND THE BORDEAUX LETTERS

The main biographical information on Lemaire was drawn from Theodore Buhl, 'Editorial Interviews: M. Theophile Lemaire', *Philatelic Record*, Vol. 21, No. 6, June 1899, pp. 123–4.

It was the editors of Stanley Gibbons's *Monthly Journal* who bemoaned the tendency of 'philatelic Rip Van Winkles' to go over old ground and who prophetically stated, 'It is extraordinary how difficult it is to get rid of a mistake which has once got well established' (Vol. 1, No. 4, 20 October 1890, p. 67).

The quotation from the *Illustrierte Briefmarken Journal* was cited in 'All about the "Post Office" Mauritius', *Stamp Collectors' Fortnightly*, 29 October 1898, p. 23, reproduced therein from English translation in *Filatelic Facts and Fallacies* (such was the merry-go-round of philatelic journalism). 'The Exhibition of the South African Colonies', *London Philatelist*, Vol. 11, No. 132, December 1902, pp. 280–81, discusses the five 'Post Office' stamps on display there.

The quotations 'her interest kindled…' and 'Many weary and dusty days…' are taken from L. N. and M. Williams, *Famous Stamps*, W. & R. Chambers, Edinburgh, revised edition 1946, p. 38. A slightly edited version, minus the youthful enthusiasm and despair, appears in Williams *Encyclopaedia* (Vol. 1, 1993, p. 197). See also the Williams brothers' letter in *Collectors Club Philatelist*, Vol. 19, No. 3, July 1940, pp. 238–9.

Much of the background information on people and locations in this chapter was derived from Bordeaux directories and censuses consulted at the Bordeaux Municipal Archives: *Almanach*, 1847; *Annuaire*, 1847, 1864, 1866, 1869, 1874, 1902; Census, 1866, 1901. Additional information on directories, routes and rates came from Peter Ibbotson, 'Arising from those Bordeaux Letters', *Gibbons Stamp Monthly*, June 1994, pp. 29–31. Marie-Laurence Sanfourche, Vignobles Marc Ducau at the Château Loupiac-Gaudiet, confirmed that the story of the Bordeaux letters and the 1847 Ducaus was unknown to them.

Georges Brunel's listing 'Mutations des Post Office de Maurice' appeared in his *Les Timbres-Poste de l'Île Maurice: Émissions de 1847 à 1898*, Editions Philatelia, Paris, 1928, pp. 25–6.

Sources on the discovery of the Bordeaux letters include Théophile Lemaire, 'Deux Nouveaux "Post-Office" de Maurice', *La Cote Réelle des Timbres-Poste*, second series, No. 9, 31 January 1903, pp. 1–7, and 'Le Numéro 23', No. 15, 15 April 1903, pp. 1–2; 'Mauritius: Discovery of Two More "Post Office" Stamps', *London Philatelist*, Vol. 12, No. 134, February 1903, p. 31; 'The Latest "Post Office" Mauritius', *London Philatelist*, Vol. 12, No. 135, March 1903,

p. 60 (source of the quotation 'novel and highly interesting discovery…'); 'The Twenty-third "Post Office" Mauritius', *Stamp Collectors' Fortnightly*, 9 May 1903, p. 38 (source of the quotation 'just by way of producing an effect…').

On the Reichspostmuseum 'as the Institute of Culture…' see 'On Postal Museums', Supplement to *Stamp Collecting*, 16 December 1922, Vol. 19, No. 11, p. xxiii. Most of the information about the 'Post Office' stamps being copied while on loan to the Reichspostmuseum comes from Williams in the *Encyclopaedia*; it was also noted in 1900 in the *Stamp Collectors' Fortnightly* (see following). The British enjoyed taunting the Germans in 'Two More "Post Office" Mauritius', *London Philatelist*, Vol. 7, No. 82, October 1898, p. 70; '"Post Office" Mauritius by the Score', *London Philatelist*, Vol. 8, No. 92, August 1899, p. 209; 'German-made "Post Office Mauritius"', *Stamp Collectors' Fortnightly*, 9 June 1900. Information about Kosack came from the exhibition brochure 'Sonderausstellung Mythos Mauritius', published by the Museumsstiftung Post und Telekommunikation, Bonn, undated.

Copies of transcribed correspondence between Hennecke and Lemaire, including the article in the *Berliner Local-Anzeiger* and the Reichspostmuseum's response, were given to me by a philatelist who specializes in Mauritius. According to the staff at the Museumsstiftung Post und Telekommunikation in Bonn, all the relevant correspondence had been destroyed during the Second World War. The provenance of the copies now in existence may be Lemaire. Another mystery in itself.

CHAPTER 9: THE BLUE MAURITIUS

Contemporary sources on the Bonar find include 'A Rarity Hidden since 1864', *Stamp Collectors' Fortnightly*, Vol. 9, No. 226, 7 November 1903; 'A Post Office for Sale', *Stanley Gibbons Monthly Journal*, Vol. 14, No. 161, 30 November 1903, pp. 87–8; 'Discovery of Another "Post Office" Mauritius', *London Philatelist*, Vol. 12, No. 143, November 1903, p. 269; 'The Last "Post Office" Mauritius', *London Philatelist*, Vol. 12, No. 144, December 1903, p. 301.

I first came across reference to Miss Thomas's story in the *Daily Mail* in the Williams brothers' correspondence with Nevile Stocken, now held in the Philatelic Collections at the British Library. The contemporary references include 'Another "Post Office" Mauritius', *Stanley Gibbons Monthly Journal*, Vol. 14, No. 161, 30 November 1903, p. 100; 'The "Post Office" Mauritius', *Stanley Gibbons Monthly Journal*, Vol. 14, No. 162, 31 December 1903, p. 124.

Mr Simpson's reminiscences are given in 'Philatelic Auctioneers. No. 2 - Messrs. Puttick & Simpson', *Stamp Collecting*, Vol. 12, No. 8, 9 August 1919, p. 414. The relationship between Alex Hastie and James Stuart Brownrigg is given in the Despatches cited in the notes for Chapter 2.

Background on the early Scottish stamp-collecting scene was derived from P. J. Anderson, 'Scottish Philatelic Literature, 1863–1923', *Stamp Collecting*, Vol. 21, No. 15, 12 January 1924, p. 394, and Vol. 21, No. 16, 19 January 1924, p. 412. Captain R. S. Chambers's anecdotes are related in 'Some Interesting Finds', *Stamp Collecting*, Vol. 13, No. 10, 13 December 1919, pp. 277–8. The 1918 treatise on the recovery and remanufacture of waste-paper was James Strachan's (pp. v–vi, 1–6, 11–14) cited in the notes for Chapter 4. Melville's 1920 talk was reported in 'Fortunes in Old Stamps: Hint to Legal Firms. Scotland a Happy Hunting Ground', *Stamp Collecting*, Vol. 15, No. 10, 11 December 1920, p. 284.

On George V as a stamp collector, see 'His Late Majesty King George V', *London Philatelist*, Vol. 45, No. 529, January 1936, pp. 1–4. Nicholas Courtney's *The Queen's Stamps: The Authorised History of the Royal Philatelic Collection*, Methuen, London, 2004, was also particularly helpful, especially pp. 83–8. I am grateful also to Michael Sefi, Keeper of the Royal Philatelic Collection (correspondence: September 2003 and March 2005). The source of the quotation 'has been on everyone's lips...' was 'Record Making', *London Philatelist*, Vol. 13, No. 145, January 1904, p. 1.

In later years several versions of the story circulated about the revelatory moment when the royal household learned the news of the purchase, a story that the King enjoyed telling against himself. Somebody (there are a number of contenders and it matters not who) telephoned or spoke to the Prince and said, 'Did your Royal Highness hear that some damned fool has just paid £1,450 for a single stamp?' to which the Prince replied that he was the damned fool. L. N. Williams's version (*Encyclopaedia*, Vol. 1, 1993, pp. 195–6), in the best tradition of tall stories ('I have the report from a lady to whom the story was related by King George V himself') had the Prince asking the question – what would the somebody say about a chap who paid £1,400 for a stamp? – and the somebody replying, 'I would call him a silly ass, Sir.' Whether a silly ass or a damned fool, the stamp-collecting King is said to have repeated the anecdote always with 'a hearty laugh'.

Some references to mention of the 'Post Office' in English-language journals was compiled by the Indian Ocean Study Circle. Others I have found, again, through much happy leafing through the journals: 'Philately in the Latest Novel', *Stamp Collectors' Fortnightly*, Vol. 2, No. 51, 5 September 1896, p. 274; C. E. Johnstone, 'Ballade of the Stamp-Collector's Paradise', *Philatelic Journal of Great Britain*, Vol. 6, No. 62, 10 February 1896, p. 30; 'The Blue Trinacria', *Stamp Collecting*, Vol. 12, No. 9, 7 June 1919, p. 199; 'Triangular Mauritius', *Stamp Collecting*, Vol. 16, No. 4, 30 April 1921,

p. 98; 'A Lay of the Blue Mauritius', *Stamp Collecting*, Vol. 18, No. 4, 29 April 1922, p. 89; 'Recent Fiction', *Stamp Collecting*, Vol. 19, No. 4, 28 October 1922, p. 86.

The source of the quotation 'Rarities, and especially in fine condition...' was 'Editorial Notes', *Philatelic Record*, March 1904.

Sources on the 'Post Office' plate include: Alexander Séfi, 'Discovery of What is Undoubtedly the Greatest Philatelic Treasure Existing', *West-End Philatelist*, 1912, pp. 114–19; 'The Plate of the "Post Office" Mauritius', *Stanley Gibbons Monthly Journal*, Vol. 20, No. 238, 31 October 1912, p. 308; Albert Rae, 'The Famous Stamps of Mauritius', in Allister Macmillan, *Mauritius Illustrated*, W. H. & L. Collingridge, London, 1914, pp. 316–23; Nevile Lacy Stocken, 'How I Found the Most Valuable Piece of Copper in the World', *Stamp Collecting*, Vol. 34, No. 24, 13 September 1930, pp. 529–33; 'Mauritius Stamp Plate Sent to Berlin for Exhibition', *The Times*, 11 September 1930, p. 8; Peter Ibbotson, 'Mauritius: Myth and Mystery – Who was Colonel Colnaghi?', *Stamp Collecting*, 21 August 1975, pp. 1,101–3; correspondence between David Beech, Philatelic Collections, British Library, and Peter Ibbotson, 1985, held Philatelic Collections, British Library; correspondence between the author and Michael Sefi, Keeper of the Royal Philatelic Collection, November 2005. 'Copy of Final Report of the Commission appointed to make enquiry concerning the plate on which the Mauritius stamps of 1847 were engraved, enclosure to Mauritius confidential despatch of 15th April 1915', is held by the Royal Philatelic Society, London.

New specimens of both values were reported found in 'News from Paris', *Stamp Collecting*, Vol. 1, No. 5, 18 October 1913, p. 77. *Stamp Collecting*, Vol. 1, No. 6, 25 October 1913, p. 88, was the source of the quotation 'It looks as though "Post Office" Mauritius will soon be as plentiful...' On other rumoured finds, see 'Reputed

Discovery of Another Post-Office Mauritius', *Australian Stamp Journal*, Vol. 3, No. 11, 10 September 1913, p. 194; 'A Supposed 1d. "Post Office" Mauritius', *Stanley Gibbons Monthly Journal*, Vol. 21, No. 251, 29 November 1913, p. 337.

The Melville quotations 'have to loosen wide...' (p. 207), 'as examples of a genuinely necessary issue...' and 'always be looked upon...' (p. 224) come from his *Chats on Postage Stamps*, T. Fisher Unwin, London, 1911.

Percy Bishop's delightful call to arms, 'Where to Hunt for Rare Stamps', appeared in the very first number of *Stamp Collectors' Fortnightly* (Vol. 1, No. 1, 20 September 1913, p. 7), and is also the source of the quotation 'All the old grandmothers' trunks...' Bishop was here quoting a sad-eyed dealer. J. Franklin wrote the letter 'The Joys of the Hunt', in *Stamp Collecting*, Vol. 22, No. 3, 19 April 1924, p. 58. The much-travelled author of *People and Places* was described by the Reverend C. S. Morton in a review, 'On Garnering', Supplement to *Stamp Collecting*, Vol. 19, No. 5, 4 November 1922, p. ix. There is indeed a chapter entitled 'Stamps' in *People and Places: A Life in Five Continents*, John Murray, London, 1922.

The *Daily Mail* story about the American stamp hunters was cited in *Stamp Collecting*, Vol. 42, No. 11, 9 June 1934, p. 255. Williams, in the *Encyclopaedia* (Vol. 1, 1993, p. 202), is the only source (and he gives no source) for the Walker and Bratt anecdote. It was included in the Williams brothers' *Famous Stamps* in 1940. Perhaps the anecdote originally appeared in one of the philatelic journals and I have missed it in my searching.

Edward Mosely's Mauritius collection is now in the British Library. His 'Combing an Island for Postal Treasures' appeared in *Stamp Collecting*, Vol. 40, No. 16, 15 July 1933, pp. 410, 413–15. Robert Walser wrote a letter about his search through the Erard archives,

'Post Office Mauritius Stamps', in *Collectors Club Philatelist*, Vol. 12, No. 1, January 1933, p. 13; L. N. Williams indicates that he searched the British and Foreign Bible Society's archives in the *Encyclopaedia* (Vol. 1, 1993, p. 201).

On more general stamp finds, see 'Finds', *Stamp Collecting*, Vol. 2, No. 17, 11 July 1914; 'Extraordinary Find of Rare Stamps', *Stamp Collecting*, Vol. 14, No. 2, 17 April 1920, p. 35.

It was Williams in the *Encyclopaedia* (Vol. 2, 1997, p. 153), and in earlier works, who described the 1917 find as 'in an old box, among a lot of valueless stamps'. Douglas Armstrong made the observation about philately weathering the storm in 'Stamp Collecting after the War', *Stamp Collecting*, Vol. 6, No. 18, 12 August 1916, p. 667.

CHAPTER 10: THE BIG-GAME COLLECTORS

Descriptions of the early Ferrary sales, reports and opinions can be found in: Fred Melville, 'The Ferrary Sale', *Stamp Collecting*, Vol. 16, No. 13, 2 July 1921, pp. 361, 363–4; 'Ferrarities', *Stamp Collecting*, Vol. 16, No. 14, 9 July 1921, p. 383; Fred J. Melville, 'The Fortunes of Ferrary', *Stamp Lover*, Vol. 14, Nos. 2-3, July–August 1921, pp. 29–40; C. J. Phillips, 'The Ferrari Sale: Its Probable Effect on the Stamp Market', *Stanley Gibbons Monthly Circular*, No. 25, September 1921, pp. 8–13, 52 (the source of 'things not likely…'); Herman Toaspern, 'The Benefits of the Ferrari Sale', *Collectors Club Philatelist*, Vol. 1, No. 4, October 1922, pp. 151–2 (the source of 'not one philatelist in a hundred…'); A. J. Séfi, 'The November Ferrari Sale', *Philatelic Journal of Great Britain*, Vol. 32, No. 384, December 1922, p. 244.

Stanley M. Bierman's *The World's Greatest Stamp Collectors*, Frederick Fell Publishers, New York, c. 1980, was used for background on Lichtenstein, Hind and Burrus, and was most useful for its bibliography. Carlrichard Brühl, *Geschichte der Philatelie*, Georg

Olms Verlag, Hildesheim, 1985, was also useful on Lichtenstein and Burrus, pp. 221–33.

Sources on Lichtenstein include 'Alfred F. Lichtenstein is Dead', *Stamps*, Vol. 58, No. 10, 8 March 1947, pp. 439–41; 'Alfred F. Lichtenstein', *London Philatelist*, Vol. 56, No. 653, April 1947, pp. 73–5 (the source for 'for other people's pleasure and instruction').

Sources on Hind include 'The American Ferrari', *Stamp Collecting*, Vol. 19, No. 8, 25 November 1922, p. 180 (the source of 'a genial, stocky, thick-set gentleman…'); Charles J. Phillips, 'Arthur Hind: Owner of the World's Highest Priced Stamp', *Stamps*, Vol. 1, No. 8, 1932, pp. 261–3, 271; A. J. Séfi, 'Obituary. A Short Memoir of Mr Arthur Hind', *Philatelic Journal of Great Britain*, Vol. 43, No. 507, March 1933, pp. 46–7 (the source of 'pure joy of possession' and 'I have watched him…'); 'Rare Mauritius Stamps; Big Prices at Sale of Hind Collection', *The Times*, 13 June 1934, p. 13; 'Hind's Stamps to be Sold', *New York Times*, 28 March 1933, p. 7.

Sources on Burrus include 'M. Burrus Sees It Through' and 'Condition and Rarity', *Philatelic Magazine* (the source of 'to reassemble the whole…'); Imre Vajda, 'Maurice Burrus: Tobacco King Turned Prince of Philatelists', *Stamps*, Vol. 103, No. 6, 1958, pp. 218–19; 'M. Maurice Burrus: A Famous Stamp Collection', *The Times*, 8 December 1959, p. 15. The anecdote about Burrus overhearing Hind's agent discussing his price and strategy for buying the 1¢ British Guiana is cited by Bierman, originally given in *Balasse Magazine*, No. 105, pp. 87–8.

'A Peep into the Maison Champion', *Stamp Collecting*, Vol. 19, No. 4, 28 October 1922, p. 85, was the source of the quotation 'brought him prominently into the limelight', on Théodore Champion.

The recent purchase of a large part of the de l'Argentière collection by Séfi, Pemberton and Co. is noted in 'Stamps of Interest', *Stamp Collecting*, Vol. 18, No. 14, 8 July 1922, p. 330; the recollections about Hind's purchase of the Bordeaux letter appear in Séfi's obituary of Hind, *Philatelic Journal of Great Britain*, Vol. 43, No. 507, March 1933, p. 46.

The anecdote 'I have a pair' was cited by Bierman, whose source appears to have been Sir John Wilson's 1952 book on the Royal Collection.

Leon de Raay, 'The Stolen "Mauritius": A True Story', *Stamp Collecting*, Vol. 13, No. 10, 13 December 1919, p. 282; Vol. 13, No. 11, 20 December 1919, pp. 360–61. Earlier sections of the story were plagiarized from 'Jabez Jones's Recollections of Continental Stamps and Stamp Countries', *Stamp-Collector's Magazine*, Vol. 2, 1 July 1864, pp. 97–9. Walter Nathan's story of fraud is related in 'Reminiscences of a Philatelist', *Stamp Collectors' Fortnightly*, Vol. 7, No. 158, 30 March 1901, p. 13; Vol. 7, No. 159, 13 April 1901, p. 22. 'Hypnotism and the Blue Mauritius' appeared in the *Philatelic Magazine*, April 1921.

On Hans Lagerloef and the Swedish Postal Museum's two 'Post Office', see James Burgeson, 'Colonel Hans Lagerloef to be Remembered at Postmuseum', *Posthorn*, Vol. 53, No. 3, August 1996, pp. 99–101; 'Collections', Swedish Postal Museum website, http://www.postmuseum.posten.se/museng/collections.html (accessed 14 March 2004). See also Erik Hamberg's *Storsamlaren Hans Lagerlöf*, Meddelanden Från Postmuseum Nr 40, Stockholm, 1996.

Both 'One of the most outstanding moments…' and 'he would almost certainly bring out…' are quoted in David Feldman's *Mauritius Classic Postage Stamps and Postal History*, 1993, p. 92. The Mohrmann advertisement appeared in *Collectors Club Philatelist*, Vol. 13, No. 4, October 1934, p. 240.

The 1947 Perth find is noted in *Stamp Collecting*, vol. 69, no. 15, 3 January 1948, p. 287, and Vol. 69, No. 17, 17 January 1948, p. 327.

L. N. and M. Williams referred to Cox's stamp as 'the unpopular black sheep' in a letter to the editor, 'Pedigree of Rare Stamps',

Collectors Club Philatelist, Vol. 19, No. 3, July 1940, p. 239. On the Royal Philatelic Society's expert committee, see *The Royal Philatelic Society London 1869–1969*, The Society, The University Press, Glasgow, 1969, p. 35, and various. Photographic records of the expert committee, held at the Royal Philatelic Society London, were consulted September 2003.

Charles J. Phillips reported Harmer's opinion on currency smuggling in 'The Pedigree of Rare Stamps', *Collectors Club Philatelist*, Vol. 18, No. 4, October 1939, p. 269, and Séfi's comment can be found in 'Market Notes', *Philatelic Journal of Great Britain*, Vol. 32, No. 380, 10 August 1922, p. 133.

CHAPTER 11: VERY MUCH IN LOVE WITH MAURITIUS STAMPS

On the 'Post Office' stamps stolen from the Reichspostmuseum, see Williams, *Encyclopaedia* (Vol. 2, 1997, p. 22); L. N. Williams, 'The Reichspostmuseum Rarities', *Stamp Collecting*, 24 November 1977, pp. 1,157, 1,159; exhibition brochure 'Sonderausstellung Mythos Mauritius', published by the Museumsstiftung Post und Telekommunikation, Bonn, undated; Dr Andreas Hahn, Museumsstiftung Post und Telekommunikation, Bonn, personal communication, 14 September 2004; David Binder, 'Rare Stamps from Nazi Hoard in Dispute', *The Times*, 12 November 1977, pp. 1, 4.

On rumoured finds in the 1950s, see 'Missing "Post Office" Mauritius', *Stamp Lover*, Vol. 47, Nos. 10–11, March–April 1955, p. 168; ' "Post Office" Mauritius', *Stamp Lover*, Vol. 49, Nos. 5–6, October–November 1956, p. 67.

The editorial in *Stanley Gibbons Monthly Journal*, Vol. 17, No. 202, 30 April 1907, p. 197, is the source of the quotation 'the discovery of fresh facts in the history...' 'On the Increase of the Timbromanie', *Stamp Collector's Magazine*, No. 11, 1 December 1863, p. 170, is the source of the quotation 'to reprint curious and obsolete stamps...'.

On philatelic forgery, and more on the Spiro and Senf brothers, and Moens and Gibbons as 'forgers', see Varro E. Tyler, *Philatelic Forgers: Their Lives and Works*, Robson Lowe, London, 1976, pp. 1-2, 11 (Elb and Moens), 17 (Gibbons), 30-31 (Moens), 43 (Senf), 45-6 (Spiro). George V's correspondence with his philatelic adviser is reproduced in Nicholas Courtney, *The Queen's Stamps: The Authorised History of the Royal Philatelic Collection*, Methuen, London, 2004, p. 88. For two examples of enhanced Mauritius covers bearing stamps of the Dardenne period (1859-60), see Dave Tarry, 'Mauritius: Beware Enhanced Classic Covers!', *London Philatelist*, Vol. 111, November 2002, pp. 326-31. For more on early 'Post Office' forgeries, see the Reverend R. B. Earée, *Album Weeds; or, How to Detect Forged Stamps*, third edition, Vol. 2, Stanley Gibbons Ltd, London, *c.* 1906, pp. 4-9.

The one penny forgeries on cover were reproduced in 'Bogus "Post Office" Mauritius: Condemned Stamps Still Being Offered', *Philatelic Magazine*, Vol. 35, No. 5, 8 March 1935. L. N. Williams pieced the history of 'Limbo I' together in the *Encyclopaedia*, through correspondence with Hiroyuki Kanai. There is also information in Kanai's *Classic Mauritius* (some of Kanai's information came from the German dealer Bartels).

In a bizarre twist to the illustrations seasoned with imagination scenario, Herpin's Sherwinized 'Post Office' was reproduced many years later in the Reverend R. B. Earée's *Album Weeds; or, How to Detect Forged Stamps* to illustrate a genuine example of a Sherwin 'Post Paid', with the caption 'Type of annexed illustration, but lettered PAID instead of OFFICE'!

Biographical detail on Louise Boyd Dale is from Bierman's *The World's Greatest Stamp Collectors* and 'Louise Boyd Dale', *Stamps*, 6 January 1968, pp. 27, 31.

The anecdote about the envelope addressed to 'M. Burrus, Philatelist, London' is given in Imre Vajda, 'Maurice Burrus: Tobacco King Turned Prince of Philatelists', *Stamps*, Vol. 103, No. 6, 1958, pp. 218–19.

On Kanai see his *Classic Mauritius*, 1981; David Feldman's *Mauritius Classic Postage Stamps and Postal History*, 1993; 'A Legend from Japan', *Stamp Magazine*, August 2001, pp. 52–3. Feldman is also the source of the quotation 'unquestionably the finer of the two recorded unused examples' (p. 29) and the source of the Gilbert anecdote (p. 30). 'The greatest number of "Post Office" stamps' is stated in *Classic Mauritius*, 1981 (p. 30) under the heading 'Owners of the unused 1d and 2d'.

Information on the Weill brothers' purchase of the Jerrom letter, and the source of the quotations from the interview, is from McCandlish Phillips, 'Two Penny Stamps Sold for $380,000', *New York Times*, 22 October 1968, pp. 1, 32.

Martina Eckart-Helm's *Die Blaue Mauritius* was published by Paul Franke Verlag, Berlin, 1939. I am grateful to Dr Andreas Hahn for bringing the film *Der Man, Der Sherlock Holmes War* (UFA, released 15 July 1937) to my attention. Google the phrases 'Blue Mauritius' and 'die blaue Mauritius' for up to date usage.

Details of the various 'Post Office' stories are Frank Richards, *Billy Bunter and the Blue Mauritius*, Charles Skilton, London, 1952; Vernon Warren, *The Blue Mauritius*, Thriller Book Club, Charing Cross Road, London, undated, first published 1954; Malcolm Field, 'The Red Mauritius', *Detective Tales*, Vol. 12, No. 1, February 1923 (this was a chance discovery through a listing of pulp fiction on the Internet; many thanks to Rob Preston in the USA for reading and providing précis of the very fragile copy in his collection); Howard Fast, *The Case of the One-Penny Orange* (writing under the pseudonym of E. V. Cunningham), first published in 1977 and republished in the omnibus Masuto Investigates, ibooks, New York, 2000.

Chapter 12: Million-dollar Questions

The papers of L. N. and M. Williams relating to their philatelic journalism are held in the Philatelic Collections, British Library. On the 'Post Office' designated 'Limbo 1' by Williams see the *Encyclopaedia*, Vol. 2, 1997, p. 135. Interviews relating to issues of forgery were held with John Rudge and David Beech, September 2003, and Vikram Chand, October 2003.

The German philatelic magazine *Briefmarken Mauritius* published an article casting aspersions on Tapling's two pence in 1971, noted in *Stamp Collecting*, 26 August 1971, p. 1,143.

The curious plate-related piece is reproduced in David Feldman's *Mauritius Classic Postage Stamps and Postal History*, catalogue lot 3. On Perron, see the photographic records of the expert committee, held at the Royal Philatelic Society London. Consulted September 2003.

Patrick Pearson's comments on provenance appeared in a note accompanying Dave Tarry's article 'Mauritius: Beware Enhanced Classic Covers!', *London Philatelist*, Vol. 111, November 2002, p. 331. Ernst M. Cohn is the expert on philatelic forgeries who cast doubt on Berlin's Bordeaux letter in 'Perspectives on Expertisers', *Fakes Forgeries Experts*, No. 6, May 2003, pp. 42–50; see also Peter Ibbotson, 'Arising from those Bordeaux Letters', *Gibbons Stamp Monthly*, June 1994, pp. 29–31. The Bordeaux letter was, naturally, described as 'truly the megastar in the philatelic firmament' in

Feldman's *Mauritius Classic Postage Stamps and Postal History*, 1993, p. 92.

Denis Vandervelde's anecdote about the Spanish franking is given in his interesting lecture 'Postal History or Postal Archaeology? Researching the Obscure', Seventh Stuart Rossiter Memorial Lecture, 2001, http://www.rossitertrust.com/rossiter_lecture_2002.html (accessed 18 April 2003).

The Reverend C. S. Morton turned up the 1861 letter from the Colonial Postmaster of Mauritius to Her Majesty's Stationery Office, speaking of his concern over the inks in use, cited in 'The Early Post Towns and Postmarks of Mauritius', *London Philatelist*, Vol. 34, No. 405, September 1925, p. 257.

Details of the scientific tests on the Tapling 'Post Office' are given in T. D. Chaplin, A. Jurado-López, R. J. H. Clark and D. R. Beech, 'Identification by Raman Microscopy of Pigments on Early Postage Stamps: Distinction between Original 1847 and 1858–1862, Forged and Reproduction Postage Stamps of Mauritius', *Journal of Raman Spectroscopy*, Vol. 35, 2004, pp. 600–604.

Kanai gave his reason for parting with the stamps ('only to satisfy the collectors who are dreaming…') in 'A Legend from Japan', *Stamp Magazine*, August 2001, p. 52. Alain Huron, of the Blue Penny Museum in Mauritius, kindly supplied me with copies of numerous news clippings from the world press about the 1993 sale of Kanai's 'Post Office', including 'Mystery Woman buys "Crown Jewel of Philately" ', *L'Express*, 5 November 1993, p. 15. Information on the Netherlands PTT Museum's purchase I took from the exhibition handout, undated, Netherlands PTT Museum, courtesy David Beech.

On the German Federal Republic Printing Office reprints, see the advertisement in *Stamp Magazine*, July 1997; copies are held by the expert committee, Royal Philatelic Society London. The statement about the 'Post Office' stamps being the Swedish Postal Museum's 'greatest treasure' is given on their website under 'Collections', http://www.postmuseum.posten.se/museng/collectio ns.html (accessed 14 March 2004).

Vikram Chand spoke with me in Singapore late in 2003. Gossip about the fourth ball envelope came to my ears at a meeting of the Royal Philatelic Society London in 2003, and is as likely to be a dealer's fantasy or wish to puff up his consequence... or not.

POSTSCRIPT

Sulieman Issany, owner of the Blue Penny shop in Quay Street, Port Louis, told me its history. Sir Anerood Jugnauth's speech was reported on the Mauritius Government Prime Minister's website, 'Prime Minister Inaugurates Blue Penny Museum', 23 November 2001, http://ncb.intnet.mu/primeminister/news1/news83.htm (accessed 2 April 2002). And it would have been so much more poetic if the Blue Penny Museum's two 'Post Office' stamps had remained unlabelled!

Time, opportunity, distance and funds meant that there were several leads I did not fully exhaust in my search for more information about Lady Gomm's ball and those who attended it. An irrefutable concrete connection between the stamps and the ball was the treasure, more than anything which I sought (apart, obviously, from an undocumented specimen of a 'Post Office' stamp).

BIBLIOGRAPHY

Adolphe, Harold, and d'Unienville, Raymond, 'The Life and Death of Joseph Osmond Barnard, Stowaway, Engraver, Stevedore and Planter', *London Philatelist*, Vol. 33, No. 985, December 1974, pp. 263–6

Anderson, Clare, *Convicts in the Indian Ocean: Transportation from South Asia to Mauritius*, 1815–53, Macmillan, London, 2000

Anderson, John, *Descriptive Account of Mauritius, Its Scenery, Statistics, &c with Brief Historical Sketch. Preceded by Elements of Geography [The Latter Designed for Youth]*, L. A. Denny, Theatre Place, Mauritius, 1858

Anonymous, 'Des Timbres de Maurice', *Le Timbre-Poste*, No. 29, May 1865, pp. 34–9

Anonymous, 'Les Timbres "Post-Office" de Maurice', *Le Timbre-Poste*, No. 35, November 1865, pp. 87–8

Bachelier, L., *Histoire du Commerce de Bordeaux depuis les Temps Plus Reculés jusqu'a nos Jours*, P. Chaumas, Bordeaux, second edition, 1863

Backhouse, James, *A Narrative of a Visit to the Mauritius and South Africa*, Hamilton, Adams & Co., London, 1844

Bartram, Alfred, Mrs, *Recollections of Seven Years Residence at the Mauritius or Isle of France*, James Cawthorn, London, 1830

Beaton, Patrick, *Creoles and Coolies; or, Five Years in Mauritius*, James Nisbet & Co., London, 1859

Bierman, Stanley M., *The World's Greatest Stamp Collectors*, Frederick Fell Publishers, New York, *c.* 1980

Bolton's Mauritius Almanac and Official Directory, 1854, 1858

Booty, Frederick, *The Stamp Collectors Guide: Being a List of English and Foreign Postage Stamps with 200 Fac-simile Drawings*, H. & C. Treacher, Brighton, 1862

Boyle, Charles John, *Far Away, or, Sketches of Scenery and Society in Mauritius*, Chapman and Hall, London, 1867

Brühl, Carlrichard, *Geschichte der Philatelie*, Georg Olms Verlag, Hildesheim, 1985

Brunel, Georges, *Ce Qu'était la Philatélie en 1867*, Yvert & Cie, Amiens, 1930

– *Les Timbres-Poste de l'Île Maurice: Émissions de 1847 à 1898*, Éditions Philatelia, Paris, 1928

Butler, A. Ronald, *The History of the Roll of Distinguised Philatelists*, British Philatelic Federation, London, 1990

Carr-Gomm, Francis Culling, ed., *Letters and Journals of Field-Marshal Sir William Maynard Gomm, G.C.B. Commander-in-Chief of India, Constable of the Tower of London &c. &c. From 1799 to Waterloo, 1815*, John Murray, London, 1881

Carter, Marina, *Servants, Sirdars and Settlers: Indians in Mauritius, 1834–1874*, Oxford University Press, Delhi, 1995

Chalmers, P. R., 'A Lay of the Blue Mauritius', *Stamp Collecting*, Vol. 18, No. 4, 29 April 1922, p. 89

Charles, Albert, *La Révolution de 1848 et la Seconde République: A Bordeaux et dans le Département de la Gironde*, Éditions Delmas, Bordeaux, 1945

Courtney, Nicholas, *The Queen's Stamps: The Authorised History of the Royal Philatelic Collection*, Methuen, London, 2004

Creeke, A. B. Jun., *Stamp Collecting: A Guide for Beginners*, Thomas Nelson and Sons, London, *c.* 1913–14 de Pitray, Alfred S., *The Post Office Mauritius and its Legend*, Editions de l'Océan Indien, Mauritius, completed 1975, published 1990

de Raay, Leon, 'The Stolen "Mauritius": A True Story', *Stamp Collecting*, Vol. 13, No. 10, 13 December 1919, p. 282; Vol. 13, No. 11, 20 December 1919, pp. 360–61

Dictionary of Mauritian Biography (Dictionnaire de Biographie Mauricienne), Societe de l'Histoire de l'Île Maurice, Port Louis, Mauritius, 1941–81

Duveen, J. H., *The Rise of the House of Duveen*, Longmans, Green and Co., London, 1957

Earée, Rev. R. B., *Album Weeds; or, How to Detect Forged Stamps*, third edition, Vol. 2, Stanley Gibbons Ltd, London, *c.* 1906

Eckart-Helm, Martina, *Die Blaue Mauritius*, Paul Franke Verlag, Berlin, 1939

Evans, E. B., 'The Stamps of Mauritius', *Philatelic Record*, Vol. 2, No. 13, February 1880, pp. 6–8; Vol. 2, No. 14, March 1880, pp. 17–20; Vol. 2, No. 16, May 1880, pp. 48–52

Ewart, John Alexander, *The Story of a Soldier's Life; or Peace, War, and Mutiny*, Sampson Low, Marston, Searle, & Rivington, London, Vol. 1, 1881

Fast, Howard, *The Case of the One-Penny Orange* (written under the pseudonym E. V. Cunningham), first published in 1977 and republished in the omnibus *Masuto Investigates*, ibooks, New York, 2000

Fenton, Elizabeth, *The Journal of Mrs. Fenton; A Narrative of Her Life in India, The Isle of France (Mauritius), and Tasmania During the Years 1826–1830*, Edward Arnold, London, 1901

Field, Malcolm, 'The Red Mauritius', *Detective Tales*, Vol. 12, No. 1, February 1923

Gradis, Henry, *Histoire de Bordeaux*, Calmann Lévy, Paris, 1888

Harrison, Michael, *Post Office Mauritius 1847: The Tale of Two*

Stamps, Stamp Collecting Ltd, London, *c.* 1947

Herpin, G., 'Des Timbres de l'Île Maurice', *Le Collectionneur de Timbres-Poste*, No. 9, 15 March 1865, pp. 50–55

Higounet, Charles, ed., *Histoire de Bordeaux*, Univers de la France et des Pays Francophones, Toulouse, 1980

Ibbotson, Peter, *Mauritius Postal History and Stamps*, Royal Philatelic Society London, London, 1991

Johnson, Stanley C., *The Stamp Collector: A Guide to the World's Postage Stamps*, Herbert Jenkins, London, 1920

Kanai, Hiroyuki, *Classic Mauritius: The Locally Printed Postage Stamps 1847–59*, Gibbons, London, 1981

Keepsake Mauricien: Mauritius Keepsake, Port Louis, Mauritius, 1839

Lallier, Justin, *Postage-Stamp Album Illustrated with Maps*, A. Lenègre, Paris, 1862

Late official resident, *An Account of the Island of Mauritius and its Dependencies*, the author, 1842

Leblanc, Marie, *Sir C. Antelme, K.C.M.G. Chevalier de la Légion d'Honneur*, Imprimerié Roussel & Cie, Mauritius, 1899

Legrand, J. A. (Dr Magnus), 'Timbres de Maurice', *Le Timbre-Poste*, January 1869, pp. 5–8; 'Les Timbres Post Office de Maurice', *Le Timbre-Poste*, No. 85, January 1870, pp. 5–8

Lumgair, G., 'Mauritius Memories', *Stamp Lover*, Vol. 1, No. 10, March 1909, pp. 253–5

Ly-Tio-Fane Pineo, Huguette, *In the Grips of the Eagle: Matthew Flinders at Ile de France 1803–1810*, Mahatma Gandhi Institute, Moka, Mauritius, 1988

Macmillan, Allister, *Mauritius Illustrated*, W. H. & L. Collingridge, London, 1914

Magon de Saint-Elier, Ferdinand, *Tableaux Historiques, Politiques & Pittoresques de l'Île de France, Aujourd'hui Maurice, depuis sa Découverte jusqu'a nos Jours*, Port Louis, 1839

Mahé, Pierre, *Les Marchands de Timbres-Poste d'autrefois et leurs Catalogues*, Yvert et Tellier, Amiens, 1908

Malim, Michael, *Island of the Swan: Mauritius*, Longmans, Green and Co., London, 1952

Matou, *Guêpes Mauriciennes*, Henri Plon, Paris, 1861

Mauritius Civil Service Almanacs, 1867–78

Mauritius Colonial Blue Books, 1840, 1847, 1848, 1853

Mauritius *Classic Postage Stamps and Postal History, Including the Entire Collection Formed by Hiroyuki Kanai, R.D.P., F.R.P.S.L,* 3 November 1993, David Feldman SA, Geneva, 1993

Melville, Fred, *Chats on Postage Stamps*, T. Fisher Unwin, London, 1911

– *The Complete Philatelist*, Philatelic Institute, London, 1924

– *New A.B.C. of Stamp Collecting*, Melville Book Company, London, 1922

Moens, Jean-Baptiste, 'Encore les Post-Office de Maurice', *Le Timbre-Poste*, No. 438, June 1899, pp. 87–93; 'Encore les Post-Office de Maurice', *Le Timbre-Poste*, No. 441, September 1899, pp. 141–2

Morton, Cyril Shadforth, 'A Study of the Early Postal Issues of Mauritius', *London Philatelist*, Vol. 33, 1924, pp. 219–23, 238–44, 264–8; 'The Post Office at the Mauritius', *Stamp Collectors' Fortnightly*, No. 779, 17 January 1925, p. 37; No. 780, 31 January 1925, pp. 46–7; No. 781, 14 February 1925, pp. 66–7; No. 784, 28 March 1925, pp. 113–14; No. 785, 11 April 1925, pp. 136–7; No. 786, 25 April 1925, pp. 149–51; No. 787, 9 May 1925, p. 168; 'The Early Post Towns and Postmarks of Mauritius', *London Philatelist*, Vol. 34, 1925, pp. 256–63

Mosely, Edward, 'Combing an Island for Postal Treasures', *Stamp Collecting*, Vol. 40, No. 16, 15 July 1933, pp. 410, 413–15

Mouat, Frederic J., *Rough Notes of a Trip to Reunion, the Mauritius, and Ceylon: with Remarks on their Eligibility as Sanitaria for Indian Invalids*, 1852, reprinted Asian Educational Services, New Delhi, 1997

Perrein, Paul, *Images d'Autrefois de Bordeaux et de la Gironde*, Pierre Fanlac, Périgueux, 1984

Pfeiffer, Ida, *The Last Travels of Ida Pfeiffer: Inclusive of a Visit to Madagascar, with a Biographical Memoir of the Author*, Harper and Brothers, New York, 1861

Pike, Nicolas, *Sub-Tropical Rambles in the Land of Aphanapteryx: Personal Experiences, Adventures, & Wanderings in and around the Island of Mauritius*, Sampson Low, Marston, Low & Searle, London, 1873

Pope, Elizabeth C., ed., *Opinions: Philatelic Expertising – An Inside View*, Philatelic Foundation, New York, 1983

Pridham, Charles, *An Historical, Political and Statistical Account of Mauritius and its Dependencies*, T. and W. Boone, London, 1849

Proud, Edward B., *The Postal History of Mauritius*, Proud-Bailey Co. Ltd, East Sussex, 2001

Rabier, Pascal, 'Regard sur la Presse Philatélique Française, T.II Les Publications Commerciales depuis 1864', Paris, 1986

Rèche, Albert, Dix *Siècles de Vie Quotidienne à Bordeaux*, Seghers, Paris, 1983

Richards, Frank, *Billy Bunter and the Blue Mauritius*, Charles Skilton, London, 1952

Robie, Lewis, *Stamp Hunting*, Donohue, Henneberry & Co., Chicago, 1898

Rothschild, Henri de, *Les Timbres-Poste et Leurs Amis*, Théodore Champion, Paris, 1938

The Royal Philatelic Society London 1869–1969, The Society, The University Press, Glasgow, 1969

Smyth, J. H., *Philately in a Nutshell*, J. H. Smyth, Sydney, 1911

Stirling, E., *Cursory Notes on the Isle of France Made in 1827: With a Map of the Island*, Baptist Mission Press, Calcutta, 1833

Strachan, James, *The Recovery and Re-manufacture of Waste-paper*, Albany Press, Aberdeen, 1918

The Stamp Collectors' Annual, C. Nissen & Co., London, 1904

Todd, T., *Stamps of the Empire*, Thomas Nelson & Sons Ltd, London, 1938

Toussaint, Auguste and Adolphe, Harold, *Bibliography of Mauritius (1502–1954), Covering the Printed Record, Manuscripts, Archivalia and Cartographic Material*, Port Louis, Mauritius, 1956

Tyler, Varro E., *Philatelic Forgers: Their Lives and Works*, Robson Lowe, London, 1976

Warren, Vernon, *The Blue Mauritius*, Thriller Book Club, Charing Cross Road, London, undated, first published 1954

Who's Who in Philately, London, 1914, 1928

Williams, L. N., *Encyclopaedia of Rare and Famous Stamps*, David Feldman, Geneva, Vol. 1, 1993, Vol. 2, 1997

– *Fundamentals of Philately*, American Philatelic Society, State College, Pennsylvania, revised edition, 1990

Williams, L. N. and M., *Famous Stamps*, W. & R. Chambers, Edinburgh, revised edition, 1946

– *The Postage Stamp: Its History and Recognition*, Penguin, Harmondsworth, 1956

JOURNALS AND NEWSPAPERS

See Notes and Sources for detailed citations.

Australian Stamp Journal, Balasse Magazine, British Guiana Philatelic Journal, Le Cernéen, Le Collectionneur de Timbres-Poste, Collectors Club Philatelist, L'Echo de la Timbrologie, L'Express, London Philatelist, Le Mauricien, Mauritius Times, Mémorial Bordelais, Mercantile Record and

Commercial Gazette, New York Times, Philatelic Journal of Great Britain, Philatelic Magazine, Philatelic Record, Philatelist, Le Philatéliste Francais, Stamp Collecting, Stamp Collectors' Fortnightly, Stamp-Collector's Magazine, Stamp Lover, Stamp Magazine, Stamps, Stanley Gibbons Monthly Journal, Le Timbre-Poste, The Times, West-End Philatelist.

Unpublished Material

Expert committee, photographic records, Royal Philatelic Society London

Mauritius Archives series: RA534, RA909, RA1800, RA2368

L. N. and M. Williams, papers, Philatelic Collections, British Library, London

ACKNOWLEDGEMENTS

Many people helped me with this book. I am indebted to David Beech at the British Library for sage counsel and trusting in my abilities. I gratefully acknowledge the support of Vikram Chand and the Chand A and Z Research Fund for Classic Philately, administered by the British Library, which supported my travel to London, France and Singapore in 2003. Melbourne philatelist and Mauritius collector John Shawley was generous with his time, his resources and thoughts on both Mauritius philately and philately in general. (He appears in these pages as the anonymous philatelist.) In Mauritius, Mico Antoine has been most helpful and encouraging and I have enjoyed our correspondence. I look forward to attending future meetings of the Mauritius Philatelic Society and joining members on one of their famed philatelic walks!

For faith in me and the book I will always be grateful to my agent, David Miller, of Rogers, Coleridge & White in London, and to Jane Bradish-Ellames. For generous and insightful advice on earlier drafts of the manuscript I thank Jill Koolmees and Dana Rowan – it has been a pleasure to share this story with them. Long ago it seems now, but also well timed, were the teaching and encouragement of Di Websdale-Morrissey at RMIT, Melbourne.

I wish to thank staff at the Archives Municipales de Bordeaux, the Bibliothèque Municipale de Bordeaux, the Mauritius Archives and National Library of Mauritius, and also members of the Royal Philatelic Societies of London and Victoria. Richard Breckon in

Melbourne and other members have been most supportive of the non-philatelist in their midst. Alain Huron at the Blue Penny Museum in Mauritius supplied copies of much material from the museum's publicity files on the stamps and took us to visit Barnard's grave.

Thanks for many things, including research assistance, answering persistent queries, photocopying, keeping an eye out for references to the stamps, a spot of translation, inspiration, sharing resources and general cheering from the sidelines go to Annette Alafaci, Bernard Behr, Pascal Behr, Richard Borek, Anne Brownrigg, Henry Brownrigg, J. F. Brun, Richard Carr-Gomm, Tony Carr-Gomm, Else Delaunay, Dr Veit Didczuneit (Museum für Kommunikation, Berlin), Monique Erkelens (Museum voor Communicatie, The Hague), Laure Fabre-Rousseau, Pascal Rabier and Patrick Thielleux (all Musée de la Poste, Paris), Jane Farago, David Feldman, Keith Fitton, Rosemary Francis, Brian Fuller, Colin Gale, Dr Andreas Hahn (Museumsstiftung Post und Telekommunikation, Bonn), Erik Hamberg (Postmuseum, Sweden), Wilson Hulme, the late Peter Ibbotson, Christopher Kelly, Patrick Kwan Cheung (Mauritius Philatelic Society – particular thanks for the gift of early society newsletters and de Pitray's book), Josh Lefers, Philip and Rachel Lindley, Pauline McGregor-Currien, David Martial, Ron Negus, Elizabeth O'Callaghan, Jason Phillips, Rob Preston, George Pursad, John Ray, Peter J. Roberts, Rosalind Robson, John Rudge, Marie-Laurence Sanfourche, Professor Hermann Schnabel, Michael Sefi, John Shaw, Ailie Smith, Emma Tinning, Rachel Tropea, Gary Watson, Elizabeth White and John Yeomans. Gavin Jones and Angela Savage have both been marvellous. My friends and colleagues at the University of Melbourne, especially Joanne Evans and Gavan McCarthy, were always encouraging and gave me time off work when I needed it.

Acknowledgements

Thanks to Toby Mundy and Clara Farmer at Atlantic Books. Clara was a wonderful editor. I enjoyed the process and learned much. Also to Lesley Levene, my copy-editor.

Finally, thanks to my family, the Morgans and Russos, who put up with a lot. To Anita Kinnoo for many divine Mauritian meals, and to my husband, Mike Pursad. Had I not met Mike, I would never have come to know and love Mauritius and I would not have written this book. For his support and encouragement, I thank him, and for willingly spending time on my behalf at the archives and library in Port Louis when he could have been at the beach.

Mauritius Philatelic Society

*The rendez-vous was fixed for 10.00am at
Manhattan (which is a stone's throw from the Town
Hall in Curepipe), but the group of eleven persons
(sixteen had subscribed) left for Mahébourg's Musée
National d'Histoire de Maurice at 10.30am in four
vehicles. One member was late; he is always late.*

Mauritius Philatelic Society News Bulletin,
No. 18, April 2001

The current incarnation of the Mauritius Philatelic Society was set up in 1989 for stamp collectors and philatelists who share an interest in Mauritius and the Indian Ocean region, to meet and exchange stamps, ideas and information. Members meet at the Collège du St Esprit in Quatre Bornes, Mauritius, on the first Saturday of the month. There is usually a stamp display and members exhibit and talk about their stamps.

I thoroughly enjoyed the two meetings of the society that I attended in 2003, roped in on the spot as I was to talk about my research, and I continue to enjoy reading their *News Items*, sent quarterly by society stalwart Mico Antoine. In much the same spirit as *Le Mauricien* in 1847, there is a delight in pointing out the occasional deficiencies of the postal authorities within these pages, and the sometimes acerbic reporting makes for good and informative reading.

I have not yet attended one of the society's outings, always philatelic in spirit, following themes and places that have appeared on Mauritius's stamps, but I hope one day to have that pleasure.

The Society may be contacted at:
Mauritius Philatelic Society
PO Box 89
Quatre Bornes
Mauritius

INDEX

Aberdeen, 127–8

Adam, Charles Félix Henry, 96–7, 112–14
  ball envelope, 97–9, 106–8, 117, 152, 171, 189, 203, 210
  ball envelope last on market, 215–16, 223

Adam, Henri, Junior, 77

Adam, Joachim Henri, 96–7

Ahmed Fuad of Egypt, King, 130

Albers, Hans, 190

Alexander of Yugoslavia, King, 130

Alfonso of Spain, King, 130

Allen, Tom, 171, 174

Altham, Emanuell, 17

Amagasaki, 186

Amsterdam, 16, 164

Antelme, Célicourt, 11–12

Appavou, Moutoussamy, 58–60, 69, 126

Argentina, stamps, 158

Armstrong, Douglas, 154

Arnold, Philipp, *see* Ferrary, Philipp von

Australia, 21, 87, 178, 185

Australian stamps, 67
  'kangaroos', 185
  'Sydney Views', 37

Avery, William, 137, 173, 187–8

Bacon, Edward, 113

Baltimore, 101

Banks, Rev. Langrishe, 89–90, 153

Barclay, Monsieur, 12

Barnard, Joseph Osmond, 57, 143, 173, 199
  engraves 'Post Office' stamps, 3, 27–9, 35, 38
  eyesight, 61–2
  production estimate, 60–1

Basle, 30

Bayeroux, François, 143

Beaupré, Alfred, 144

Beech, David, 212

Behr, Bernard, 216

Belgium, 130
  stamps, 44

Bell Telephone, 119

Berlin, 121, 158, 177
 International Stamp
  Exhibition, 145, 204
 missing 'Post Office' stamps,
  177, 191–2
 Museum für Post und
  Kommunikation, 192, 203,
  207–9, 211
 Reichspostmuseum, 5, 118–21,
  126, 129, 141, 164, 170, 177,
  191, 208

Berlingin, René, 184, 202

Bernichon, Jules, 106

Bilbao, 210

*Billy Bunter and the Blue
 Mauritius* (Frank Richards),
  192–4, 196

Bishop, Percy, 148–9

Black River, 25

Blanchard, Colonel, 14

Blondel, Monsieur, 152

Bloss, Bill, 122

Blue Mauritius, The (Vernon
 Warren), 194–6

'Blue Mauritius' tea, 222–3

Bombay, 87–90, 107, 157, 188

Bonar, James, 122–31, 138, 174,
  181, 183
 and genuineness of 'Post
  Office' stamp, 197, 205, 212

price attained for 'Post
  Office' stamp, 129, 131, 136,
  147, 149, 197

Bond, Rev. H. C., 65

Bonn, 192

Booty, Frederick, 33–4, 38, 46,
  65

Borchard, Adolphe, 45, 48–9,
  109, 207, 223

Borchard, Madame, 44–6,
  48–53, 81, 116, 223
 ex-Borchard 'Post Office'
  stamps, 68, 84, 87, 99, 126,
  128, 137, 163–4
 'Post Office' stamps, 44–52,
  65–6, 114, 120, 125, 161, 170,
  173, 175, 186, 188
 provenance and genuineness
  of 'Post Office' stamps, 207,
  209, 211, 213

Bordeaux, 6, 41–54, 66, 73, 120,
  125, 173, 212, 219, 223
 Annuaire, 45, 51, 53, 114–15
 Borchard firm, 47, 54, 84, 90,
  114, 148, 152
 Ducau and Lurguie firm,
  108–11, 114–16, 152, 191, 209
 postal system, 42
 Quai des Chartrons, 41–2, 44,
  109, 114–16
 stamp collecting, 44–6, 52–3

stamp issues, 185
trade with Mauritius, 47-8,
    54, 87, 207
wine trade, 42, 108, 110,
    114-15, 209
Bordeaux letters, 126, 129, 136,
    162-3, 172-3, 186, 189
    discovery, 107-21
    last on market, 214, 223
    suspected forgeries, 203, 205,
        207-9
'Boscawen' stamp, 170
Boulogne-sur-Mer, 110-11, 208
Boy's Own Magazine, 122-3
Boyle, Sir Cavendish, 140
Bradford, 159
Bratt (American tourist), 150
Brazil, stamps, 30, 42
Breitfuss, Frederick, 137
Britain, 6, 21, 72
    philatelic press, 179
    trade with Mauritius, 125
    uniform postal rate, 65
    see also England
British and Foreign Bible
    Society, 89, 153
British Commonwealth, stamps,
    187
British Guiana, stamps, 67, 76,
    121, 147, 150, 177, 191
    1¢, 101, 154, 161-2

British Library, 61, 202, 212,
    215-16, 218
    Tapling Collection, 76, 156,
        203, 207, 213
British Museum, 61, 65, 76, 145,
    164, 173
British North America, stamps,
    158
British stamps, 42, 67, 79, 153
    Penny Black, 28, 30, 53, 217
Brooklyn, 158
Brownrigg, James Stuart, 18, 20,
    23, 57, 89
    irregularities and
        resignation, 26, 58
    letter to Colonial Secretary,
        61-2, 137
    support for, 125
Brunel, Georges, 111-12, 154
Brussels, 36-7, 43, 50, 67, 164
Burrage, A. M., 135-6
Burrus, Maurice, 104, 157,
    159-64, 172-3
    collection sold, 185-6, 189
    tally of 'Post Office' stamps,
        185, 187, 189
Byron, Lord, 14

Caillebote, Monsieur, 74
Calais, 110
Calcutta, 218

Calebasses, 92

Canada, stamps, 153

Canberra, 223

Cape of Good Hope, 16, 21
  stamps, 133–4, 158

Carlist Wars, 210

Carmenteuil, Monsieur, 164

Carol of Romania, King, 171, 184

Case of the One-Penny Orange, The, 198–200

Caunten fragment, 77, 81, 157, 188–9, 214

'Cerne', 93–5

Chalmers, P. R., 134

Chambers, Captain R. S., 126–8

Champion, Théodore, 158–9, 163–4, 171, 198, 215

Chand, Vikram, 217–18

Charade, 41

Charlotte of Monaco, Princess, 130

China, 10

Cole, Governor, 22

Colnaghi, Colonel Dominic Henry, 140–2, 203–5

Colnaghi's (art dealers), 203

Colombo, 173

convicts, 18

Coutures, Albert, 44–5, 52, 66, 84

Cox, Mr, 164, 175–6

Crawford, Earl of, 140–1

Crawford, J., 5, 129–30

Creoles, 10

Crippa, A., 31

Curepipe, 24

Daily Mail, 123, 150

Dale, Louise Boyd, 185, 188
  Dale-Lichtenstein collection, 188, 204

Dardenne, Louis, 175

Darwin, Charles, 9

de l'Argentière, Brunet, 118, 162

de Pitray, Alfred, 29

de Raay, Leon, 164–7

de Robillard, Edouard, 143

de Robillard, Madame, 12

de Silva, Ernest, 173, 185, 187

Delmestre, Monsieur, 54

D'Epinay, Madame, 12

Depression era, 171, 173

Der Man, Der Sherlock Holmes War, 190

Desbois, Madame, 46–7, 49–53, 72, 81, 84, 116, 205
  'Post Office' stamps, 46, 52–3, 62, 66, 68–9, 82, 170, 188

Detective Tales, 197–8

Dick, Madame, 12

Die Blaue Mauritius, 190, 192

dodos, 4, 8, 17

Dublin, 42

Dupré, 144

Durant St André, Monsieur, 12

Duveen, Henry, 86, 137, 140,
147, 173, 180, 187–8

death, 162

prices paid, 98–9, 128

Duvivier, Aimé, 92–3, 95

Duvivier, Edmond, 92, 96

Duvivier, Émile, 92

Duvivier, Madame, 92, 95, 114,
116, 152

ball envelope, 92–3, 95–8,
107, 117, 131, 210

Edinburgh, 122, 126–7

Edward VII, King, 129

Egypt, 218

Eisleben, 177, 191

Elena of Italy, Queen, 130

England, 87, 110–11, 120, 131, 175,
183

stamp collecting, 43, 74

English language, 11

Evans, Major Edward
Benjamin, 74, 94, 106, 146,
149, 165, 178

articles published, 55–6

collection sold, 75

in Mauritius, 55–7, 60–3, 103,
149, 151

and 'Post Office' plate, 137,
141–2, 144

'Post Office' stamps, 63, 68–9,
75, 84, 93, 151

Evening News, 155

Evening Standard, 90, 100

Ewart, Sir John, 13–15, 56

Fast, Howard, 198–9

Fédération Internationale de
Philatélie, 205

Feldman, David, 214

Fenton, Mrs, 9

Ferrary, Philipp von, 69–83, 101,
104, 168, 181

buys Rothschild collection, 81

death and fate of his
collection, 82–3, 154

'Post Office' stamps, 69, 73,
81, 147, 157, 161, 163, 170,
189

sales, 155–64, 171, 186, 198

Field, David, 138, 140–1, 144, 204

Field, Malcolm, 198

Figaro, 85

First World War, 82, 145, 154,
204

Folkestone, 174

*Forged Stamps: How to Detect
Them*, 178–9

Fouqueraux, Monsieur, 14

France, 38, 41, 71, 94, 96, 116, 152, 172, 183, 208
    anonymous 'Post Office' stamp find, 153–4
    and Ferrary collection, 154, 156–7
    postal system, 51
    rumoured 'Post Office' stamp, 219
    South of France, 68
    stamp collecting, 43
    stamps, 44–5
    trade with Mauritius, 47–8
Franco-Prussian War, 67
Franklin, J., 149
Franz-Joseph, Emperor, 79
Fraser, Monsieur, 12
French East India Company, 8
French language, 8–9, 11–12
French Revolution, 79

Galliera, Duke and Duchess of, 70–1, 79
Garonne, River, 41
Geneva, 30
Genoa, 70, 79
George V, King (Prince of Wales), 80, 136, 151, 157, 163
    acquires 'Post Office' stamps, 5–6, 129–31, 147, 197, 212

and genuineness of stamps, 180–1
    'Notes on the Postal Issues of the United Kingdom', 130
    and Mauritius stamp plates, 140–1
George VI, King, 175
Germany, 4, 70, 82–3, 145, 154, 172, 176
    and 'Post Office' stamps, 119–21, 131, 190–2
Gilbert (stamp collector), 187
Gilbert & Sullivan, 201
Giroux, Hector, 103
Glasgow, 122–3, 125
Gomm, Lady Elizabeth, 7–8, 11, 140, 221
    arrival in Mauritius, 7–8
    ball invitations, 1–3, 15, 29, 93–6, 106–8, 110, 112, 148, 171, 208, 219
    fancy-dress ball, 1–3, 13–15, 20, 48, 61
Gomm, Sir William, 7–8, 10–11, 13, 93, 95, 140
    and postal service, 25–6
Grain d'Or, 18, 59
Grand Port, 8, 25
Gray, Dr, 65
Great Thoughts, 134
Greece, stamps, 82, 186

Greibert, Hugo, 129, 161–2

Guadeloupe, 42

Gustavus Adolphus of Sweden, Crown Prince, 130

Hamburg, 179

Hammarskjöld, Dag, 102

Hampstead, 122

Hanciau, Louis, 36–8

Harmer, H. R., 145, 176, 204

Harmers, 153, 172, 187

Hawaii, stamps, 67, 76, 121, 177, 191

'Missionaries', 103, 147, 154

Haydock, R., 175

Hennecke, Herr, 120–1, 208

Herpin, George, 32, 35–6, 38, 40, 72, 182

Hill, Sir Rowland, 65

Hind, Arthur, 136, 157, 159–64, 180, 184, 187, 198, 217

death and will, 171, 174

sales, 171–4, 188

Hiroyasu of Japan, Prince, 130

Howard, Charles, 87–8, 90–1

Humbert of Piedmont, Prince, 130

hypnotism, 168–9

Ibbotson, Peter, 111, 140, 208

Île aux Tonneliers, 16

Île Bourbon (Réunion), 42

Image, W. E., 75

India, 6, 90–1, 152, 172

immigrant labour from, 10, 218

stamps, 50, 101

trade with Mauritius, 21, 48, 87

Indian Ocean, 8, 190, 215, 219

Indians, 10, 18

Ireland, 87

Italy, 38, 70–1, 172

Jamaica, 8

Japan, 186, 217

stamps, 187

Jerrom letter, 98, 107, 136, 153, 157, 163, 188–9

discovery, 88–91

returns to market, 216

Johnstone, C. E., 132

Jones, Jabez, 167

Jugnauth, Sir Anerood, 224

K, Monsieur, 151

Kanai, Hiroyuki, 186–90, 204, 209, 217–18

collection sold, 214–15, 223

visits Mauritius, 223

Kintore, Earl of, 98, 131

Kosack, Philipp, 119, 121, 129, 137

la Rénotière von Kriegsfeld,
  Emmanuel, 70
Lagerloef, Hans, 164, 170
Lalanne, Émile, 173
  'Post Office' stamps, 66–7, 69,
    73, 85, 158, 188, 211
  collection sold, 81–2
Lallier, Justin, 46, 178
Lamartine, Alphonse Marie
  Louis de, 48
Lataudrie, Piet, 81, 85, 188
Lausanne, 159, 185
Le Cernéen, 7–8, 11, 13, 24–6, 93
Le Havre, 165
Le Mauricien, 11–12, 24, 26
Le Pouce, 7, 221
Lea, W. E., 184, 187
Legrand, Jacques Amable, 36–7,
    72, 94, 165
  collection sold, 81–2
  'Post Office' stamps, 67–8, 81,
    87, 99, 105, 116, 119, 211
  and 'Post Paid' stamps, 39
Leipzig, 179
Lemaire, Théophile, 105, 158
  and 'Post Office' stamps,
    97–8, 105–6, 112–14, 116,
    118, 129, 153, 162, 164, 203
  dealings with Reichspost-
    museum, 119–21, 126
  and suspected forgeries,
    207–8
Leroux, Gaston, 103
letters in bottles, 16
Lewes and Pemberton, 122
Lichtenstein, Alfred, 157–60,
    162–4, 185, 217–18
'Limbo I', 184, 197, 201–3, 205
Lionnet, Monsieur, 53
Livermore, W. Bernard, 105
Lloyd, Madame, 12
Lloyd's Magazine, 135
Loder, Sydney, 138, 144–5
Lowe, Robson, 191
London, 4, 25, 81, 89, 91, 107, 168
  Almack's balls, 12
  Army and Navy Stores, 139,
    142
  auctions, 153, 172, 186–7
  Birchin Lane, 32, 43
  City of, 148
  Drummond's Bank, 139–40
  International Jubilee
    Philatelic Exhibition, 140
  Leicester Square, 129
  'Post Office' stamp
    discovered, 124
  'Post Office' stamp
    rumoured, 145–6
  (Royal) Philatelic Society,
    55, 67, 73–7, 113, 129–30,
    140–2, 146, 176, 181, 183, 187

South African exhibition, 123
Strand, 98
Long Mountain, 7
Loupiac, 115
Lowe, Robson, 173
Lumgair, Mr, 58, 60, 63, 89–90

Madagascar, 8, 10, 21
Madagascar fir trees, 23–4
Madras, 18, 58
Mahé, Edward, 82
Mahé, Pierre, 52, 71–2, 82
Mahebourg, 143
Maison Champion, 158–9
    *Bulletin Mensuel de la Maison
        Théodore Champion & Co.*,
    154
Maison Erard, 152–3
Malta, 55
Manchester, 106
Manus, Henry, 137, 147, 164, 171,
    215
Mapou, 143
Margerison, John, 136
Marquay, Monsieur Alcide, ball
    envelope, 63, 69, 75, 93, 96–7,
    213
Marseilles, 113
Martineau (stamp collector), 52
Mauritius
    air service, 26

balls, 1–2, 12
British community, 12–13,
    221
cholera epidemic, 97
colonial history, 8–9
exports, 151
Dutch colonists, 8, 215
financial crises, 11, 25
French community, 2, 9–10,
    12–13, 47–8, 212
government, 85
as Île de France, 8–9
immigration, 10, 18, 218–19
impact of stamp sales, 96
imports, 11
Legislative Council, 94
mail ships arrive, 21–2
maps, 215
missionaries, 89
naval blockades, 9, 17
official language, 9, 11–12
plantocracy, 10–11
population, 10
Portuguese name, 93
and 'Post Office' plate, 138–
    44
postage stamps introduced,
    2–3, 20, 27–30, 52
postal history, 190, 202,
    217–18
postal rates, 111, 209

postal system, 1–3, 15, 17–27, 51, 94

private collections, 77

racial and cultural mix, 10

soldiering in, 14, 56

stamp discoveries in, 53–4, 87, 92–4

stamp hunting in, 150–2

sugar industry, 8, 10, 22, 57

trade with Britain, 125

trade with France, 47–8

Mauritius Agricultural Department, 143

Mauritius Archives, 38, 61, 92

Mauritius Commercial Bank, 97, 223

Mauritius Illustrated, 92, 140, 152

Mauritius Institute, 92

Mauritius Postal Museum, 221–4

Mauritius stamps, 33–5, 38, 67, 151, 158, 190–1

  'Britannias', 34

  cancellations, 211–12

  commemorative, 15, 174–5, 216

  Dardenne issue, 34–5, 185

  dating, 33–5, 40, 56–7

  difficulty of, 187

  De La Rue issue, 34–5

  introduced, 2–3, 20, 27–30, 55

  Lapirot issue, 34–5

  newspapers bearing, 53

  rarity, 57, 99

  Sherwin issue, 34–5, 182

  see also 'Post Office' stamps; 'Post Paid' stamps

Mauritius Treasury, 85, 142, 144

Maurits van Nassau, Prince, 8, 215

Melville, Fred, 80, 128, 147, 157

Mémorial Bordelais, 47

Mercantile Record and Commercial Gazette, 56

Miami, 171

Miller, Frank, 164, 166–7

Moens, Jean-Baptiste Philippe Constant, 36–40, 46–7, 66, 72, 90, 211

  death, 82

  and history of 'Post Office' stamps, 36, 49–51, 84, 91, 95–6, 106, 112–13

  'Post Office' stamps, 44, 52–4, 67–9, 73, 81–2, 117

  publisher of *Le Timbre-Poste*, 36, 44, 77, 182–3, 206

  retirement, 201

  and stamp values, 81–2, 91, 96, 98–9

  and suspected forgeries, 180, 202, 205–7

Mohrmann, Edgar, 172
Moka, 1
Monitor, 84
Monte Carlo, 68
Montevideo, 42
   stamps, 44, 46
Montferrand, 110
Monthly Journal, 90, 106, 124
Morel, Bernard, 143
Mors family, 158
Morton, Rev. C. S., 1, 16, 177
Mosely, Edward, 151
Mozambique, 18
Mulhausen, 118
Mulready, William, 132
Murray, John, 41

Napoleon, Emperor, 79, 220
Napoleonic Wars, 17
Nash (artist), 15
Nathan, Walter, 100, 168–9
Neapolitan government,
   stamps, 133
New Orleans, 185, 188
New South Wales, 37
New York, 42, 89–90, 171–2,
   188–9
   Collectors Club, 185
   Stock Exchange, 187
New Zealand, 21, 38
Nicolas, Madame, 71–2

Nissen, Harry, 184, 187–8
Noirel, Monsieur, 53–4, 67, 170

paintings, 187
Paris, 25, 70–2, 82, 110, 113, 119,
   145, 152, 166
   Austrian Embassy, 79
   Avenue de l'Opéra, 105
   fair, 66, 69
   Ferrary sales, 155–64
   Hôtel Matignon, 79–80, 83
   Luxembourg gardens, 43,
     165
   origins of philately, 32
   reprints, 204
   Tuileries, 43
Pauillac, 42, 51
Pearson, Patrick, 205
Peckitt, W. H., 91, 96–9, 105–7,
   116–17, 136–7, 188
   early stamp collecting, 158
   and stamps on cover, 97–8
   'Thousand-pounder', 107
Pemberton, Edward Loines, 55
Peninsular Wars, 8
People and Places, 149–50
Perce, Mr, 17
Perinelle (stamp collector),
   68–9, 73, 75, 170
Perrissin, Monsieur, 77–8
Perron, Victor, 204, 213

Perth, Western Australia, 145–6, 174

Philadelphia, International Philatelic Exhibition, 191

philatelic exhibitions, 190–1

Philatelic Fraud Squad, 191

philatelic journals, 32, 118, 154
  illustrations, 181–2
  see also stamp collecting magazines and journals

philatelists, 5–6, 32–3, 112

philately, 32, 103, 111, 125, 218
  see also stamp collecting

Philbrick, Frederick Adolphus, 66–8, 70, 73–4, 78, 80, 90, 161, 211

Philippe, Leon, 143–4

Philippines, stamps, 36

Phillips, Charles, J., 5, 73, 79–80, 91, 101, 129, 162, 172

Pieter Both, 7, 221

Piggott, Francis, 144

Pike, Nicolas, 21

Plaines Wilhems, 25

Plymouth, 55, 110

Pneumatic Tube, 119

Pope, T. A., 96

Port Louis, 1, 6, 11, 15, 30, 41, 53, 77, 97, 218
  Blue Penny Museum, 223–4
  cholera epidemic, 89
  heat, 18–19, 40
  early postal system, 25–7
  Edward Francis & Co., 110–11, 209
  French character, 9–10
  Government House, 2, 7–8, 14–15, 20, 93–4, 221
  Grand Hôtel d'Europe, 27
  history and topography, 92
  international trade, 87
  Masonic Lodge, 12
  merchants, 125
  newspapers, 17, 26, 48, 143
  origins, 16
  pianos, 23, 152
  Place d'Armes, 2, 20–2, 24, 220, 223
  post office, 20–1, 40, 51, 58, 60, 90, 110, 142–4
  Royal Society of Arts and Sciences, 56
  street names, 22–3
  volcanic mountains, 7

Portsmouth, 27

'Post Office' stamps, 3–4, 27–30, 34–6
  achieves highest philatelic prices, 89, 96, 118, 131, 184, 187, 214
  auctioned, 4–5, 89–90, 124–5, 129–31, 172–4, 184, 186–9,

214–15
and ball invitations, 1–3, 15, 93–5
'black sheep', 175–6
'Blue Mauritius' phrase enters vernacular, 134
copies, 119, 151–2, 216, 224
crime and, 167–9, 192
dating, 51, 62–3
design, 28–9
dies, 182
discontinuation, 29
discovery, 36, 44
engraving, 3, 27–8
in fiction, 131–6, 190, 192–200
first American owner, 137
first discovery in Britain, 124
first discovery in Mauritius, 53–4
first discovery outside Mauritius, 87–8
first entire discovered, 108
introduction, 27–30, 48
legitimacy affirmed, 60–3, 103
limited availability, 47, 89–90, 101
missing from Reichspost-museum, 177, 191–2
number of impressions, 61–2
ownership (1913), 147; (1923), 164; (1997), 216;

ownership kept confidential, 217
ownership listings, 87
paper, 143, 213–14
plate(s), 39–40, 85, 137–45, 199, 202–5, 216
prestige, 87, 147, 159, 216
prices settle, 137
production estimate, 28, 60–1
provenance, 203, 206–13
public awareness of, 107, 147
rarity, 4, 28–9, 40, 53, 62, 77–8, 87, 101–3, 147, 152, 159
relative rarity of different values, 132–3, 197
relative value of different values, 99, 118, 133, 136, 174
reprints, 141–2, 202, 204–5
reproductions, 204, 213
rising value, 5, 44, 50, 54, 66, 77, 81–2, 98–9
rumoured finds, 145–7, 219
scientific analysis, 213–14
stories concerning, 91, 106, 164–7
survival rates, 219
suspected forgeries, 176, 183–4, 201–13, 218
values, 3, 38–40
'Post Paid' stamps, 3, 28, 30, 34,

146, 168

forgeries, 213

one penny, 35, 50, 53, 86

PENOE error, 29

plates, 29, 35–6, 39–4, 62–3, 140–3

rarity, 50, 99

reprints, 144

two pence, 29, 99

value, 50

Potiquet, Alfred, 33, 43

Pouget, Marcel, 84–5

Pridham, Charles, 21

Prince of Wales, *see* George V, King

Provence, 161

Prussian blue, 213

Punch, 31

Puttick and Simpson, Messrs, 4, 123–5, 128–30, 172

Raaber, Franz, 169

Rae, Albert, 53, 76–7, 84, 140, 142, 152

Rae, William, 142

Raman microscopy, 213

Rawson, Monsieur, 12

Réunion, stamps, 85–6

Revue Historique et Littéraire, 92

rhinoceros, 11

Richards, Frank, 192

Robert Hastie & Co., 125

Robert, Henri, 143

Robert, Pierre, 143–4

Robert, Victor, 85

Roll of Distinguished Philatelists, 185

Rothschild, Baron Arthur de, 67–8, 71, 80–1

  L'Histoire de la Poste aux Lettres, 68

  'Post Office' stamps, 52, 54, 67–8, 81, 117, 163, 170

  sells collection, 68, 81

Rothschild, James-Edouard de, 67

Rothschild, Nathaniel de, 67

Roussel, Leopold, 143

Royal Archives, 141

Royal Artillery, 55–6

Royal College of Surgeons, 75

Royal Engineers, 140

Royal Philatelic Collection, 130, 164, 173, 203, 212, 215–16

Royal Sussex Regiment, 13

Rudelle, Monsieur, 12

Rühmann, Heinz, 190

Sachim, Nawab of, 130

St-Croix-aux-Mines, 160

St Helena, 38

St Louis, 101

Sandringham, 131

Schiller (stamp owner), 84, 87, 175

Scotland, 122, 126–8, 164, 175, 212

Scott, Walter, 14

Scout magazine, 136, 197

Second World War, 177, 191, 215

Séfi, Alexander, 138, 141, 160, 163, 176

Séfi, Pemberton and Co., 162–3

Senegal, 42

Senf brothers, 179

Serizier and Lafitte, Messieurs, 47, 54, 109

Seychelles, 57

Sherman, Leonard, 102

ships

  Arab, 48

  Augusta Jessie, 48

  Beagle, 9

  Braemer, 218

  Centaur, 218

  Champion, 218

  Cleopatra, 7

  Emily, 218

  Equateur, 110

  Hopewell, 17

  Intrepid, 218

  Jane-Greene, 47

  John King, 110–11

  London, 48

  SS *Majestic*, 172

  Mischief, 111, 120, 208

  Norfolk, 47–8

  Nussur, 218

  Portly, 218

  HMS *Rattlesnake*, 18

  Reliance, 47–8

  Sirène, 48

Sicily, stamps, 82

Signal Mountain, 7

Singapore, 217

Slater, H. G., 90–1

slavery, 8, 10

Smith, Sir Lionel, 8

Smithsonian Institution, 170

Société Française de Timbrologie, 68

South Africa, 48, 87, 123, 219

Spain, 211

  stamps, 210–11

Speranza, Lieutenant, 55

Spiro brothers, 179

stamp albums, 46, 49, 178

stamp catalogues, 33, 43

stamp clubs, 178

stamp collecting, 3–6, 31–2, 43–4, 76

  'amateur', 112

  changes in, 78–9, 82

chequebook, 217
children and, 122–3
criticisms of, 99–101
and First World War, 154
growing popularity, 65, 87,
    136, 156
inclusive, 65, 78–9
instructive value, 5, 65, 218
literature on, 31
practices, 181
in Scotland, 128, 212
stamp hunting, 149–53
timbromanie, 32
women and, 31, 47, 72
stamp collecting magazines and
    journals
Australian Stamp Journal,
    145–6, 175
Collectors Club Philatelist, 162,
    172
Gazette des Timbres, 51
*Illustrierte Briefmarken
    Journal*, 106
*La Cote Réelle des Timbres-
    Poste*, 112–13, 116, 120
*Le Collectionneur de Timbres-
    Poste*, 35
Le Philatéliste Français, 106
Le Timbre-Poste, 36, 38, 44, 77,
    90, 96, 182–3, 206
London Philatelist, 1, 16, 76, 78,

    82, 87, 113, 118–19, 131
New Stamp Magazine, 123
*Philatelic Journal of Great
    Britain*, 86, 93, 132
Philatelic Magazine, 169, 183
Philatelic Record, 28, 55–6, 75,
    78, 94, 100, 136, 142
Philatelist, 32
Postage Stamp, 98
Stamp Collecting, 31, 65, 118,
    122, 126, 133–5, 138, 145,
    151, 154, 158, 164, 177, 220
*Stamp Collector's Herald and
    Advertiser*, 123
Stamp Collectors' Fortnightly,
    85, 100, 107, 118–20, 132,
    148, 168
Stamp-Collector's Magazine,
    40, 167, 178
Stamp Lover, 58
*Stanley Gibbons Monthly
    Journal*, 123, 141, 146, 201
West-End Philatelist, 138
stamp dealers, 36, 43, 98–9, 216
stamps:
    auction prices, 5, 99–100, 131,
        153, 161, 184, 187–9, 214
    beauty in, 100
    clean, 51–2
    colour errors, 196
    countries issuing, 3, 32–3

dies, 182

'entires', 49, 72, 209

facsimiles, 178–80, 182

forgery, 178–83

high prices, 100–1

historic associations, 103–4

intrinsic values, 99–100

margins, 124

on newspapers, 53

numbers of issues, 102

perforations, 32, 37, 39, 51

plating, 39

press interest in, 89, 99, 106, 152, 214

provenance, 104

rarities, 78, 98, 101–3, 136, 147–8, 157, 159, 161, 191, 214

repairs, 181

reprints, 180

survival rates, 219

'tied together', 46

'unused', 51

value, 49, 100–4

watermarks, 32, 37

world's rarest, 101

Standley, Samuel, 142

Stanley Gibbons, 55, 81, 85–6, 95, 137, 188–9

Stanley Gibbons, Edward, 55, 74, 180

Stavely, Madame, 12

Stephan, Herr, 118

Stocken, Nevile Lacy, 123–5, 138–42, 145, 204

Stockholm, 223

Swedish Postal Museum, 126, 170

Sugar Duties Bill, 25

Surrey, 73, 90

Sweden, 48, 87, 219

Switzerland, 82, 159, 185

stamps, 30, 158

Sydney, 48, 219

Talleyrand, Charles Maurice de, 79

Tapling, Thomas Keay, 73–80, 82, 217–18

Collection, 76, 156, 207, 213

'Post Office' stamps, 75–6, 96, 203, 207, 213

The Hague, 215

Thomas, Miss D., 123–4

Thompson, Thomas Henry, 57, 60, 142–4

Tilleard, J. A., 130–1

Times, The, 31, 99, 125, 145, 172, 174

tortoises, 16

United States of America, 119, 159–60, 172, 181

Depression era, 173
  'Post Office' stamps in, 137,
    147
  and Reichspostmuseum
    stamps, 191–2
  stamps, 30, 67, 101–1
Uruguay, stamps, 158
  Montevideo 'suns', 44, 46
US Postmaster General, 102
Utica, New York, 159–60

Vandervelde, Denis, 210
Ventom, Bull and Cooper, 99
Vera Cruz, 42
Vereenigde Oost-Indische
  Compagnie (United East
  India Company), 16
Verhoeff, Pieter Willemsz, 16
Victoria, Queen, 2–3, 5, 11, 28,
  30, 35, 99
Vienna, 82, 169, 178
Vigoureux, Monsieur, 14
Ville Bague, 24

Walker (tea planter), 150
Walser, Robert, 152–3
waste-paper, 49, 54, 116, 127–8,
  148
Waterloo, Battle of, 8
Weill, Raymond H., 185–6,
  188–9

Weill brothers, 89, 189
Westminster Gazette, 93
White, F. M., 132, 134
Whitfield King & Co., 77
Who's Who in Philately, 130
Williams, Norman, 152, 201–2,
  205
Williams brothers, 107, 114, 150,
  162, 175, 191, 201–3
Worthington, George, 137, 147,
  157–8, 162

Young Men's Buddhist
  Association, 185

Zurich, 30, 214